REGIONAL INEQUALITY AND STRUCTURAL CHANGES

For my father

Regional Inequality and Structural Changes

Lessons from the Brazilian experience

EDUARDO A. HADDAD
Fundação Instituto de Pesquisas Econômicas (FIPE),
University of São Paulo, Brazil
Regional Economics Applications Laboratory (REAL),
University of Illinois, USA

Routledge
Taylor & Francis Group
LONDON AND NEW YORK

First published 1999 by Ashgate Publishing

Reissued 2018 by Routledge
2 Park Square, Milton Park, Abingdon, Oxon, OX14 4RN
711 Third Avenue, New York, NY 10017, USA

Routledge is an imprint of the Taylor & Francis Group, an informa business

A Library of Congress record exists under LC control number: 99073640

ISBN 13: 978-1-138-32718-4 (hbk)
ISBN 13: 978-0-429-44940-6 (ebk)

Contents

List of Figures and Maps

List of Tables

Preface

The role of regions in the economic development process is gaining more attention in the last few years. Regional issues are being rediscovered by economists, especially those interested in international trade theory. Krugman (1991a) suggests that one of the best ways to understand how the international economy works is to start by looking at what happens *inside* nations. The location of production and consumption in space should not be ignored. As Frankel (1998) observes, most of international trade research in the past has ignored the geographic dimension. International trade models, whether empirical or theoretical, whether based on small-country or large-country assumptions, and whatever else their attributes, tended until recently to have one curious thing in common: they treated countries as disembodied entities that lacked a physical location in geographical space.

Recent changes in the world economy are having direct effects on the Latin American countries. Transformations induced by technological changes are responsible for a new world order, in which global competition plays a major role; the opening of markets is a process that is occurring in many countries in the region, and has brought about significant impacts on their productive structures. As these countries present internal heterogeneity in their resources allocation, these impacts are perceived differently across regions within these national economies.

The liberalization process of the 1990s in Latin America resulted in the increase and diversification of trade in the region. Brazil, as a major player, strengthened its insertion into the world economy through the adoption of strategies for opening up markets adopting new production technologies, complemented recently by the creation of a broadly-based stabilization plan. The latter plan has been a familiar strategy for Latin-American countries: it involves monetary and fiscal reforms, and privatization processes that stimulate private investment and inflow of foreign capital, spurred by interest rates that are more attractive than those of other international markets (Arocena, 1995).

In this context, issues related to structural changes in the economy, such as those involving the complexity of new international trading agreements (e.g. Mercosul, AFTA, WTO) and their impacts on the Brazilian economy, deserve special attention. Brazil's economy, like many developing countries, is not homogeneous internally, presenting strong variations across regions, sectors, and income groups. Consequently, macro policy changes have differential regional impacts, as well as differential impacts on producers and consumers. Thus, as Higgins and Savoie (1995) argue, the designing of policies to assure good performance of national economies requires thorough understanding of the behavior of the regional economies of which they are composed, and formulating specific policies for each region on the basis of that understanding.

The discussion of regional and sectoral impacts of alternative strategies of regional development in the present macroeconomic context of the Brazilian economy has often lacked a formal analytical framework. Hence, if policy analysis is to be based on sound, consistent economic data, it is important that an analytical framework be developed to provide this capability. Accordingly, the primary analytical focus of this book is to build an interregional computable general equilibrium model (ICGE) for the Brazilian economy. The model is to be used to capture the role of interindustrial and interregional relations in the economic development process through the evaluation of the regional impact of different economic policies. The use of this modeling approach is very relevant to the Brazilian case as well as to the analysis of similar economic issues in other developing countries. Its ability to handle detail – both in terms of its disaggregation level and in terms of its theoretical specification – is useful for the analysis of the evolution of Brazil's productive structure. The choice of the policy simulations to be carried out is heavily motivated by both theoretical and historical relevance in the Brazilian case. Recent contributions to this debate, raised by Azzoni (1995, 1996) and Zini Jr. and Sachs (1996), on the pattern and direction of regional income convergence in Brazil in the new cycle of economic growth, are considered in the context of macroeconomic, sectoral and structural policies, and their differential impacts on the patterns of regional imbalances. The theoretical framework to support the analytical results is rooted in alternative theories used to explain regional inequalities in the economic development process.

Plan of the Book

The remainder of the book is organized as follows. Chapter 1 introduces a brief discussion of the dynamics of regional inequality, followed by an historical review on the process of spatial formation of the Brazilian economic territory. Attention is directed to three issues: the pattern followed in the evolution of regional imbalances; social distributive dimensions of regional growth; and the spatial impacts of macroeconomic, structural and sectoral policies.

Chapter 2 discusses recent developments in the field of regional modeling, focusing on CGE models built for sub-national territories. Initially, a stylized interregional general equilibrium model of a private ownership economy is formally introduced. The purpose is to show the essential structure of an interregional bottom-up CGE model, from a theoretical perspective. Following that, some issues in regional and interregional modeling are analyzed, with emphasis on those related to CGE modeling, relevant to the Brazilian model.

The theoretical structure of the **B**razilian **M**ultisectoral **A**nd **R**egional/**I**nterregional **A**nalysis Model (B-MARIA) is presented in Chapter 3. The functioning mechanisms of the model are delineated and some of the contributions to regional modeling are highlighted. Technical details have been considered in such a way that the model can be adapted to a large group of developing economies.

Chapter 4 provides a comparative analysis of the economic structure of the regional setting adopted in the analysis. The interregional input-output table, especially built for the calibration of the model, is used, and traditional input-output methods are used in an attempt to uncover similarities and differences of the regional economies.

B-MARIA is used in Chapter 5[1] for supporting the discussion of alternative strategies of regional development in the present macroeconomic context of the Brazilian economy. Simulations are carried out in this part of the study, showing the regional impacts of different economic policies. Different instruments of public policy are used to demonstrate the flexibility of the model to give support to decision-makers in relation to strategies for the economic development of the country. Theoretical and historical relevance to the Brazilian case motivates the choice of policies to be analyzed. Attention is directed to three different issues: the effects of trade liberalization (tariff reductions), reductions in transportation costs reflecting changes in a specific component of the so called *Custo Brasil*

[1] Chapter 5 is partly based on a paper that will appear in *Oxford Development Studies*, and another paper that was presented at the International Workshop on "Theories of Regional Development", in Uddevalla, Sweden, in June 1998, and will appear in a volume with the proceedings of the meeting.

(factor productivity growth in the transportation sector), and the regional impact of a development project (new investments in the automobile sector). A thorough discussion of the issues is added, emphasizing their significance to regional development in Brazil, in accordance with the theories considered in Chapter 1, and theoretical aspects of the fields of international trade, regional economics (location theory), and economic development (industrialization policies).

Finally, Chapter 6 presents the main conclusions of this book, as well as provides policy implications drawn from the study. The future agenda for research is also outlined in the last chapter; this agenda can eventually be extended to other developing countries.

Acknowledgements

This book is a modified version of my Ph.D. dissertation submitted in partial fulfillment of the requirements for the degree of Doctor of Philosophy in Economics in the Graduate College of the University of Illinois at Urbana-Champaign, in December 1997. I would like to acknowledge the following institutions for their help in the course of this book: the Regional Economics Applications Laboratory at the University of Illinois for providing financial support and the proper intellectual and physical environment for the development of my research; the *Conselho Nacional de Desenvolvimento Científico e Tecnológico* – CNPq – for the financial support; the Inter-American Development Bank (IADB), where I spent the Summers of 1995 and 1996 working at the RE1/OD1 and returned in September of 1997 for a short period to work on my dissertation; the Department of Economics and the Department of Geography at the University of Illinois; the University of Oxford's Centre for Brazilian Studies (CBS) and the School of Geography, also in Oxford, where I spent the calendar year of 1998; and the *Fundação Instituto de Pesquisas Econômicas* (FIPE), at the University of São Paulo.

While at the University of Illinois, there were two people who were directly responsible for my training as a professional economist: Professors Werner Baer and Geoffrey J. D. Hewings. They both have supervised my work during the Ph.D. program and have given me great support in my studies in that institution, providing a friendly environment. Their positive attitude towards my work, their belief in my abilities, and their precious friendship gave me the strength to succeed. To them, I owe my deepest gratitude.

I am also grateful to Prof. Bill Williamson, who served as a member of my committee, and, although he began advising me after I was well into the research, gave me much insight, constructive criticism and guidance. James Dinsmoor, at the IADB, was not only my mentor at the Bank but also my friend, whose belief in my work gave me the confidence necessary to complete my Ph.D.

After receiving my Ph.D., I was engaged in post-doctoral research, from January to December 1998 at the University of Oxford. I would like to thank Prof. Leslie Bethell, Prof. Edmund Amann, and Prof. Bill MacMillan for their support.

In November 1998, in a meeting of the *Regional Science Association International* in Santa Fe, New Mexico, USA, Prof. Walter Isard easily persuaded me to try to publish my Ph.D. dissertation. I am very grateful for his encouragement and also his comments on an early draft of the dissertation.

Currently, back to Brazil, I have undertaken research and teaching duties at FIPE at the University of São Paulo. I would like to express my gratitude in particular to Professors Carlos Azzoni and Evaldo Comune for their advice and support.

Some other people deserve my gratitude: Prof. Joaquim Guilhoto, for invaluable assistance, who first stimulated me in the field of CGE modeling and kindly shared his research with me; Prof. Michael Sonis, who has greatly inspired and encouraged me with his vast knowledge; the staff at the Centre of Policy Studies and the IMPACT Project at the Monash University, Australia, especially Professors Matthew Peter, Ken Pearson, Peter Dixon and Brian Parmenter, who gave great support during my stay at that institution and, after I returned, provided the technical assistance to the development of B-MARIA; Prof. Eric McVittie, who read Chapter 2 and with whom I had insightful discussions on the research; and the staff and friends at REAL, the Department of Economics and the Department of Geography at UIUC, the CBS and FIPE.

Last but most importantly, I would like to acknowledge the wonderful support I received from my family. My father, to whom this book is dedicated, has always been the source of inspiration to my life, serving as a great role model for me. As an economics professor, I would like to thank him for his suggestions and constructive criticism on the argument and methods of analysis as well as his guidance throughout my studies; as a father, I would like to thank him for his love. The model developed in this book was named after my mother and my wife, my "two Marias". I am deeply indebted to my beloved mother for her huge and endless understanding, enduring love and unconditional support of various kinds that make my life meaningful. I must also express my heartfelt appreciation to my brother, my sisters and my exceptional parents-in-law for their long-distance support and encouragement during my stay in the USA and UK. Finally, to my lovely wife and to our baby; my wife has always been there to help me maintain a proper perspective of life and living. I can do no more than reaffirm my eternal devotion and look forward to even happier moments together with our first child.

Eduardo Amaral Haddad

1 Regional Development and Regional Inequality: An Overview of the Brazilian Economy

The present configuration of Brazil's economic space is heavily rooted in the development path followed by the country since colonial times. The uneven distribution of wealth in the Brazilian territory is characterized by a high concentration of resources in the Center-South portion of the country. In the classification adopted in B-MARIA, in which the regional setting consists of three different regions – North, Northeast, and Center-South (Rest of Brazil), the latter comprises the more dynamic regions of the Southeast and South, as well as the Center-West (Map 1.1).[1] This classification, heavily constrained by data availability, considers the Southeast, South and Center-West regions as a single region, precluding the analysis of each of these regions individually. However, the regional delimitation still offers a great range of analytical possibilities focusing on the less developed regions of the North and Northeast Brazil.

The degree of regional inequality in Brazil can be gauged from Table 1.1 below, which shows the proportion of the average per capita output of each region to the national average per capita output. While the Northeast presented, in 1994, an average per capita output 50% below of the national average, and the North reached only 68.0% of the national average, the other regions, especially the Southeast, showed indicators substantially above the national average.

These differences in regional wealth are accompanied by impressive differences in regional social indicators as well, which can be summarized by the *poverty incidence indicator* estimated by IPEA: in 1990, 40.9% of the population in the Northeast were considered to be indigent, in contrast to 13.9% in the North, 12.4% in the Southeast, 18.1% in the South, and 16.1% in the Center-West (Guimarães Neto, 1995).

---

[1] In B-MARIA, the North includes the following states: Acre, Amazonas, Pará, Rondônia, Roraima, Amapá, Tocantins, and Mato Grosso.

Map 1.1 Regional Setting in B-MARIA

Table 1.1 GDP and GRP per capita: Brazil and Regions, 1994 (R$)

	GRP/GDP per capita	% of national
North	2299.94	68.0
Northeast	1635.13	48.4
Southeast	4490.83	132.9
South	3983.42	117.8
Center-West	3650.90	108.0
Brazil	3380.14	100.0

Source: IPEA/DIPES

A more recent study, commissioned by UNO, provides further insights into this issue. The estimates of the *Human Development Index* (HDI) for the Brazilian states and regions reveal other aspects of regional inequality in the country. The HDI[2] is a new way of measuring development which

[2] The HDI is a composite of three basic components of human development: longevity, knowledge and standard of living. Longevity is measured by life expectancy. Knowledge is measured by a combination of adult literacy (two-third weight) and mean years of schooling (one-third weight). Standard of living is measured by purchasing power, based on real GDP per capita adjusted for the local cost of living (purchasing power parity, or PPP). The HDI

combines indicators of life expectancy, educational attainment and income. One way the use of the HDI has been improved is through disaggregation. Using disaggregated HDIs at the national and sub-national levels, for instance, helps highlighting the significant disparities and gaps among regions. Table 1.2 presents the HDI values for Brazil and its macro regions for the period 1970-1996, and Table 1.3 shows the progress of its dimensions over time.

Table 1.2 Human Development Index: Brazil and Regions, 1970-1996

	1970	1980	1991	1996
North	0.425	0.595	0.676	0.727
Northeast	0.299	0.483	0.557	0.608
Southeast	0.620	0.795	0.832	0.857
South	0.553	0.789	0.834	0.860
Center-West	0.469	0.704	0.817	0.848
Brazil	0.494	0.734	0.787	0.830

Source: UNDP (1998)

Table 1.3 Dimensions of the Human Development Index: Brazil and Regions, 1970/1996

	Life Expectancy		Education		Income	
	1970	1996	1970	1996	1970	1996
North	0.484	0.706	0.567	0.777	0.223	0.697
Northeast	0.323	0.658	0.433	0.714	0.142	0.452
Southeast	0.532	0.730	0.702	0.875	0.625	0.966
South	0.588	0.753	0.688	0.870	0.384	0.957
Center-West	0.516	0.726	0.614	0.860	0.277	0.959
Brazil	0.461	0.710	0.611	0.825	0.411	0.954

Source: UNDP (1998)

Throughout the period, it is clear that all the regions presented improvements in their HDI values. However, the relative situation did not change, with the North and Northeast regions showing performances

sets a minimum and a maximum for each dimension and then shows where each country or region stands in relation to these scales – expressed as a value between 0 and 1.

systematically below the national average. The analysis of the evolution of the dimensions of the HDI in the regions reveals an overall improvement. It is interesting to notice that the income component for the less developed regions (North and Northeast) more than tripled in the 1970-1996 period, but income continued to be the dimension with the greatest differential to the other regions. Nevertheless, the other two dimensions, life expectancy and education, which represents closely the human capital in the regions, still offers significant gaps among regions.

This chapter includes two other sections. The next section introduces a brief discussion of the dynamics of regional inequality, followed by an historical review of the process of spatial formation of the Brazilian economic territory.

Economic Development and Regional Inequality

Economic development is spatially unequal everywhere. At the national level, it is always possible to identify more developed and less developed regions. In general, almost all socio-economic indicators of development apply in the same direction; leading economic regions present higher standards of economic and human development.

The description of the patterns of regional inequality and the process of economic development has been the focus of attention of prominent economists (e.g. Myrdal, 1957; Hirschman, 1958; Williamson, 1965; Alonso, 1968; and more recently, Krugman, 1991b; and Barro and Sala-i-Martin, 1995). It is agreed that, at the early stages of the development process, growth is, in the geographical sense, necessarily unbalanced. Because of agglomeration externalities, there can be little doubt that an economy, to lift itself to higher income levels, must and will first develop within itself one or several regional centers of economic strength (Hirschman, 1958, p. 183). Historical evidence confirms these hypotheses, be it verified for developed or less developed countries (Williamson, 1965). In some cases, it dictates the directions of regional policies. For instance, the concept of growth poles (Perroux, 1955), worldwide utilized in the formulation of regional development projects, is based on the conflictive idea that the "cake" has to grow before it can be split.

In the analysis of regional disparities, it is usually assumed that the regional dualism is initially determined by geographical and historical *accidents*. Thus, the initial pattern of regional concentration encountered in different countries depends on particularly favorable natural conditions for the economic activities concentrated in a given location which give the specific region competitive advantage at a certain period of time.

Myrdal (1957) and Hirschman (1958) were interested in the interregional interactions derived from the growth process in a region and their implication to national development. Once growth takes place in one locality, the interaction of two different forces will determine the movements of the national economy towards/against regional inequality. First, there will be a tendency towards inequality. Given the initial dualistic setting, expansion of the rich region increases inequality through migration, capital movements and trade. Selective migration takes place, draining skilled labor force from the poor regions; capital also tends to migrate to the growing regions, driven by higher rates of return connected to agglomeration economies; regional specialization in manufacturing goods in the expanding region, protected by tariff barriers, creates a deterioration of the terms of trade unfavorable to the peripheral area, generating recurrent interregional trade deficits.

These effects were called by Myrdal "backwash" effects, also characterized by Hirschman as "polarization" effects; they work in a cumulative way in a process of circular causation, and might be strengthened through the interplay of non-market forces as well. Actions by the government can also contribute towards regional inequality. If government policy is intended to maximize national growth, the regional allocation of public investments will be concentrated in the rapidly developing region, in order to meet the demands for public infrastructure by the private sector. In addition to direct investment in social overhead capital, the favored regions tend to benefit from implicit regional policies carried out by the central government.[3] This has been the case of protectionism policies that benefit the growing industrial regions, precluding the poor regions from the consumption of similar goods from abroad, at lower prices.

The second force has beneficial effects to the backward areas. The "spread" effects, also denominated "trickling-down" effects, operate as positive spillovers of the expansion from the centers of economic growth to the other regions. Regional integration might arise from the regional division of labor; as the peripheral regions supply the central regions with agricultural products and raw materials, conditions for growth start to be created in the former from the income generated in those sectors. Thus, the spread effects from a center of industrial expansion to the other localities

[3] These are essentially macroeconomic or sectoral development policies whose differential regional effects depend on the regional economies' structures under consideration.

and regions, operating through increased demands for their products and in many other ways, weave themselves into the cumulating social process by circular causation in the same fashion as the backwash effects, in opposition to which they set up countervailing changes (Myrdal, 1957, pp. 43-44).

However, more important as a growth stimulator in the less developed regions is the action taken by the government. The trickling-down effects generated by market forces are very unlikely to overtake the polarization effects in the early stages of the development process. The lack of economic infrastructure that facilitates the flows of goods, such as transportation and communications, represents an obstacle for the operation of the forces for the centrifugal spread of economic expansion in developing countries. Free play of market forces in those countries, thus, has an inherent tendency to create regional inequalities. In this case, deliberate economic policy comes into play to correct this situation. The interference by the state, in order to reverse regional inequality, takes the form of provision of social overhead capital for the physical integration of the regional markets, tax incentives, and, in some cases, direct investments in productive plants.

The interaction of the adverse and favorable direct economic repercussions from the rich regions to the poor ones will determine the direction of regional inequality in the national economy. Empirically, Williamson (1965) did not reject the long-run hypothesis that the early stages of national development generate increasing income differentials, as the spread effects are very weak. Somewhere during the course of development, as the forces for the centrifugal spread are strengthened due to improved transportation and communication systems, and higher levels of education, for instance, the disequilibrating tendencies diminish, causing a reversal in the pattern of interregional inequality. Thus, instead of divergence in interregional levels of development, convergence becomes the rule, with the backward regions closing the development gap between themselves and the already industrialized areas.

As far as the effects of business cycles are considered, industrialized regions are more affected by changes in the path of economic growth, i.e., boom periods are led by the dynamic sectors in those regions, which are also more intensively affected by recession periods. If during a boom period the relative strength of the spread effects increases, the emergence of the depression period drives regional inequality down, as the poor regions are less susceptible to the cyclical changes and have received stimuli to grow in the previous period. Even though depression decreases the strength of the spread effects, its pervasive effects are felt less intensively by the lagging regions, which benefit from a less integrated economic structure. This fact suggests a cyclical pattern of regional concentration, with short run implications, where the differential behavior of the regions lies on the differential intensity of the expansion/depression phases on those economies.[4]

The circularity story was recently reinforced by Krugman (1991b), embodied in a simple yet rigorous model. More important than providing new ideas to the debate on the emergence of regional inequalities, his work brought up the attention of mainstream economics to issues neglected for a long time, with some exceptions, by the profession.[5]

Finally, the subject of regional inequalities has returned to the stage under the impact of the New Growth Theory. The incorporation of growth-determining factors endogenous to the regions (e.g. human capital, information, R & D, institutions) helps to explain the pattern of regional growth, emphasizing the role of such non-traditional locational factors in determining differential regional growth. Economic growth is not constrained by decreasing returns to capital and, therefore, there is a possibility for regional inequality to increase over time. Using this framework, many country studies proliferated in the last years trying to analyze the problem of convergence and divergence of regional income levels over time. The results challenge the traditional inverted U-shaped hypothesis, showing that regional disparities have increased in mature economies (e.g. Amos, 1989; Barro and Sala-i-Martin, 1995). Studies for the Brazilian economy (Azzoni, 1995; Zini Jr. and Sachs, 1996) point to a recent convergence of regional income without any reliable indication of its future trend. In the next section, the path of regional inequality in Brazil is examined in the light of historical developments and the theoretical background outlined above.

---

[4] See, for instance, Guimarães Neto (1996) for empirical evidence in the Brazilian case. The study shows that, up to the 1980s, whenever the Brazilian economy experienced rapid growth, the Northeast followed the increasing trend, but at a slower pace, increasing regional imbalances; in recession periods, the adverse effects were felt less intensively by the Northeastern economy.

[5] In general, the rediscovery of the spatial dimension by economists has greatly ignored the work developed in the field of Regional Science. Some of the contributions of researchers in the field are documented in Malecki (1991) and Higgins and Savoie (1995); other sources of information are the specialized academic journals.

Regional Inequality in Brazil

The process of spatial formation of the Brazilian economic territory can be divided into four different stages. First, as early as the colonial times until the first decades of the twentieth century, development was based on the external linkages of the regional economies through international trade. Before the sources of economic growth became internalized with the industrialization process, economic growth was induced by exports of primary products. Regional growth was constrained by the availability of export commodities. Internal linkage effects would not expand further than the surroundings of the production and commercialization geographical centers.

At that time, the pattern of regional concentration was determined by the location of primarily export-oriented products, in these regions. Alternate growth cycles benefited the regions where the production of export commodities took place; they included the sugar cycle in the Northeast, the gold and the coffee cycles in the Center-South, and the rubber boom in the North. However, the historic shifting of favored economic regions came to an end in the early years of the twentieth century, when the emerging industrial sector in the Center-South of the country established its position as the leading region of Brazil's economy (Baer, 1995).

In general, it is assumed that geographical and historical facts determine the initial concentration pattern in a country. In the case of Brazil, it can be argued that the facts determining the North-South dualism took place in the late nineteenth century. As Denslow (1978) observes, the economic differences between the Northeast and South of Brazil could not be easily perceived in the 1870s. At that time, the economy of the Northeast was heavily based on the exports of sugar and cotton, while the South depended on its coffee exports. Export revenues in both regions were very similar.

In an open economy depending on external linkages derived from trade of a few primary products, as was the case of Brazil in the last century, external exogenous shocks dictated the trends of national growth. At the regional level, the export composition, or more precisely, the leading regional export products – sugar and cotton, in the Northeast, and coffee, in the South – were strongly subject to the fluctuations in the international markets. In addition, supply-side considerations were somehow important to determine the spurt in coffee exports *vis-à-vis* the relative stagnation of the Northeastern exports.

From 1840 to 1910, coffee demand increased by an average of almost 5% per year. Increases in demand for coffee in the last half of the last century and the first decade of this century were accompanied by supply responses from Southern producers. British investments in infrastructure, the better human capital of the European immigrants, and the technological progress in the sector established Brazil as the main world supplier of coffee. The weight of coffee in the country's exports increased dramatically bringing prosperity to the producing region; the incoming revenue was decisive in speeding development and finance industrialization in the region. Moreover, trade policies carried out in the last years of the nineteenth century included a serie of currency devaluation and tariff protection, benefiting coffee exporters and the incipient manufacturing sector in the São Paulo area (see Baer, 1965).

On the other hand, the development in the Northeast lagged behind in that period. Sugar production faced competition of substitutes (sugar beets) and, more strongly, competition of Caribbean cane sugar, that took over the U.S. market. Regional production, hampered also by the decrease in international prices, did not follow the new technological developments of the sector, resulting in declining shares in international markets; sales shifted towards national markets in the South. World demand for cotton almost stagnated in the last decades of the nineteenth century, and the producers in the South of the United States, with better technology and lower internal transportation costs, dominated the main markets in Britain. The production of the Northeast shifted towards the markets of the South, where a protected textile industry emerged. By the turn of the century, internal trade became an important component in the uphold of the productive structure of the Northeast.

In the first decades of the twentieth century, regional dualism was already established in the Brazilian economy. Estimates from the *Inquérito Industrial*, for the year 1907, show that the Southeast accounted for 58.2% of the total industrial output; the Northeast had a share of 16.7%, and the North 4.3%. In 1900, the population shares for the Southeast, Northeast, and North were, respectively, 44.5%, 39.0%, and 4.0%.

The second stage in the process of spatial economic formation in Brazil is characterized by an increasing share of the industrial sector in the GDP. Industry became the leading growth sector, bringing about important structural changes in the economy. However, the Southeast was the main beneficiary from the industrialization process, which contributed to a higher degree of regional concentration. This is a transitional period in which the economy, primarily agricultural and based on the coffee sector, with a relatively high degree of free trade, embarked on a path of inward-oriented growth, with a rigid control of the external transactions. Until the 1930s, agriculture was still the leading sector of the economy, presenting higher rates of growth. Spurts of industrial growth were common in the three decades preceding World War II; by the early 1930s, the industrial sector already presented consistent higher rates of growth, leading the national economic development.

Regional equity was not part of the country's development agenda, and central government policies contributed to worsen regional imbalances. In the 1920s, the formulation of coffee support policies, whose main beneficiaries were the producing regions of the South, represented one of the main government actions. In one of the first attempts at planning in Brazil, in 1942-43, the Cooke Mission provided the first analysis, for policy purposes, of the Brazilian economy from a regional point of view. Efforts should be concentrated in the South, so that spread effects would operate towards the other regions (Baer, 1965, 1995). That seems to agree with the implicit beliefs of policy-makers in the import substitution industrialization era.

When import substitution industrialization expanded, especially in the post World War II period, the regional distribution of income in the country became more concentrated. In the 1950s, the focus of attention of the central government was the development of the industrial sector in the Center-South in order to solve balance-of-payments problems and promote an industrial complex. It harmed the less developed regions of the country, which subsidized somehow the industrialization process. By facing protection walls, these regions were constrained to the consumption of the more expensive manufactures produced in the South. In the case of the Northeast, which continued to depend on its exports of primary products to generate foreign trade surplus, an artificial deterioration of its terms of trade was imposed by its interactions with the Center-South, characterizing an income transfer towards the latter (see Furtado, 1963, and Baer, 1965, 1995).

Efficiency concerns were translated into government actions in the period. For instance, the main goal of the *Plano de Metas* (1956-60) was to increase the rate of industrialization of the country, and it did not contain any explicit regional concern. The net result was to accentuate the regional concentration of the economic activities in the Southeast (Maimon *et al.*, 1977). The country grew at high rates in the period, providing an example in which the choice of investment in the leading sector of the economy, i.e. the choice of maximizing national development, may tend to increase still further the degree of regional inequality. By the end of the 1950s, regional disparities reached a critical level, calling the attention of the government to the less favored regions, especially to the Northeast. In 1960, the Southeast's share in the national population was 43.7%, and its share in the national income 62.8%; Northeast's share in the national income was only 14.8%, with 31.7% of the Brazilian population living in the region.

The period from the early 1960s to the 1980s represents the third stage of the economic spatial formation of Brazil. The explicit concern of public authorities with regional imbalances was manifested in actions such as direct investments in regional development projects and tax incentives in the poorer regions of the country. These efforts helped to reverse the regional concentration trend, promoting more development in the North, Northeast and Center-West.

Before 1960, the economic base of the North relied only on rubber production as the source of external linkages. The rubber boom in the last decades of the nineteenth century gave some push to the development of the Amazon region. However, international competition resulted in the loss of almost its entire share of the world market. Since then, regional production, lagged technologically and locationally, survived from the low revenues from its rubber exports. In the 1960s, motivated by the appropriation and access to natural resources, and the occupation of the territory, public authorities began to give more attention to the region. Federal government intervention in the 1970s, in the form of tax and financial incentives to the private sector, public investments in infrastructure (especially roads connecting the region with the rest of the country), and direct investments of state enterprises, was crucial to the development of dynamic spaces in the region. Even though environment degradation and income distribution worsening accompanied the regional economic growth, the issue of regional equity achieved positive results. The regional share in the national GDP increased from 2.16% in 1970, to 4.36% in 1985. In the same period, population share moved from 3.87% to 5.54%; GDP per capita grew from 44.7% of national average, to 73.64%.

Azzoni (1995) shows that the states of the North and Northeast experienced increasing differentiation in terms of per capita income in the last decades. In the case of Brazil's North, growth in the region was eminently uneven across space. Three dynamic areas, which benefited directly from government intervention, can be identified (Buarque *et al.*, 1995). First, the western agricultural pole in Rondônia, an area characterized by a recent population settlement whose production is oriented to the regional and national markets, became viable after the access to the cheap lands was facilitated by public investments in infrastructure in the region, especially in roads. Second, following the basic orientations of the regional policies to the Amazon region in the late 1960s, which determined the creation of development poles and the establishment of population settlements in the region, a free trade zone was created in Manaus. The industrial sector benefited from huge tax incentives and was responsible for a spectacular growth in the 1970s and 1980s. Today, the *Zona Franca de Manaus*, as it is known, presents an industrial profile heavily concentrated in the electric and electronic sectors oriented to the domestic markets outside the region, especially to the Southeast. Finally, the third dynamic area in the region is located in the state of Pará. Even though the state has a mixed economy, with relatively strong agricultural and industrial sectors, the mining-metal complex of Carajás represents its most dynamic center. The existence of natural resources in the region, valuable in international markets, attracted heavy government investments in infrastructure, in a first stage, and, later, direct investments by public enterprises in the development of an economic complex which induced growth in the region. These three areas were the main sources of economic growth in the North in the 1970s and 1980s, and in the case of Carajás and Manaus, structural changes accompanied growth, in that the share of the industrial sector in the North's GRP increased from 15.1%, in 1970, to 39.8%, in 1985.

In the Northeast, government intervention contributed to growth by providing the region with artificial locational advantages in the form of tax and financial incentives. Direct investments of state enterprises also were carried out in the region, especially in intermediary goods (petroleum refining and chemicals).

Segmented regional spaces also appeared in the region, strengthening the dual character of the economy; areas of intense modernization coexist with traditional economic structures, reluctant to technical changes. On one hand, the Northeast encompasses dynamic regional poles developed from private investments reinforced by government incentives, as well as from government investments; they include the petrochemical complex of Camaçari, the textile and clothing pole in Fortaleza, the mining-metal complex of Carajás, in Maranhão, which also encompasses part of the Brazil's North, and scattered areas of modern agriculture. On the other hand, the sugar cane and cocoa plantations represent areas resistant to changes, incorporating traditional methods of land cultivation with low standards of productivity (Araújo, 1995).

It is important to point out that the redistributive role the government played through the federal fiscal system was a common practice in the 1970s and 1980s. As is apparent from Tables 1.4 and 1.5 below, the regional shares of the central government revenues in the poorer regions were recurrently smaller than the shares of central government expenditures in those regions. These figures suggest an effective redistribution of public funds to the North and Northeast over the period.

Table 1.4 Brazil: Regional Shares of Central Government Revenues

	1970	1975	1980	1985	1991
North	1.4	1.5	1.7	2.2	2.3
Northeast	10.0	8.2	7.2	8.3	9.9
Center-South	88.6	90.3	91.1	89.5	87.8

Source: SUDENE, Boletim Conjuntural, August 1996, p. 397

Table 1.5 Brazil: Regional Shares of Central Government Expenditures

	1970	1975	1980	1985	1991
North	3.2	2.5	3.0	3.5	3.6
Northeast	13.4	10.9	10.3	10.4	11.2
Center-South	83.4	86.6	86.7	86.1	85.2

Source: SUDENE, Boletim Conjuntural, August 1996, p. 400

The pioneering efforts by Rolim *et al.* (1996) provide a more complete interpretative scheme on interregional flows in Brazil, based on available statistics on trade balance, government accounts, investments by the public sector, and savings. The preliminary results for 1985 are summarized in Table 1.6, and reinforce the character of interregional government transfers suggested above. Even though the analysis covers only one year, it can give a rough idea on how interregional flows were oriented in the years preceding 1985. The repeated pattern of government fiscal transfers depicted in Tables 1.4 and 1.5, together with the estimates of interregional and international trade balances for the Northeast and North in the same period, support the following generalization of the results presented in

Table 1.6.[6] The North and Northeast presented trade deficits recurrently over the period. In the case of the Northeast, the perennial interregional trade deficits were partially compensated by international trade surpluses, indicating a transfer of foreign exchange earnings to other regions of the country. The continual overall interregional trade deficits of these two regions had to be financed by public and/or private savings, so that the conditions for macroeconomic balance were met.[7]

The conjecture, taking 1985 as a typical year, is that the transfers of federal resources to the Northeast, for instance, had to be greater than the trade gaps in order to compensate the interregional flows of private capital oriented towards other regions. Even though the figures show a net outflow of private capital from the Center-South, less aggregated figures, for 1985, show a tendency of net private capital gains to the states of São Paulo and Rio de Janeiro, as well as the Center-West. The orientation of public capital to the less developed regions has often been offset by the flight of private capitals. Rolim *et al.* (1996) argue that this represents the synthesis of bad allocation of government funds from the point of view of an efficient regional policy. However, it might be argued, based on the previous discussion, that government transfers to the North and Northeast, during the 1970s and early 1980s were necessary to build the social overhead capital in those regions in order to strengthen the potential spread effects from the Center-South and create self-reinforcing mechanisms in the regions to generate their own sustainable growth. In other words, government transfers might have achieved a greater relevance in the less developed regions by creating the necessary infrastructure to foster development and attract, in a second moment, private investments to directly productive activities. This hypothesis would be better tested by looking at estimates of investments in the region; if it is somehow relevant, the relation between the share of public investments in the target region to the share of public investments in the country should show an increasing trend during the 1970s with an inflection point after the necessary time for

---

[6] The Northeast presented a recurrent surplus in the international trade balance in the period: 1970 (US$229 M); 1975 (US$796 M); 1980 (US$707 M); 1985 (US$1,692 M). In the same period, the North achieved repeated deficits: 1970 (-US$27 M); 1975 (-US$173 M); 1980 (-US$312 M); 1985 (-US$55 M). Even though estimates for interregional trade flows are not systematically available, it is acknowledged that the Northeast presents historically deficits in relation to the rest of the country (Araújo, 1995).

[7] This condition establishes that income inflows should equal outflows, in equilibrium. Thus, if a region presents trade deficit with the rest of the country and the rest of the world, in equilibrium, it has to be compensated by net inflows of resources from government expenditures and/or private investments (see Rolim *et al.*, 1996).

the economic infrastructure to have matured. From the estimates for the Northeast, however, an increasing path in the share of public investment in the region, compared to the national average, is apparent from 1973 to 1989 (Figure 1.1). Even though there seems to be a declining tendency towards the national average in the first years of the1990s, empirical evidence to support the conjecture on the existence of a change in gears is very weak.

Table 1.6 Interregional Flows by Regions, 1985 (in Cr$ billions)

	North	Northeast	Center-South
1. Interregional trade balance	-2016	-13071	15088
2. International trade balance	-207	4383	56573
3. Government current account balance	4208	13651	-117273
4. Government capital account balance	2269	16874	80470
5. Allocation of government resources (3+4)	6477	30525	-36803
6. Private capital flows (1+2+5)	4254	21873	34898

Source: Rolim *et al.* (1996)

Hence, in the three first stages identified here, there was clearly a pattern delineated, initially, by increasing spatial concentration, followed by a reversion in this tendency in the last decades, as can be seen from Figure 1.2. It should be mentioned, however, that the decrease in regional inequality has been accompanied by a remarkable increase in the concentration of both intraregional and personal income distribution in those regions, in the same period (Azzoni, 1995 and 1996).

Finally, the fourth stage encompasses deep structural changes in the Brazilian economy. After 1988, with the *new* Constitution, the central government was hampered by a profound loss in its revenues to the state and municipal governments. Nevertheless, the fiscal crisis reached all levels of government, decreasing their financial capability for carrying out new investment ventures. The lack of investment in economic infrastructure increased the average cost of production; producers were facing increasing costs due to the inefficient mechanisms of trade and transportation, which lagged technologically. A new paradigm of development had to be defined, in the context of increasing globalization, high rates of inflation in the country, and the fiscal crisis of the State. In 1994, the Brazilian government introduced a so-far successful stabilization program in order to stop inflation. This action, together with trade liberalization measures introduced since the early 1990s, made the country more attractive to foreign investments again. Direct investments in high linkage industries, such as the automobile sector, increased in the last years. Brazil is now going through a new expansion cycle, whose directions should be analyzed carefully.

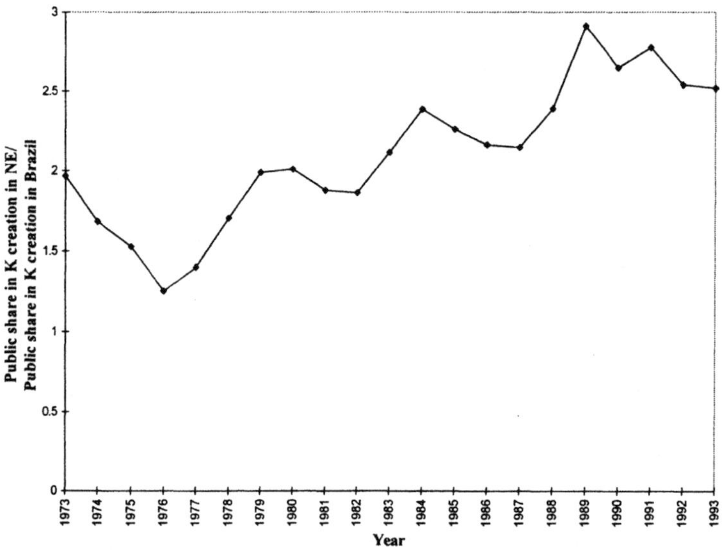

Source: SUDENE, Agregados Econômicos Regionais, 1996 and FIBGE, Anuário Estatístico, several years.

Figure 1.1 Northeast: Ratio of the Public Share in Regional Investment to the Public Share in National Investment for Capital Creation: 1973-1993

Estimates of regional shares in the GDP for the period 1985-1994 show an unchanged picture in the decade. North's share oscillated slightly around its average 4.75%, the same occurring to the Northeast (average of 14.10%) and the Center-South (81.15%) [Table 1.7].[8] Regional inequality, as measured by the Williamson's coefficient, also presented a stable behavior (Figure 1.2).

[8] Disaggregated estimates for the Center-South show that there was a gain of approximately 2% for the Center-West, in the period, in the same proportions of the loss of the Southeast (Lavinas *et al.*, 1997).

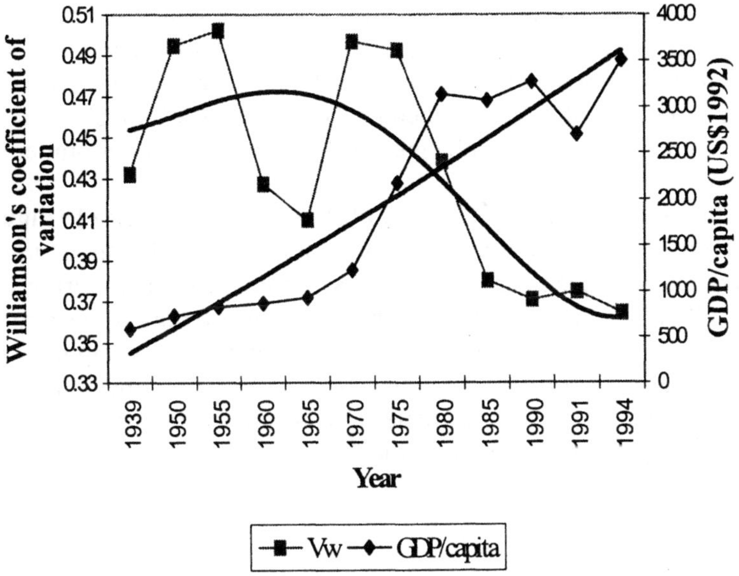

Source: Author's calculations using data from Anuário Estatístico, several years.

Figure 1.2 Brazil: Time Path Relating Regional Inequality and GDP per capita

Table 1.7 Regional Share in GDP

	North	Northeast	Center-South
1985	4.36	13.93	81.71
1986	4.52	14.18	81.30
1987	4.65	14.09	81.26
1987	4.80	14.10	81.10
1989	5.06	14.29	80.65
1990	5.02	14.02	80.96
1991	4.89	14.15	80.96
1992	4.63	13.90	81.47
1993	4.79	14.32	80.89
1994	4.82	13.97	81.21

Source: IPEA/DIPES

The effects of the new growth cycle of the Brazilian economy have generated renewed debate on the future of the regions. The stable regional setting shown above is not likely to persist; estimates from the national accounts point to a weak tendency of regional divergence of state per capita income after 1992 (Lavina *et al.*, 1997). The possible reversal of the secular tendency of regional income convergence established in the late 1960s coincides with the changes in the economic environment of the economy.

At the macro regional level, similar questions are raised (Figure 1.3). Will the regional concentration continue its downward path, as implied by the inverted U-shaped curve hypothesis, which states that, during the early stages of development, the per capita income of regions becomes more unequal, but during the later stages, more equal – as suggested in the Brazilian case up to the mid-1980s? Or will there be a new concentration period, suggesting a cyclical pattern, with alternating cycles of regional inequality expansion and contraction?

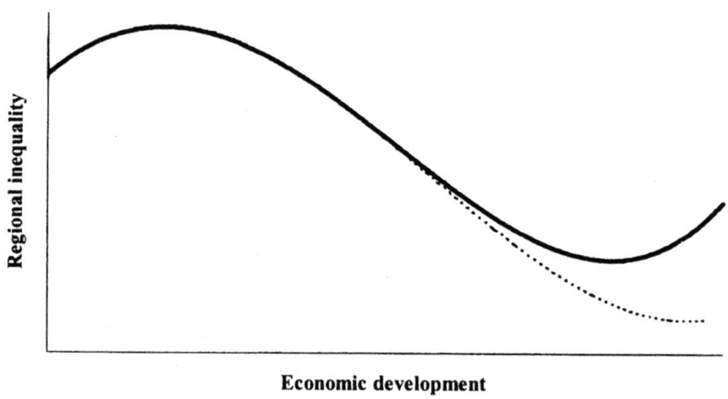

Figure 1.3 Brazil: Alternative Paths Relating Regional Inequality and Economic Development

In this context, *the main objective of this book is to examine the effects of the changing economic environment of the Brazilian economy on the patterns of regional concentration and structural changes*. Trade liberalization policies, the infrastructure component of the *Custo Brasil* – the extra costs of doing business in Brazil – and the new industrial investments will be examined through the use of simulation exercises, focusing on their impacts on regional inequality and structural changes. The simulations will be carried out using an interregional computable general equilibrium model, described in Chapter 3. Before, modeling issues are discussed in the next chapter.

2 Interregional Computable General Equilibrium Models: A Survey on Specification and Implementation Issues

The theory of general equilibrium in economics has its origin in the work of the classical economists. The perception of its most important implication, that competitive markets can achieve an allocation of resources that is efficient in some sense, is present in Adam Smith's *The Wealth of Nations*, 1776. Although Leon Walras (1874) and Edgeworth (1881) are considered to be the precursors of the theory, as we know it today, many other authors are recognized to have given their contribution to its theoretical development. Thomas Malthus, David Ricardo and John Stuart Mill can be regarded as early expositors of general equilibrium theory. Stanley Jevons and Carl Menger also contributed to the development of important neoclassical elements present in the general equilibrium theory.

Modern theorists of general equilibrium did not emerge until the 1930's. The main issues examined related to the existence, uniqueness and stability of equilibrium, and comparative statics. The classic works by Debreu (1959) and Arrow and Hahn (1971) formalized the main results of the field and established general equilibrium as a recognized field in economics. [For an historical introduction to the development of general equilibrium analysis, see Arrow and Hahn (1971); for recent developments, see Eatwell *et al.* (1989).]

The general equilibrium approach treats the economy as a system of many interrelated markets in which the equilibrium of all variables must be determined simultaneously. Any perturbation of the economic environment can be evaluated by recomputing the new set of endogenous variables in the economy. This methodological feature of general equilibrium analysis attracted many researchers to develop its applied dimension. The desire to convert general equilibrium theory into a practical tool for the evaluation of economic policy motivated the construction of algorithms for computing solutions to numerically specified general equilibrium models.

Scarf (1967, 1973) conceived the first description of a successful attempt to provide this link between theory and operational models. Johansen (1960) is also regarded as a benchmark in the literature of computable general equilibrium (CGE) modeling. His model for Norway is considered to be the first CGE model developed based on the premises of general equilibrium theory (Dixon and Parmenter, 1994).

In the last twenty years, stimulated by the work of Johansen and Scarf, a large number of computable general equilibrium models has been applied to a great variety of economic questions in different geographical areas [reviews are found in Dervis *et al.* (1982), Shoven and Whalley (1984), De Melo (1988)]. The broad spectrum of applications and theoretical issues envisaged by researchers in the area contributed to the substantial differences encountered in the CGE models around the world.

In this chapter, attention is directed to Walrasian-type models built for sub-national territories. It precludes the analysis of Marshalian-type general equilibrium models[1] (e.g. Israilevich *et al.*, 1997) and models whose regional setting considers national economies as regions in a multicountry framework. Although such models provide interesting insights for issues related to interregional CGE modeling, which is the ultimate focus here, they are not considered.

In the next section, a stylized interregional general equilibrium model of a private ownership economy is formally introduced. The purpose is to show the essential structure of an interregional bottom-up CGE model, from a theoretical perspective. Following that, some issues in regional and multiregional economic modeling are analyzed, with emphasis on those related to CGE modeling; comparisons of regional CGE models are established based on published studies of operational models. Final remarks follow.

A Stylized Theoretical Interregional General Equilibrium Model

The purpose of this section is to show the essential structure of an interregional bottom-up CGE model, from a purely theoretical perspective. The starting point is the characterization of a private ownership economy.

---

[1] The Chicago Regional Econometric Input-Output Model (CREIM) incorporates the idea of the Marshallian equilibrium adjustment process (quantity adjustment process) to overcome the unavailability of regional prices of goods and services. As an input-output econometric model, a time series of regional prices would be necessary to estimate price-related parameters.

Results from general equilibrium theory are drawn from the literature (Mas-Colell *et al*., 1995; Varian, 1992; Eatwell *et al*., 1989); proofs are found elsewhere (Mas-Colell *et al*., 1995; Arrow and Hahn, 1971). The assumptions for the economy follow:

Regions

A.1. There are R regions, r = 1, ..., R, which exhaust the space of the economy. Economic interactions take place inside and outside the region (intraregional and interregional trade).

Commodities

A.2. There are L commodities, l = 1, ..., L, provided by R different sources. A list of quantities of all commodities are given by a vector in IR^{LR}.

Consumers

A.3. There are I consumers, i = 1, ..., I, spatially distributed in the R regions. In each region r, the population is given by $I^{(r)}$, so that $0 < I^{(r)} < I$ and $\sum_{r=1}^{R} I^{(r)} = I$.

A.4. Each consumer i is characterized by a convex consumption set $X^i \subset IR^{LR}$.

A.5. Consumers preferences are assumed to be rational (complete and transitive), continuous, convex, and locally nonsatiated.

Firms

A.6. There are J firms, j = 1, ..., J, spatially distributed in the R regions. In each region r, the number of firms is given by $J^{(r)}$, so that $0 \leq J^{(r)} \leq J$ and $\sum_{r=1}^{R} J^{(r)} = J$.

A.7. Each firm j is characterized by a production set $Y^j \subset IR^{LR}$. We impose a further restriction in Y^j, that the firms produce only regional commodities related to their specific location. Thus, if j is located in region r, j's production of commodity ls, $s \neq r$, is zero. Production vectors available for each firm j in region r are denoted by $y^j = (0,...0, y_{1r},..., y_{Lr}, 0,...,0) \in IR^{LR}$.

A.8. Y^j is a closed, strictly convex set containing 0. Moreover, Y^j is bounded above.

Endowments

A.9. Consumer i has an initial endowment vector of commodities $\omega^i \in X^i \subset IR^{LR}$ and a claim to a share $\theta^{ij} \in [0,1]$ of the profits of firm j, where $\sum_i \theta^{ij} = 1$ for every j.

A.1 defines the regional setting of the model. A.2 suggests that the source of each commodity matters, and spatial heterogeneity is taken into account in the model. A.3-A.5 describes the consumers' characteristics: A.3 distributes the population across the regions so that in each region there is at least one consumer; A.4 and A.5 are technical assumptions. A.6-A.8 refer to the firms: A.6 is connected to the regional productive structure; A.7 says that the source of production is directly connected to the location of the firm where the commodity is produced, while A.8, again, is a technical assumption. Finally, A.9 outlines the initial distribution of wealth among consumers.

Definition 1 Given a private ownership economy specified by A1-A.9, an allocation (x^*, y^*) and a price vector $p = (p_{11},..., p_{L1},..., p_{1R},..., p_{LR})$ constitute a Walrasian (or competitive) equilibrium if:

(i) For every j, y^{*j} maximizes profits in Y^j; that is,

$$p \cdot y^j \leq p \cdot y^{*j} \quad \text{for all } y^j \in Y^j$$

(ii) For every i, x^{*i} is a preference-maximizing choice in the budget set $\left\{ x^i \in X^i : p \cdot x^i \leq p \cdot \omega^i + \sum_j \theta^{ij} p \cdot y^{*j} \right\}$

(iii) For every r, $\sum_{i=1}^{I^{(r)}} x^{*i} + \sum_{i=I^{(r)}+1}^{I} x^{*i} = \sum_{i=1}^{I} \omega_r^i + \sum_{j=1}^{J^{(r)}} y^{*j}$

Definition 1 is precisely what Walrasian general equilibrium models are about, the determination of equilibrium quantities and prices in a system of perfectly competitive markets and maximizing behavior by the agents. *(i)* defines the producer's supply of each regional commodity based on profit-maximizing behavior; *(ii)* states that each consumer's demand arises from utility maximization subject to budget constraint; *(iii)* is a market clearing equation, that equates aggregate demand for each regional commodity to its aggregate supply (including initial endowments of each commodity). The existence of a Walrasian equilibrium in our economy is assured by the set of assumptions above. We need an additional claim to pursue the main properties of a spatial general equilibrium model.

Claim Given a private ownership economy specified by A1-A9. Let b_r be the trade balance of region r. Walrasian equilibrium implies that

(i) For every r, $b_r = \sum_{l=1}^{L} p_{lr} y_{lr}^{*} - \sum_{l=1}^{L} \sum_{s=1}^{R} p_{ls} x_{lsr}^{*}$

(ii) $\sum_{r=1}^{R} b_r = 0$

This claim is easily proved by contradiction. For sake of exposition, it is assumed from now on that consumers living in the same region are equal, and that the population in each region is known. In addition, the economic structure of each region is also known and firms within a region adopt the same technology. By using these assumptions, a representative agent approach can be used, implying a dramatic reduction in the size of the model. The number of equations and variables in the model are reduced proportionally from the order of $(I+J)$ to $2R$. Rewriting *(i)-(iii)* in *definition 1* in functional form, and redefining the trade balance in each region for general flows, we have:

$$Y_{lr} = \sum_{j=1}^{J^{(r)}} y_{lr}^{j} = \varphi\left(p^{(r)}\right), \quad l = 1,\ldots,L \quad r = 1,\ldots,R \tag{2.1}$$

where Y_{lr} is the output of commodity l supplied by producers in region r, and $p^{(r)}$ is the price vector referring to the L commodities produced in region r.

$$X_{lrs} = \sum_{i=1}^{I^{(s)}} x_{lrs}^{i} = \gamma\left(p, \omega^{(s)}, \theta^{(sr)}\right), \quad l = 1,\dots,L \quad r,s = 1,\dots,R \tag{2.2}$$

where X_{lrs} is the demand by consumers in region s for commodity l produced in region r, p is the price vector which includes all LR commodities, and $\omega^{(s)}$ and $\theta^{(sr)}$ reflect the aggregated wealth of consumers in region s. In this case, $\omega^{(s)}$ is the vector of initial endowments of consumers in region s, and $\theta^{(sr)}$ is the claim to a share of profits of firms in each region, r, from consumers in region s.

$$Y_{ls} = \sum_{r=1}^{R} X_{lsr} \quad l = 1,\dots,L \quad s = 1,\dots,R \tag{2.3}$$

$$b_r = \sum_{l=1}^{L} p_{lr} y_{lr} - \sum_{l=1}^{L}\sum_{s=1}^{R} p_{ls} x_{lsr}, \quad r = 1,\dots,R \tag{2.4}$$

Together with equations (2.1)-(2.4), the introduction of equation (2.5), determining the interregional aggregate price level – fixing arbitrarily the sum of prices to unity – is sufficient for finding a solution for the model.

$$\sum_{l=1}^{L}\sum_{s=1}^{R} p_{ls} = 1 \tag{2.5}$$

The interregional model consists of $LR^2 + 2LR + R + \left(R^2 + R\right)$ variables and $LR^2 + 2LR + R + \left(1\right)$ equations. The closure of the model requires $\left(R^2 + R - 1\right)$ variables to be determined exogenously. One suggestion is to set the $\theta^{(sr)}$s exogenously together with all but one of either the $\omega^{(s)}$s or the b_rs. Once the closure is determined, the equilibrium solution to the model is achieved when a vector of prices is found that clears the markets for all regional commodities.

The simple stylized model depicted above is rooted in established microeconomic concepts. Optimizing behavior of consumers and producers is explicitly specified, as well as the institutional environment (competitive markets). Thus, demand and supply functions are derived consistently with prevalent consumer and production theories.

Interesting insights for regional analysis can be gathered from the properties of this stylized model. First, regional interactions are captured through interregional trade. Interregional linkages have an important role in interregional CGE models, as it will become clearer as some modeling aspects are analyzed below. Secondly, the behavior of agents is specified in all regions, which characterizes the bottom-up approach in regional modeling. Outcomes for the economy as a whole are summations from their regional counterparts. Thirdly, one can describe, *ex ante*, the regional economic structure of the economy, based – in the case of the stylized model – on the assumptions of the model. This is a somehow neglected issue in most of the CGE applications, but it is an important component for the understanding of such complex models.

More sophisticated theoretical general equilibrium systems are described in the literature. Incorporation of different features, such as factor markets, are very usual, but it would not add much to the discussion above, given the scope of our exposition. Open economy models with taxes and tariffs are presented in Shoven and Whalley (1992). Harris Jr. (1988) describes a dynamic spatial economic system without recontracting, that includes governments as separate decision-making units, allows for foreign trade, and allows the possibility of externalities and monopolistic power. A wide range of possible extensions is one of the major attractiveness of general equilibrium models. The examples cited above only give a light taste of it. Many issues might be addressed through the general equilibrium framework, and this feature has been being developed by many researchers in both theoretical and applied analysis. In the next section, some issues related to applied models focusing on regional economies are addressed.

Regional and Interregional Computable General Equilibrium Modeling

Regional economic models reveal systematic and quantitative representations of spatial economic systems. Different modeling approaches have been developed for understanding regional economies and interactions among them. Traditional methodological approaches include economic base methods, input-output analysis, gravity-type models, shift-share analysis, econometric models and programming models (Nijkamp *et al.*, 1986). A large literature on the development of such models is available [e.g. Anselin and Madden (1990), Harrigan and McGregor (1988a), Hewings and Jensen (1986), Nijkamp *et al.* (1986), Bolton (1985)]. More recently, a new approach of regional modeling has been gaining the attention of regional scientists, and efforts have been being increasingly concentrated in order to develop its vast possibilities of addressing regional economic issues. Contrasts between traditional fixprice methods, such as input-output, and flexprice methods (e.g. CGE) appear in that relative prices play a central role in the latter as a means of allocating resources [see Batten and Westin (1988), and West (1995) for a comparison of fixprice and flexprice models]. CGE modeling constitutes nowadays one of the main research frontiers in regional modeling. The main aspects related to its recent developments are discussed below.

Regional Setting and Data Constraints

Many of the issues related to regional CGE modeling, as will be seen, are general issues of the broader field of regional modeling. In general, the construction of an operational CGE model follows two basic steps: a) the specification of the model; and b) the calibration of the model, using input-output data and elasticities estimates. More general features of the model should be tackled at first. The choice of the regional setting is of major interest since it implies data availability and relevance of the policy simulations. On the one hand, data availability not only restricts enormously the regional aggregation of the model, but it also contributes to the proliferation of studies for a few regions for which consistent data are available. In the first case, researchers are constrained to define their object of study. Regions are almost always defined based on statistical divisions (Haddad, 1978, Adams and Dixon, 1995), which in most cases do not accompany the dynamism of changes in space. More comprehensive (Markusen, 1987) or economic-oriented (Boudeville, 1961) definitions of regions remain to be implemented, and, in the rare cases in which they have been, the method follows an *ad hoc* (dis)aggregation of statistical divisions data.

In the case of the examined regions, more in academic research and less in government studies, there seems to be an inclination among researchers to minimize their efforts in data collection by selecting the regional setting putting a heavy weight on data availability. Selection always falls on those regions for which government agencies have consistently estimated regional data bases. In regional CGE modeling, this procedure can be justified on the grounds of the novelty of the field (data are used just to illustrate the new ideas). Harris Jr. (1988) suggests that for such models to be useful to policy makers, data effort is necessary. The point here is that those regions for which information exists have benefited from academic studies in a cumulative way.

Finally, the choice of a region embeds the policy simulations to be carried out. It is important to define the regional setting in accordance with the economic issues to be addressed. Model results should also encompass consistent estimates for the main variables of the region under consideration. Not only spatial limits should be carefully defined, but also the number of regions in the model and their interactions. Single-region and multiregional CGE models provide different perspectives of policy simulations. Single-region models, in most cases, adapt the structure of existing national models; feedback effects from the region are not considered. The regional economy is modeled in the same way as small open economies in the international trade literature: trade has an important role and the economy is assumed to be a price-taker. Examples of single-region CGE models are: Despotakis and Fisher (1988), Harrigan *et al.* (1992), Dixon *et al.* (1993), Koh *et al.* (1993). The alternative to single-region models are multiregional models. They allow for interregional imbalances to be captured and are preferred to single-region models in the sense that regional interactions can be introduced. The discussion that follows focuses mainly on such models.

Bottom-Up and Top-Down Approaches

Closely related to the policy implementations and results is the specification of linkages between the national and regional economy. Two basic approaches are prevalent – top-down and bottom-up – and the choice between them usually reflects a trade-off between theoretical sophistication and data requirements (Liew, 1984b).

The top-down approach consists of the disaggregation of national results to regional levels, on an *ad hoc* basis. The disaggregation can proceed in different steps (e.g. country-state → state-county), enhancing a very fine level of regional divisions.[2] The desired adding-up property in a multi-step procedure is that, at each stage, the disaggregated projections have to be consistent with results at the immediately higher level (Adams and Dixon, 1995). The starting point of top-down models are economy-wide projections. The mapping to regional dimensions occur without feedback from the regions. In this sense, effects of policies originating in the regions are precluded. In accordance with the lack of theoretical refinement in terms of modeling of behavior of regional agents, most top-downs CGE models are not as data demanding as bottom-up models.

Examples of CGE models that rely on a top-down approach in their analysis of regional questions include ORANI [Dixon *et al.* (1982)], and Horridge *et al.* (1995). In ORANI, an adaptation of the method proposed by Leontief *et al.* (1965) for regional disaggregation of national input-output outcomes is used. The method is very economical in its data demand, in the sense that the necessity of interregional trade flows is avoided. It consists of three stages: a) in the first stage, the ORANI model is run to obtain projections for different national aggregates; b) then, constant-regional-share assumptions are used to allocate economy-wide outputs of national goods to the regions; c) in the third stage, the condition that regional outputs of local goods equal regional demands is imposed. Thus, regional outcomes capture differences in the economic structures of the regions and the local multiplier effects. Consistency with the economy-wide ORANI results can be checked: by reaggregating the regional results, initial economy-wide results are reproduced.

In the bottom-up approach, agents' behavior is modeled at the regional level. A fully interdependent system is specified in which national-regional feedback may occur in both directions. In this way, analysis of policies originating at the regional level are facilitated. The adding-up property is fully recognized, since national results are obtained from the aggregation of regional results. In order to make such highly sophisticated theoretical models operational, data requirements are very demanding. To start with, an interregional input-output data base is required, with full specification of interregional flows. Data also include interregional trade elasticities and other regional variables, for which econometric estimates are rarely available in the literature.

[2] Adams and Dixon (1995) report regionally disaggregated projections for 56 statistical divisions in Australia derived from national forecasts of the MONASH model.

Alternatives to the theoretical appealing bottom-up and the data-saving top-down CGE models are available. In Higgs *et al.* (1988), a partially regionalized CGE model is used to drive a top-down regional equation system. Using the fact that in most national CGE models agents are defined at a sectorally disaggregated level, the authors propose a further sectoral disaggregation in which regional sectors are explicitly specified. Although this procedure ameliorates the model's ability to handle some regional shocks, analysis of region-wide shocks still requires the more demanding bottom-up approach.

A different hybrid approach is proposed by Liew (1995). In this model, national-regional interactions are restricted to strategic interactions over money creation between the central and regional governments. The CGE core of the model remains purely top-down in essence. Interactions that drive one of the components of final demand is deliberately taken as generating important feedback from the regions.

Comparisons of operational models using the different approaches show that the construction of bottom-up models does not always justify the extra effort involved. Liew (1984b) compares regional results of a change in tariffs from the ORANI model (top-down) with regional results from a model constructed adopting the bottom-up approach, an extension of ORANI involving, essentially, the application of the same approach to regional agents. He finds that the introduction of interstate commodity flows, under very restrictive assumptions (constant technology and sales patterns across states, uniformity of price and expenditure elasticities for each commodity across states) does not contribute significant insights beyond those drawn from the top-down procedure. However, this conclusion is not valid when the interest is on individual regional-industry results, which seems to be one of the most desirable results in interregional multisectoral models. Moreover, when less restrictive assumptions about interregional feedback are used (McGregor *et al.*, 1996), some exogeneity assumptions may induce considerable bias in the measurement of regional variables.[3]

Defining an hypothetical input-output data base, Parmenter *et al.* (1985) use three skeletal models for performance comparison of three methods for regionalizing CGE models: top-down, bottom-up and hybrid. The hypothetical data base minimizes data differences, in the sense that the

[3] McGregor *et al.* (1996) compare a single-region version of a CGE model for Scotland with an interregional extension of it, in which the behavior of agents in the Rest of UK is explicitly modeled. In this case, exogeneity of regional prices and quantities, in the former model, for the Rest of UK is considered.

same economy-wide picture is depicted in the three models. This comparison allows only for national policies, given the restrictive features of the top-down and hybrid approaches. Although other dimensions of regional economies are not taken into account (for instance, regional commodity distinctions are minimal), results exhibit some illuminating differences.

Operational Models

Albeit the very heavy data requirement for bottom-up CGE models, they do not seem to have been neglected in favor of data-saving top-down model for the purpose of regional impact analysis. Regional CGEs based on the former approach have been developed in different contexts. Examples of operational interregional bottom-up CGE models are: Liew (1982, 1984a, 1984b), Ko (1985), Ko and Hewings (1986), Harrigan and McGregor (1988b), Morgan *et al.* (1989), Jones and Whalley (1988, 1989), Kraybill *et al.* (1992), Gazel (1994), McGregor *et al.* (1996), Naqvi and Peter (1996), Watanuki (1996).

Two different models for the U.S. are reported in Morgan *et al.* (1989), and Kraybill *et al.* (1992). The latter analyzes regional and sectoral impacts of macroeconomic imbalances, focusing on the economy of Virginia. Seemingly aspatial national policies – changes in the Federal government deficit, and in the international trade balance – are showed to be an important source of shifts in the geographic distribution of output and income. In a six region general equilibrium model for the U.S., Morgan *et al.* (1989) assess the potential long-run effects of tax policies on regional production patterns.

Jones and Whalley (1988, 1989) developed an interregional CGE model for the Canadian economy. The model is used for comparative statics, dealing with the evaluation of regional impacts of government policies. Applications of different variants of the model are reported in the literature and refer primarily to tax policies. Whalley and Trela (1986) exhaustively applied the model to a variety of policies elements within Confederation with regional impacts.

An interregional multicountry model was developed by Gazel (1994) on the premises of the skeletal version of a single-country CGE model developed at the U.S. International Trade Commission. The author expanded that model incorporating two different regional dimensions to it: firstly, the model was divided into three trading blocks (U.S., Canada and Rest of the World); secondly, the American economy was regionalized, being specified four regions.[4] The model was designed specifically for the analysis of the effects of the Free Trade Agreement (FTA) between U.S. and Canada. The impacts of the elimination of all tariff barriers between U.S. and Canada were measured and showed that Canada gains more than the U.S. in relative terms as the result of the FTA. However, gains are regionally concentrated and they are not proportional to regional income. These results provide a taste of interregional CGE models, showing their capability of capturing region-specific impacts in an integrated framework.

AMOS (Harrigan *et al.*, 1992) is a regional CGE model for the Scottish economy; its interregional version, AMOS-RUK, developed by McGregor *et al.* (1996), consists of two complete models of regions, each of which is very similar to AMOS. MONASH-MRF (Naqvi and Peter, 1996) is an interregional multisectoral model of the Australian economy. The model is fully documented: reports on the theoretical structure (Peter *et al.*, 1996b), the implementation (Naqvi and Peter, 1995), the construction of the data base (Peter *et al.*, 1996a), and application of the model (Peter, 1996) are available. This model has been used as the basis for the Brazilian model developed in this book.

Examples of interregional CGE models for developing economies are presented in Ko (1985), Ko and Hewings (1986), Watanuki (1996), and Harrigan and McGregor (1988b, 1989). Ko (1985) and Ko and Hewings (1986) expanded the national model for Korea developed by Adelman and Robinson (1978) adopting a five-region bottom-up approach. The model is based on region-specific equations, comprising of five highly interdependent CGE models. Watanuki (1996) presents a model for Indonesia, in which the Indonesian economy is divided into two regions: Java (central and developed region), and the Outer Islands (peripheral and underdeveloped region). The stylized model for Malaysia described in Harrigan and McGregor (1988b, 1989) provides a very rich contribution in terms of modeling issues to be addressed in interregional CGEs.

Interregional Linkages

Interregional linkages play an important role in the functioning of interregional CGE models. These linkages are driven by trade relations (commodity flows) and factor mobility (capital and labor migration). In the first case, interregional trade flows should be incorporated in the model. Interregional input-output data bases are required to calibrate the model,

[4] In an intermediary step, the American economy was divided into two regions.

and interregional trade elasticities play an important role. In the second case, labor mobility has received more attention from modelers.

In the CGE context, interregional feedback, when explicitly modeled, has proven to provide more refined results. The scale of feedback effects is also relevant. In the interregional CGE model for UK (McGregor *et al.*, 1996), preclusion of feedback effects from the Rest of UK to Scotland in the model, albeit its modest scale, generates considerable long-run bias in the measurement of employment effects. In a CGE experiment for Indonesia (Watanuki, 1996), in which interregional trade and factor mobility are incorporated, it is shown that new investments in a less developed, dependent region (Outer Islands) benefit, through feedback effects, relatively more the more developed, more dynamic region (Java). Similar results were found using an interregional input-output model (Hulu and Hewings, 1993); however, when disaggregated results are considered, the CGE model provides more insights on the regional economies.

The degree of interregional interaction of all markets includes different dimensions, as indicated above. One possible dimension of "openness" of regional economies is encompassed in the elasticities of substitution between similar commodities produced in different regions. A common assumption widely used in interregional CGE models, the Armington assumption, considers similar commodities produced in different regions as close substitutes, but unique goods (Armington, 1969). It allows for the incorporation of estimates of elasticities of substitution between domestically produced products and similar imported products, and between regionally produced products and similar products from other regions, suggesting nested multiple stage demand functions. Spencer (1988) points out that this assumption is extraordinarily convenient for [interregional] CGE work, since it admits the presence of cross-hauling in a standard neoclassical model and reduces concern about small changes having big effects on the pattern of trade and production (ruling out specialization in consumption). However, econometric estimates for such elasticities for interregional substitution are extremely rare, and modelers have often to extrapolate from estimates for their equivalent estimates for substitution between domestic and foreign commodities.

Factor mobility also plays an important role. Factors might be allowed to move intersectorally, interregionally, and internationally. Models vary in the treatment given to mobility of capital and labor. Capital is commonly assumed immobile in short-run simulations. In the long-run, capital movements are conventionally stimulated by rates-of-return differentials across sectors and regions, and productivity differentials. The basic stimulator of labor migration present in CGE models is regional wage differentials.

Differences in the treatment of labor mobility have been shown to have major impacts in model results (Harrigan and McGregor, 1988b). Simulations using AMOS-RUK (McGregor *et al.*, 1996) confirmed, at the interregional level, the results achieved through experiments with AMOS (Harrigan *et al.*, 1992) showing that specific treatment of labor markets heavily affects the properties of the system as a whole. Three aspects of regional labor markets were individually considered. First, the determination of wages was addressed through a variety of perspectives, including labor market closures with both aggregate and disaggregate regional labor markets, with different theoretical orientation (e.g. neoclassical, Keynesian). Second, net migration was assumed to respond to any induced changes in wages and unemployment in the regions. Finally, labor demand was consistently derived from firms' optimizing behavior. Empirical simulations in Morgan *et al.* (1989) include the extreme case of no labor mobility as well as the intermediate cases, through the imposition of different elasticity values of interregional migration response to real wage gap. Values used for interregional migration elasticity were set at 100 (perfect mobility), 0.1 (partial mobility), and 0 (immobility). Labor mobility was found to be an important determinant of regional growth, because less capital is attracted if the labor force cannot expand.

Some unconventional modeling attempts to include other variables affecting migration decision include Ko (1985), Ko and Hewings (1986), Jones and Whalley (1988, 1989), and Gazel (1994). In Ko (1985) and Ko and Hewings (1986), supply of labor is assumed to depend not only on the wage differentials across sectors and regions but also on adjusted differences in expected wages over some horizon plan, incorporating the Harris-Todaro hypothesis. In Jones and Whalley (1988, 1989), labor is assumed to be partially mobile across regions. This assumption is incorporated into the model through an ingenious mechanism. They assume that individuals in each region differ only by their intensity of locational preference, and then specify the utility function for any agent in any region as the maximum of two separate subutility functions. These functions represent the utility from consuming the same bundle of goods inside and outside the region, and, thus, it is possible to base an individual's choice of migrating on a trade-off between differences in income across regions and locational preference. Partial mobility of labor is justified against polar cases based on the latter's inability to capture appropriate welfare effects of policies pursued under Confederation.

Individuals would either have no direct association with specific regions – in the case of perfect mobility of labor – or not respond to policies on fiscally induced migration – in the case of interregional labor immobility. In Gazel (1994), labor mobility was given special attention. In a variant of the basic model – in which labor is immobile – labor was allowed to move following the utility-equalization-across-space hypothesis of open city models in urban economics. Labor supply in each region responds to wage and price differentials up to the point when utility is the same in all regions.

Theoretical Specification

In the elaboration of a CGE model, different blocks of equations have to be specified. The basic structure comprises three blocks of equations determining demand and supply relations, and market clear conditions. In the stylized model depicted in the last section, it implies the algebraic specification of the demand functions, φ, and the supply functions, γ. Production technology and structure of household demand determine these functional forms, and, in interregional models, they are commonly based on multilevel structures, which enable a great number of substitution possibilities. Models that have been produced so far share common features in such nesting structures.

Figure 2.1 illustrates the basic variations of production technology encountered in most models. Dotted-lined boxes represent standard functional forms used at each stage. Two broad categories of inputs are recognized: intermediate inputs and primary factors. Producers in each regional industry choose inputs requirements per unit of output through optimizing behavior (e.g. cost minimization). Constraints are given by the nested production technology. In the first level, primary factors and an intermediate-input bundle are combined, either assuming fixed proportions (Leontief) or some degree of substitution between them (Cobb-Douglas or CES). The use of CES production functions at the top level of the production structure dominates modeling procedures. Fixed proportion combinations of intermediate inputs are assumed in the second level, on one side, and substitution between capital and labor, on the other side. The third level involves substitution between domestically produced and imported intermediate inputs. At the fourth level, bundles of domestically produced inputs are formed as combinations of inputs from different regional sources.

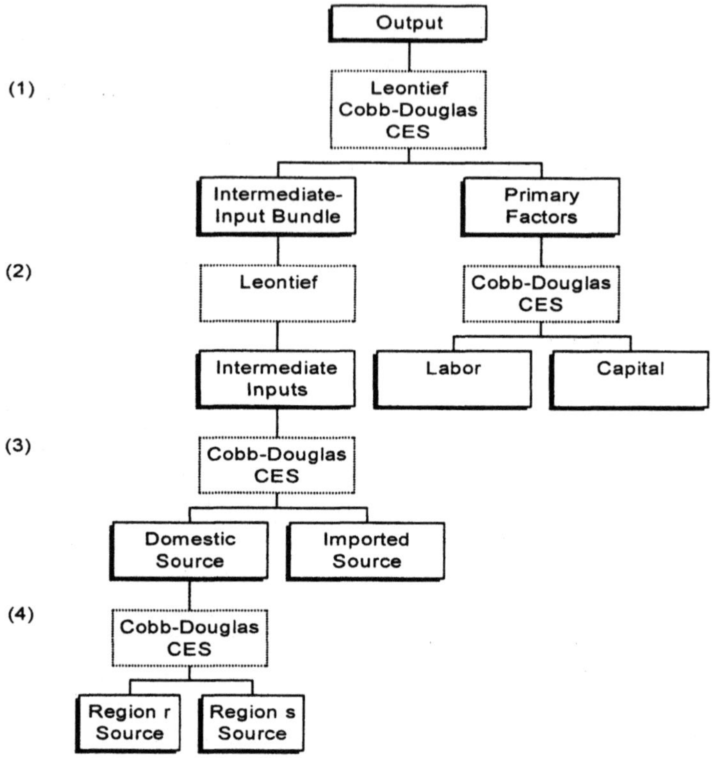

Figure 2.1 Standard Nesting Structures of Regional Production Technology in Interregional CGE Models

Standard modeling procedures use either Cobb-Douglas or constant elasticity of substitution (CES) functions in the lower levels to combine goods from different sources. More flexible functional forms have been rarely attempted in regional models, due to data availability. One exception in regional CGE modeling is the model developed by Despotakis and Fisher (1988) for California. In that model, a generalized Leontief specification is adopted. Dixon *et al.* (1982) propose the use of constant ratios of elasticities of substitution, homothetic (CRESH) functions, a generalization of CES which allows for elasticities of substitution between different pairs of inputs to differ. However, the estimation procedure was not satisfactory, leading the authors to adopt CES estimates.

The treatment of household demand structure, depicted in Figure 2.2, is also standard in most of the interregional CGEs. It is based on nested

Cobb-Douglas (or CES)/linear expenditure system (LES) preference functions. Demand equations are derived from an utility maximization problem, whose solution follows hierarchical steps. It resembles the utility tree and multiple-stage budgeting problem analyzed in Deaton and Muellbauer (1980), in which separable preferences enable stepwise choices according to different group levels of commodities. In the interregional context, group dimensions refer to regional sources of commodities. The structure of household demand follows a nesting pattern which enables different elasticities of substitution to be used. At the bottom level, substitution occurs across different regional domestic sources of supply. Utility derived from the consumption of domestic composite goods is maximized. In the subsequent upper level, substitution occurs between domestic composite and imported goods.

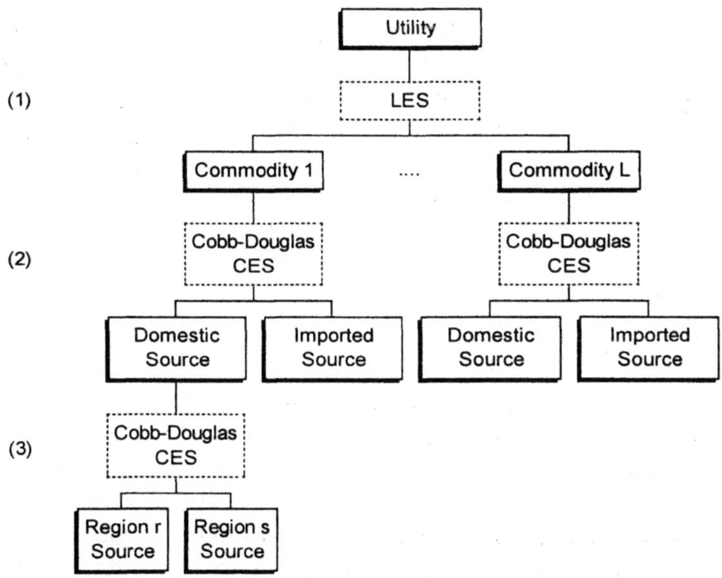

Figure 2.2 Standard Nesting Structure of Regional Household Demand in Interregional CGE Models

The generalized use of Leontief, Cobb-Douglas and CES specifications in the production side of regional CGE models, and LES in the household demand side is partly explained by the structural properties of such functions [see Dixon *et al.* (1983) for a detailed theoretical analysis]. These functional forms have been conveniently used in empirical applications. Their low requirements for parameters determination is the main attractiveness for modelers, specially when calibration of large-scale models is to take place (Koh *et al.*, 1993).

Calibration

The calibration of regional CGE models, i.e., the assignment of values to the relevant parameters and coefficients of the model, is a very demanding process. It consists of fitting the model specification to a consistently adjusted basic data set for the economy for a single year. This procedure determines the parameters values of the model for a benchmark equilibrium. [Shoven and Whalley (1992), and Koh *et al.* (1993) discuss the calibration procedure of CGE models.] Interregional input-output tables provide the various production and consumption estimates. Specification of exogenous elasticities values is also needed.

Interregional commodity flows data are seldom available. It has been common practice in regional CGE modeling to use nonsurvey techniques to estimate them, which might incorporate bias in the model estimates. Gravity-type models (Leontief and Strout, 1963), contingency table method (Batten, 1982), and a combination of Round's method (Round, 1978, 1983) and *ad hoc* splits of rows and columns of national tables based on extraneous regional shares (Hulu and Hewings, 1993) are examples of techniques utilized. In Gazel (1994), great attention was given to the estimation of the interregional trade matrix. The method developed by Hulu and Hewings (1993) was adopted, and sensitivity analysis for the interregional trade flows data was carried out in which a 10% increase in imports was assumed. Remarkable differences were noted for labor and capital incomes, but not for the aggregated income.[5]

Even though consistent non-survey techniques for the estimation of interregional trade flows are available, the quality of regional data has always been a problem. A validation test was carried out in Ko (1985), showing that results for the national aggregates are far better than those for regional variables. The improvement of the regional results would involve the availability of better data.

---

[5] The choice of input-output data for regional models is an important issue in regional modeling. A recent paper by Israilevich *et al.* (1996) reveals that differently constructed input-output tables would have a significant effect on the results of a regional econometric model, both in forecast and impact analyses; Haddad *et al.* (1998) evaluate the choice of the input-output data embedded in an interregional CGE system, showing differences for different closures.

Bias in the estimates of the MONASH-MRF model (Naqvi and Peter, 1996) is compromised by the estimation procedure of the interregional input-output. The spatial disaggregation of the national input-output table relied on *ad hoc* column and row splits based on regional shares. The use of other non-survey techniques that carry the theoretical background essential to a more reliable construction of regional input-output tables under limited information, widely available in the literature, should be considered [see Round (1978, 1983), Hulu and Hewings (1993)].

Another data-related problem that modelers frequently face is the lack of trade elasticities at the regional level. The pocket rule is to use international trade elasticities as benchmarks for "best guess" procedures. Other elasticities are commonly borrowed from econometric studies; in this case, more reliable estimates are available. Sensitivity analysis for key parameters are sometimes performed, providing a more reliable range of model results.

Closure

The selection of the set of exogenous variables determines many features of the use of the model. Closure reflects the theoretical orientation and the type of simulation of the experiment being undertaken. In regional models, specifically, they define the settings that will determine the interactions among regional markets. McGregor *et al.* (1996) consider a range of alternatives on wage determination by using different labor market closures. In the neoclassical closure, regional wage adjusts so as to continuously clear the region's labor market, while in the Keynesian closure, nominal wages are fixed. It is shown that, by alternating closures representing contrasting macroeconimc visions of a regional economic system, the direction and scale of the interregional transmission of disturbances are affected.

The determination of regional investment in Peter *et al.* (1996b) is specified by different closures, implying distinct experiments: short-run and long-run comparative statics, and forecasting. In short-run experiments, capital stocks in regional industries and national aggregate investment are exogenously determined; aggregate investment is distributed among the regional industries on the basis of relative rates of return. In long-run comparative statics experiments, it is assumed that the aggregate capital stock adjusts to preserve an exogenously determined economy-wide rate of return. Further, it is assumed that the allocation of capital across regional industries adjusts to satisfy exogenously specified relationships between relative rates of return and relative capital growth; industries' demands for investment goods are determined by exogenously specified investment/capital ratios. Finally, in forecasting experiments, regional industry demand for investment is determined by an assumption on the rate of growth of industry capital stock and an accumulation relation linking capital stock and investment between the forecast year and the year immediately following the forecast year. Forecasting closure demands that changes in all exogenous variables over the simulation period be taken into account. In general, this information has to be taken from extraneous sources. Time is also taken into consideration in historical closures, which might be utilized to update the input-output data base.

One important issue raised when one moves to the interregional context refers to the macroeconomic closure of such systems. It becomes more complicated when compared to single-region models, in which the small-economy assumption holds, implying the exogeneity of prices and demands from the rest of the economy, as well as interest and exchange rates. Regional prices and quantities are taken care of in the bottom-up approach, but a more precise specification of interest rate and exchange rates still remains to de defined. In AMOS-RUK (McGregor *et al.*, 1996), this issue is extensively discussed, but a solution for the treatment of nationwide prices seems to await further work.

Solution Method

A final remark on model specification and implementation refers to the solution method. Not so long ago, computational costs were always cited as a huge constraint in CGE modeling. The inclusion of a regional dimension to sectorally disaggregated CGE models increases the size of the system dramatically. Interregional models increase in size with the square of the number of regions. Some sacrifice in terms of sectoral aggregation and/or the range of intersectoral relationships to be included in interregional models was usually advocated and almost always necessary (Parmenter, 1983). Nowadays, computational costs do not play such a crucial role anymore. The recent developments in the computer industry allied to the development of software designed specifically for implementing and solving general and partial equilibrium models (e.g., GEMPACK, GAMS) reduced the limits of model sizes to memory requirements.

Solution methods adopted for regional CGE models fall into the same two broad classes as those for general CGEs: modifications of the Scarf algorithm, and the Johansen procedure for linearized models. One of the first modifications of the Scarf solution for regional models was discussed in Kimbell and Harrison (1984). The Johansen procedure is widely used in the Australian tradition, in the work by Dixon, Liew, Parmenter, and Peter, among others. Harrison *et al.* (1994) describe the implementation of Johansen-type multiregional models via GEMPACK. Special features of the software facilitates the work of model builders, increasing the flexibility of their models.

Final Remarks

The development of regional and interregional CGE modeling has experienced, in the last ten years, an upsurge in interest. Different models have been built for different regions of the world. Research groups, located especially in Australia, North America and the UK, and individual researchers contributed to these developments through the specification and implementation of a variety of alternative models. However, much effort is still needed in the field. Issues such as the integration of disaggregated regional labor markets, the incorporation of financial markets, and different institutional frameworks including imperfect competition are examples of important theoretical issues to be operationally addressed in future work.

The use of CGE models in the regional context should be appealing for policy makers. Data availability has always been of great concern to regional scientists, and regional econometric models often encounter severe problems in their specification and implementation. First, reliable time-series data for sufficiently long periods are not available at the regional level, and, when available, the data often present inconsistencies which affect econometric estimation procedures. Second, regional structural changes appear to be very dynamic, which call for different structural models, thereby reducing the time span available for hypothesis testing with a selected econometric model (see De Melo, 1988). However, CGE models are not without their limitations – especially their limited ability to handle dynamics. Hence, they should be viewed as complement to existing models rather than as replacement.

The interregional CGE model for the Brazilian economy (B-MARIA) developed in this study tackles many of the issues discussed above. B-MARIA is the first fully operational interregional CGE model for Brazil, containing three regions and forty sectors in each region, which makes it a relatively detailed interregional CGE model. The model is used to analyze regional imbalances and structural changes in the Brazilian economy emphasizing the role of backwash and spread effects, which are qualitatively described in the regional development literature as the mechanisms driving regional (in)equity (e.g. Myrdal, 1957, Hirschman, 1958). The results are driven by price effects and the operation of internal and external multipliers in the regional economies.

The interregional input-output table used in the calibration of the model is derived from published regional tables, which are integrated in an interregional system consistent with the national tables. The estimation of the interregional trade flows is based on the method proposed by Hulu and Hewings (1993) and benefits from the existence of aggregate regional trade estimates. It is shown that a deep understanding of the relations presented in the benchmark data base facilitates the analysis of the model's results.

In many instances, the way the input-output data are compiled enables theoretical innovations in the specification of the models. The availability of key information for the calibration of specific coefficients motivates experiments with the structure of the model. For instance, the nature of the input-output data base used in this book enables the isolation of the consumption of public goods by both the Federal and regional governments, which encourages the experimental specification of the government demand for public goods.

Another instance in which data availability induces theoretical experimentation in B-MARIA relates to the group of equations defining the government accounts. The existence of a previously developed data base for regional government accounts (Dinsmoor and Haddad, 1996) accommodates a common budget structure which enhances the disaggregation and specification of the revenue and expenditure components of government accounts. However, in most cases, experiments with different structures of the model do not pay the extra modeling effort. In the Brazilian model, the existence of a group of equations, theoretically specified, that contains accumulation relations to facilitate forecasting with the model, does not produce reliable results. Unavailability of consistent time series at the regional level for Brazil precludes this specification to be operationalized.

A unique feature of B-MARIA is the explicit modeling of the transportation services and the costs of moving products based on origin-destination pairs. The model is calibrated taking into account the specific transportation structure cost of each commodity flow, providing spatial price differentiation, which indirectly addresses the issue related to regional transportation infrastructure efficiency.

One way to overcome the scarcity of estimates of regional trade elasticities (and any other key parameter), suggested here, is to estimate policy results based on different qualitative sets of values for the parameters. Starting with international trade estimates, if available, the calibration should be based on the specific characteristics of each commodity. The characteristics of each sector have to be considered individually and the commodities can, thus, be grouped. Through the judgment of the modeler, a range of alternative combinations reflecting differential technological hypothesis for the regional economies can be used to achieve a range of results for a policy simulation. This method, hereafter called *qualitative or structural sensitivity analysis*,[6] provides a "confidence interval" to policy makers, and incorporates an extra component to the model's results which contributes to increased robustness through the use of possible structural scenarios. As data deficiency has always been a big concern in regional modeling, one which will not be overcome in the near future, this method tries to adjust the model for possible parameter mispecification. Qualitative sensitivity analysis should be used on a regular basis in regional CGE modeling in order to avoid, paradoxically, speculative conclusions over policy outcomes. If the modeler knows enough about the functioning of the particular national and regional economies, the model achieves a greater degree of accuracy when such procedure is adopted. These issues are further discussed throughout the book. In the next chapter, the theoretical structure of the Brazilian model is delineated. Attention is directed to the main equations determining the functioning mechanisms of the model.

[6] The term "qualitative sensitivity analysis" is used as opposed to "quantitative sensitivity analysis", which is the common practice adopted by modelers to define confidence intervals for the simulations' results. Usually, the parameters are allowed to deviate over a range centered in the initial assigned values, or to present small increases/decrease in one direction, which does not address the likely cases of structural mispecifications (see Haddad *et al.*, 1998).

3 The Theoretical Specification of B-MARIA

The **B**razilian **M**ultisectoral **A**nd **R**egional/**I**nterregional **A**nalysis Model (B-MARIA) is the first fully operational interregional CGE model for Brazil. The model is based on the MONASH-MRF Model, which is the latest development in the ORANI suite of CGE models of the Australian economy. B-MARIA contains over 200,000 equations, and it is designed for forecasting and policy analysis. Agents' behavior is modeled at the regional level, accommodating variations in the structure of regional economies. The model recognizes the economies of three Brazilian regions: North, Northeast, and Center-South (Rest of Brazil). Results are based on a bottom-up approach – national results are obtained from the aggregation of regional results. The model identifies 40 sectors (industries) in each region producing 40 commodities; there is a one-to-one correspondence between sectors and commodities, i.e., industry *j* produces only commodity *j* and is the sole producer of that commodity. Two commodities (trade and transportation) are used as margins. The list of sectors/commodities is presented in Table 3.1.

The model also identifies a single household in each region, regional governments and one federal government, and a single foreign consumer who trades with each region. Special groups of equations define government finances, accumulation relations, and regional labor markets. In the Brazilian tradition of modeling, it benefits from the work by Guilhoto (1986, 1995), whose PAPA model represented a computable national model of the Johansen type with the solutions given in growth rates. Besides the Moreira and Urani (1994) model for the Northeast Brazil, which is rooted in the requirement analysis framework, and, therefore, does not provide any supply-side constraint, B-MARIA is the first attempt to model the Brazilian economy in an interregional general equilibrium framework, taking into account both demand and supply constraints. [For a survey of CGE models applied for the Brazilian economy, see Guilhoto and Fonseca (1990), Moreira and Urani (1994), and Guilhoto (1995).]

Table 3.1 Sectors of B-MARIA

S1	Agriculture
S2	Mining
S3	Nonmetallic Minerals
S4	Steel
S5	Nonferrous Metals
S6	Other Metal Products
S7	Machinery
S8	Electrical Equipment
S9	Electronic Equipment
S10	Transportation Equipment
S11	Wood Products and Furniture
S12	Paper Products and Printing
S13	Rubber
S14	Chemicals
S15	Petroleum Refining
S16	Other Chemicals
S17	Pharmaceuticals and Veterinary
S18	Plastics
S19	Textiles
S20	Clothing
S21	Footwear
S22	Coffee
S23	Processed Vegetables
S24	Meat Packing Plants
S25	Dairy Products
S26	Sugar
S27	Vegetable Oil Mills
S28	Other Food Products
S29	Other Manufacturing
S30	Electric, Gas, and Sanitary Services
S31	Construction
S32	Trade
S33	Transportation
S34	Communication
S35	Financial Institutions
S36	Personal services
S37	Business Services
S38	Real Estate
S39	Public Administration
S40	Community Services

The historical development of the model is presented in Figure 3.1. The starting point is the pioneering work by Johansen (1960). In his study, a multisectoral model for the Norwegian economy was presented, based on cost-minimizing industries and an utility-maximizing household sector. In the early 1970s, a group of Australian researchers, led by Professors Peter Dixon, Alan Powell and Brian Parmenter, developed the ORANI model as part of an ambitious government-funded research project, the IMPACT Project. Its aim was to develop a framework for policy studies of the Australian economy which would improve the quality and consistency of the policy advice available to the government (Kenderes, 1990). The ORANI model, a Johansen-type CGE model for the Australian economy, is now considered a benchmark in the applied general equilibrium literature. Its continuing development and evaluation have brought about important contributions to theory and computational methods in the field of applied economics. The model has been used as the basis of national models for different countries, including Brazil (Guilhoto, 1986 and 1995), and South Africa (Horridge *et al.*, 1995).

The MONASH model and its interregional version, the MONASH-MRF, represent the results of the latest full cycle of development of ORANI. They are both designed for comparative-static and forecasting simulations; in the latter case, annual projections over medium-run periods are made available (e.g. Adams and Dixon, 1995). B-MARIA is a policy information system which benefits directly from the theoretical structure of MONASH-MRF. It also benefits from the PAPA model – the Brazilian version of ORANI – by using some shortcuts in the modeling process, especially in the search for parameters stage.

In this chapter, an overview of the theoretical structure of the model is presented. The complete model specification is available in Haddad and Hewings (1997). Excerpts from the TABLO input file, which contains the equations of the model written down in a syntax which is very similar to ordinary algebra, will be presented in an appendix.[1] Prior to the description of the model, an overview of the mathematical structure of B-MARIA and an introduction to the Johansen/Euler solution method are provided. Comments on the closure and the test of the model are presented in the final section.

[1] For a complete description of TABLO input files and their use in the implementation of CGE models via GEMPACK, see Harrison and Pearson (1996).

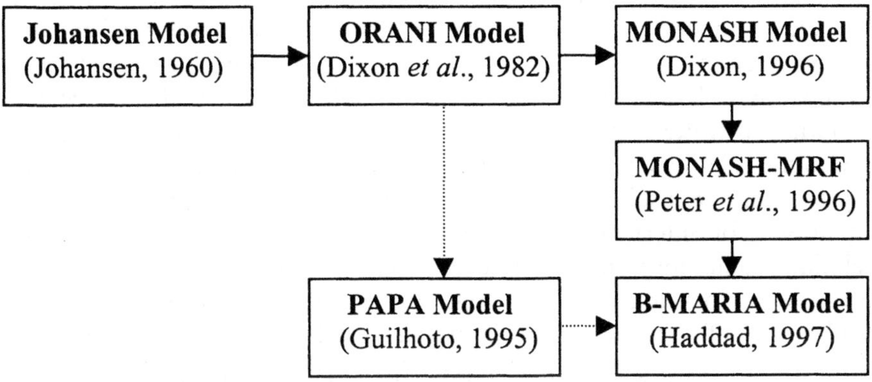

Figure 3.1 Historical Development of B-MARIA

Mathematical Structure and Solution Method

B-MARIA is based on the interregional version of the MONASH Model, the MONASH Multiregional Forecasting Model – MONASH-MRF (Naqvi and Peter, 1995; Peter *et al.*, 1996b). The equations of the CGE core module of the model are defined following the structure of the ORANI Model (Dixon *et al.*, 1982), with a regional subscript added, when appropriate. It qualifies as a Johansen-type model in that the solutions are obtained by solving the system of *linearized* equations of the model. A typical result shows the percentage change in the set of endogenous variables, after a policy is carried out, compared to their values in the absence of such policy, in a given environment.

The schematic presentation of Johansen solutions for such models is standard in the literature. What follows is a summary of its contents in order to see how these models work. More details can be found in Dixon *et al.* (1982, 1992), Harrison and Pearson (1994, 1996), and Dixon and Parmenter (1994).

In the Johansen approach, the system of linearized equations of the model can be written as

$$F(V) = 0 \tag{3.1}$$

where V is an equilibrium vector of length n (number of variables), and F is a vector function of length m (number of equations), which is assumed to be differentiable. Regarding the dimensions, *n* and *m*, it is assumed that the total number of variables is greater than the total number of equations in the system, i.e., $(n > m)$. Thus, $(n - m)$ variables must be set exogenously. Examples of economic variables contained in the vector V include quantities, prices, taxes, and technological coefficients. The economic relations depicted in the system (3.1) are comprised of equations representing household and other final demands for commodities, equations for intermediate and primary-factor inputs, pricing equations relating commodity prices to cost, and market clearing equations for primary factors and commodities, among others. For the purpose of calibration of the system, it is fundamental to assume that an initial solution, V^*, is known. In other words, $\exists V = V^* s.t.\ F(V^*) = 0$.

For B-MARIA, part of the vector V^* is read from the interregional input-output data base especially designed from the regional input-output tables for the North and Northeast regions, and from the national input-output tables for Brazil, for the year of 1985. Given the initial solution, V^*, the basic approach used to compute a new set of solutions to the model starts with assigning the variables to the exogenous and endogenous categories.[2] Let V_1 be the vector of *m* endogenous variables, and V_2 be the vector of $(n - m)$ exogenous variables. Equation (3.1) can be rewritten as

$$F(V_1, V_2) = 0 \tag{3.2}$$

By totally differentiating (3.2), we get

$$F_1(V^*)dV_1 + F_2(V^*)dV_2 = 0 \tag{3.3}$$

where F_1 and F_2 are matrices of partial derivatives of F evaluated at V^*. Solving (4.3) for dV_1,

$$dV_1 = \underbrace{\left[-F_1^{-1}(V^*)F_2(V^*)\right]}_{B\left(V^*\right)} dV_2 \tag{3.4}$$

or

$$dV_1 = B(V^*)dV_2 \tag{3.5}$$

[2] The following describes the one-step Johansen/Euler solution.

It is assumed that the relevant inverse, $F_1^{-1}(V^*)$, exists.

In the B-MARIA model, the specification of *F*, i.e., the specification of the equations of the model, is presented in five different integrated blocks of equations: the CGE core module, the government finance module, the capital accumulation and investment module, the foreign debt accumulation module, and the labor market and regional migration module.

Linearization Errors. Because $B(V^*)$ is the matrix of first-order partial derivatives of *F*, evaluated at the initial values of the model's variables, V^*, the solution achieved by the procedure described above represents an approximation of the "true" solution. As one moves away from V^*, the partial derivatives of *F* are also moving. This fact produces errors between the model solution and the "true" solution derived from any change in the initial set of exogenous variables, due to the linearization of the equations of the model.

To solve this problem, and, thus, get more accurate results, a multi-step computation procedure is introduced, in which the exogenous shock is divided into *p* equal parts. Hence, a sequence of Johansen-style computations is used, in which the matrix *B* is reevaluated at each step. The question that arises concerns the manner in which the model solution converges to the "true" solution as *p* goes to infinity, and, if so, to the number of steps, i.e., the size of *p*, that is necessary to obtain an accurate solution of the model. Dixon *et al.* (1982) shows that one can be confident that as *p* approaches infinity, multi-step Johansen/Euler method will produce an exact model solution. Moreover, the experience with ORANI and MONASH reveals that highly accurate solutions are obtained by applying this method with very few steps, say $p \leq 4$, supplemented by an extrapolation procedure.

The two-step Johansen/Euler computation ($p = 2$) is illustrated in Figure 3.2, for the two-variable case. The change in the exogenous variable, V_2, is divided into two equal parts. Accordingly, the first step in the computation of the solution for the exogenous change, dV_2, produces the value $V_1^* + dV_1$ for the endogenous variable. At point *D*, the slope of the function is reevaluated, and the second step takes place. It is clear that this procedure reduces the computation errors as the number of steps increase (in the example, the error is reduced by $\overline{BC}$).

Figure 3.2 Two-Step Solution Method to Reduce Linearization Error: Two-Variable Illustrative Diagram

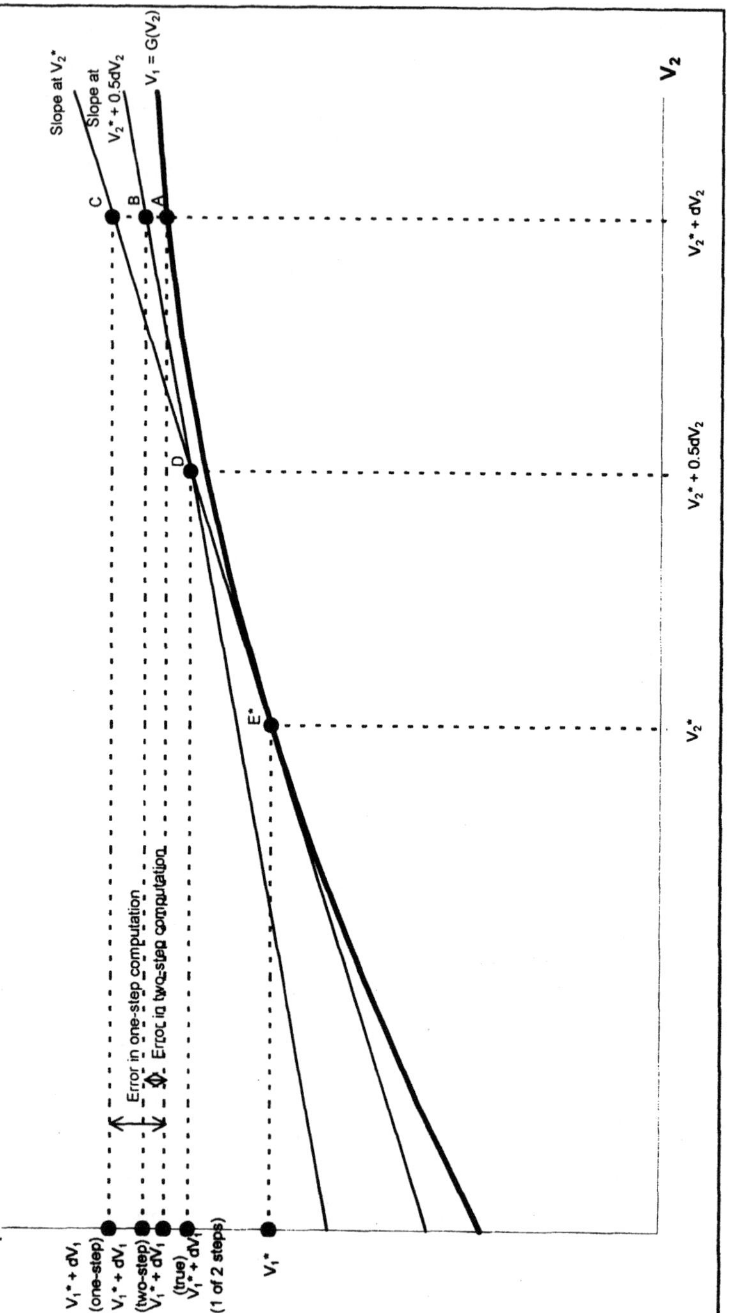

GEMPACK provides alternative solution methods in order to minimize linearization errors. The default method used by the software is Gragg's method which uses an even more accurate method than Johansen/Euler method for calculating the direction to move at each step. When the shocks are broken into p parts, Euler's method does p separate calculations while Gragg's method does $p+1$. At step 1, Gragg and Euler are identical, following a tangent along the curve from the initial solution. At other steps, both methods take their direction from the tangent at the current point; the difference is that Gragg's method follows this direction starting from the previous point, while Euler's method follows the tangent from the current point. GEMPACK also makes available the midpoint method, which is very similar to Gragg's method. Hence, one way of increasing accuracy is to increase the number of steps. It turns out, however, that the best way to obtain an accurate solution is to carry out 2 or 3 different multi-step calculations with different numbers of steps and then to calculate the solution as an appropriate weighted average of these; this is what is meant by the extrapolation solution (Harrison and Pearson, 1996).

Model Specification

The basic structure of the CGE core module comprises three main blocks of equations determining demand and supply relations, that are derived from optimizing assumptions, and market clearing conditions. In addition, various regional and national aggregates, such as aggregate employment, aggregate price level, and balance of trade, are defined here. There are, in total, nineteen groups of equations.

Figure 3.3 illustrates the basic production technology adopted in B-MARIA, which is a common specification in regional models. Dotted-line boxes represent functional forms used at each stage. Two broad categories of inputs are recognized: intermediate inputs and primary factors. Producers in each regional industry choose input requirements per unit of output through optimizing behavior (cost minimization). Constraints are given by the nested production technology. Fixed proportion combinations of intermediate inputs and primary factors are assumed in the first level. The second level involves substitution between domestically produced and imported intermediate inputs, on one side, and substitution between capital, labor and land, on the other side. At the third level, bundles of domestically produced inputs are formed as combinations of inputs from different regional sources. The modeling procedure adopted in B-MARIA uses constant elasticity of substitution (CES) specification in the lower levels to combine goods from different sources.

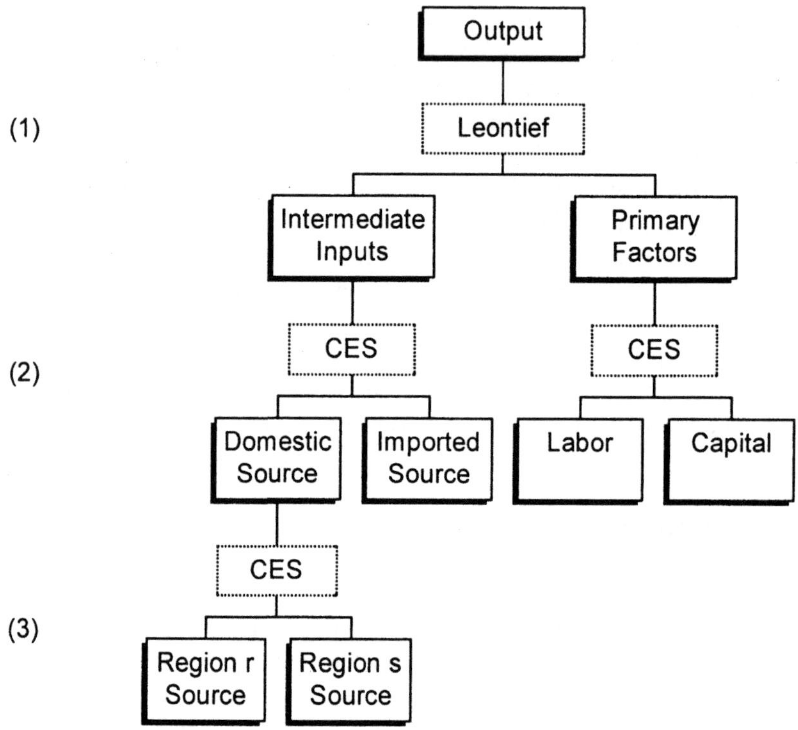

Figure 3.3 Nesting Structure of Regional Production Technology

The treatment of the household demand structure, depicted in Figure 3.4, is based on a nested CES/linear expenditure system (LES) preference function. Demand equations are derived from a utility maximization problem, whose solution follows hierarchical steps. The structure of household demand follows a nesting pattern that enables different elasticities of substitution to be used. At the bottom level, substitution occurs across different domestic sources of supply. Utility derived from the consumption of domestic composite goods is maximized. In the subsequent upper-level, substitution occurs between domestic composite and imported goods.

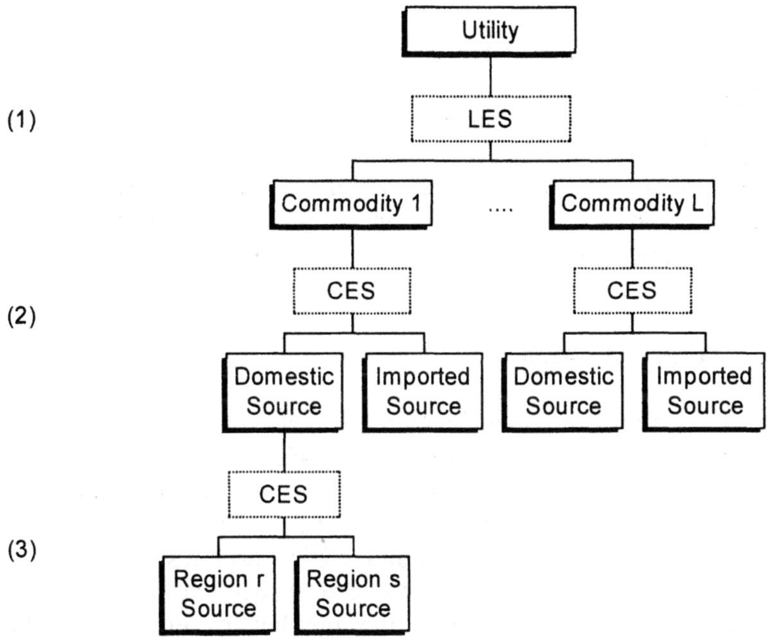

Figure 3.4 Nesting Structure of Regional Household Demand

Equations for other final demand for commodities include the specification of export demand and government demand. Exports are divided into two groups: traditional exports (agriculture, mining, coffee, and sugar), and non-traditional exports. The former faces downward sloping demand curves, indicating that traditional exports are a negative function of their prices in the world market. Non-traditional exports form a composite tradable bundle, in which commodity shares are fixed. Demand is related to the average price of this bundle.

One new feature presented in B-MARIA refers to the government demand for *public goods*. The nature of the input-output data base enables the isolation of the consumption of public goods by both the federal and regional governments. However, productive activities carried out by the public sector cannot be isolated from those by the private sector. Thus, government entrepreneurial behavior is dictated by the same cost minimization assumptions adopted by the private sector. This may be a very strong assumption for the Brazilian case but the liberalization process of the 1990's offers some enhanced credibility for this assumption. Public good consumption is set to maintain a (constant) proportion with regional private consumption, in the case of regional governments, and with national private consumption, in the case of the federal government.

Other definitions in the CGE core module include: tax rates, basic and purchase prices of commodities, tax revenues, margins, components of real and nominal GRP/GDP, regional and national price indices, money wage settings, factor prices, and employment aggregates. The description of the main groups of equations is described at the end of the book in a technical appendix, in thematic order.

Closing and Testing the Model

The system of equations provides the theoretical structure of the model. B-MARIA contains 243,754 equations and 246,901 variables. In the implementation of the model, the linearized version of the model was condensed by eliminating some equations and variables, generating a reduced version with 4,831 equations and 7,243 variables. To close the model, values for 2,412 variables have to be set exogenously (the number of endogenous variables must equal the number of equations). The condensation procedure, i.e., the reduction of the size of the model, is carried out by substituting out variables that are to be endogenous and are of less interest to the analysis and presentation of the simulation results, and by omitting variables that are to be exogenous and not shocked in the simulations. Given the dimensions of the original specification of B-MARIA, this step had to be applied to solve the model. The high degree of endogeneity of the model, as represented by the relative small number of exogenous variables required in the closure of its complete version, allows for such reduction in size.

The choice of the set of exogenous variables is very flexible in B-MARIA. Different economic environments can be set up by different choices of exogenous and endogenous categories. Even though there are many legitimate possibilities of assigning variables to the endogenous and exogenous sets, not all possible combinations of variables are acceptable. Some care is necessary to avoid inconsistencies. B-MARIA can be closed to reflect short-run and long-run comparative-static, as well as forecasting simulations. Although a forecasting closure might be theoretically delineated (Peter *et al.*, 1996b), availability of reliable, consistent time series at the regional level for Brazil precludes this option to be operationalized. At this stage, two standard closures for alternative time frames of analysis in single-period simulations are available. A distinction between the two closures relates to the treatment of capital stocks encountered in the standard microeconomic approach to policy adjustments. In the short-run closure, capital stocks are held fixed, while, in the long-run, policy changes are allowed to affect capital stocks.

Short-run. In addition to the assumption of interindustry and interregional immobility of capital, the short-run closure would include fixed regional population and labor supply, fixed regional wage differentials, and fixed national real wage. Regional employment is driven by the assumptions on wage rates, which indirectly determine regional unemployment rates. These assumptions describe the functioning of the regional labor markets as close as possible to the Brazilian reality. First, changes in the demand for labor are met by changes in the unemployment rate, rather than by changes in the real wage. This seems to be the case in Brazil, given the high level of disguised unemployment in most of the areas of the country; excess supply of labor has been a distinct feature of the Brazilian economy. Secondly, interregional immobility of labor in the short-run suggests that migration is not a short-term decision. Finally, nominal wage differentials in Brazil are persistent, reflecting the geographical segmentation of the workforce (Savedoff, 1990). On the demand side, investment expenditures are fixed exogenously – firms cannot reevaluate their investment decisions in the short-run. Household consumption follows household disposable income, and government consumption, at both regional and federal levels, is fixed (alternatively, the government deficit can be set exogenously, allowing government expenditures to change). Finally, since the model does not present any endogenous-growth-theory-type specification, technology variables are exogenous (Peter, 1997).

Long-run. A long-run (steady-state) equilibrium closure is also available in which capital is mobile across regions and industries. Capital and investment are generally assumed to grow at the same rate. The main differences from the short-run are encountered in the labor market and the capital formation settings. In the first case, aggregate employment is determined by population growth, labor force participation rates, and the natural rate of unemployment. The distribution of the labor force across regions and sectors is fully determined endogenously. Labor is attracted to more competitive industries in more favored geographical areas. While in the same way, capital is oriented towards more attractive industries. This movement keeps rates of return at their initial levels.

The proposed closures do not exhaust the possibilities of specifying the economic environment under which the exogenous shocks take place.[3] As mentioned above, the choice of exogenous variables can be made in different ways. B-MARIA, following the ORANI tradition of modeling, allows a great degree of freedom to reclassifiy variables between the exogenous and endogenous categories, which is very useful for policy and other applications of the model.

Finally, after B-MARIA was implemented and calibrated,[4] a test of the model was carried out to check for computational errors. Given the theoretical structure of the model, the expected results of a homogeneity test are already known: by shocking the *numéraire* by one per cent, since the model is homogeneous, it is expected that all nominal variables increase by one per cent, and all quantity variables remain unchanged. A test simulation for the B-MARIA model under the standard short-run closure was carried out, and the results confirmed expectation.

---

[3] The closures are further discussed in Chapter 5, together with the model's applications.

[4] Calibration is discussed in the next chapter.

4 Linkage and Interdependence in the Brazilian Economy: The B-MARIA Data Input Files

The calibration of the model, i.e., the assignment of values to the relevant parameters and coefficients of the model which produce an initial solution, is based on the data files described in this chapter. By working with percentage changes rather than absolute changes, the coefficients of the model are often readily interpretable cost and sales shares, and they can be derived from input-output tables. Together with values of substitution elasticities, and some supplementary data on values of capital stocks, depreciation rates, demographic variables, and some other variables, the initial solution V^* can be deduced.

In order to generate the interregional input-output table necessary to calibrate the model, published tables for the North (SUDAM, 1994), Northeast (BNB, 1992) and Brazil (FIBGE, 1995) were used; estimates refer to 1985, the year of the last economic censuses for the country. They provide a good picture of the Brazilian economic structure before the policy changes analyzed in this book, which is an essential requirement for counterfactual exercises as the ones to be carried out in the next chapter. An attempt to reconcile the national and the regional tables in an integrated regional system was made, using a similar procedure to the one proposed by Hulu and Hewings (1993), preserving the original properties of the data set. The basic procedure was to disaggregate the national tables using the published regional estimates as starting points. Data for a third region (Center-South) were estimated by residual, using the national tables as the desirable adding-up total. The structure of the derived input-output data base for the CGE core of the model is shown in Figure 4.1; the labels assigned for each block in the absorption matrix represent the corresponding matrix of the values of flows of commodities, margins, indirect taxes, and primary factors. For instance, BAS1 is a four-dimensional array showing the flows of 40 commodities, produced in 4 different regions, to be used as inputs in the production of 40 industries in each of the 3 Brazilian regions.

			ABSORPTION MATRIX															
			1			2			3			4	5			6		
			Producers			Investors			Household			X	Regional Govt.			Federal Govt.		
		Size	40	40	40	40	40	40	1	1	1	1	1	1	1	1	1	1
	Size	Source	N	NE	CS	N	NE	CS	N	NE	CS		N	NE	CS	N	NE	CS
Basic Flows	40	N	BAS1			BAS2			BAS3			BAS4	BAS5			BAS6		
	40	NE																
	40	CS																
	40	IM																
Margins (Trade)	40	N	MAR1			MAR2			MAR3			MAR4	MAR5			MAR6		
	40	NE																
	40	CS																
	40	IM																
Margins (Trans.)	40	N	MAR1			MAR2			MAR3			MAR4	MAR5			MAR6		
	40	NE																
	40	CS																
	40	IM																
Taxes	40	N	TAX1			TAX2			TAX3			TAX4	TAX5			TAX6		
	40	NE																
	40	CS																
	40	IM																
Labor	3		LABR															
Capital	1		CPTL															
Land	1		LAND															
OCT	1		OCTS															

OCT = other cost "tickets"
Note: Adapted from Peter *et al.* (1996b)

Figure 4.1 The CGE Core Input-Output Data Base: Data Files for B-MARIA

In the next section, the general structure of the absorption matrix is described in terms of summary indicators specifying agents' sales and purchases orientations, and output composition. An evaluation of the production linkages follows, based on the BAS1 flows, providing a comparative analysis of the economic structure of the three regions. Traditional input-output methods are used in an attempt to uncover similarities and differences in the structure of the regional economies. Finally, a brief description of the additional data set used to calibrate the model is presented.

The Structure of the Absorption Matrix

To better understand the results of the model, a thorough analysis of the structure of the economy is needed. A close inspection of the benchmark data base is necessary, conducted not only on the relationships in the input-output data base, but also on the other relevant parameters of the model. The latter will be discussed in the next chapter. In this section, some of the main structural features of the economy are revealed through the use of indicators derived from the absorption matrix. These indicators draw on the idea developed by Chenery and Watanabe (1958), which states that a hierarchy of sectors can be proposed based on ratios of intermediate purchases to total input, and intermediate sales to total output. An analysis of output composition, and sales and purchases shares is presented, considering intermediate demand, final demand, and value added transactions.

Output Composition

Tables 4.4, 4.8, and 4.12 present the output shares for the North, Northeast, and Center-South, respectively. The Center-South region dominates the national production, with a share of 83.32% in total output, followed by the Northeast (12.91%) and the North (3.78%). It is important to notice that, in the benchmark data base, regional population shares estimates are the following: 65.58% (Center-South); 28.77% (Northeast); 5.64% (North).

The relative distribution of output by sector for the three regions is shown in Figure 4.2. The dominant role of agriculture (1), mining (2), and electronic equipment (9) in the North stands out *vis-à-vis* the Northeast and Center-South, while Northeast's specialization in petroleum refining (15) and agriculturally-based production systems (like processed vegetables [23] and sugar [26]) is apparent. In the case of the Center-South, industrial production (3 to 29) is responsible for a higher share in total output. The remaining distributions of the services sectors are rather similar.

Moreover, the regional shares in the output by sector reveal the specialization of Brazil's North in electronic equipment (25.09% of the national output), mining (11.48%), wood products and furniture (9.53%), and agriculture (9.14%). The Northeast specializes in sugar (29.25%), community services (26.78%), mining (23.00%), processed vegetables (21.85%), and personal services (21.37%). It is interesting to point out that the weight of community services is heavily influenced by the adoption of compensatory policies in the region, while personal services reflect the regional orientation to tourism activities. The concentration of industrial activities in the Center-South is evident from the results in Table 4.12. Leading sectors include transportation equipment (97.71%) and the heavy industry (like steel, other metal products, and machinery).

Sales Shares

For each sector, the distribution of sales was calculated based on the different destinations of output. Sales-orientation indicators are very important in the discussion of the model results, since changes in different markets will have differential impact on producers' decisions. Thus, for instance, an export-oriented sector will be more affected by changes in external demands than a sector that sells all its production locally.

Tables 4.1, 4.5, and 4.9 show the sales structure for each sector in the three regions. Regional aggregated results, presented at the bottom of each table, reveal important features of the regional economies. For the Center-South, the high share of sales to intermediate production within the region suggests a high degree of intraregional linkages, which might generate potentially higher internal multipliers. The lower values presented by the North and Northeast suggest a less integrated regional structure in those regions. The share of total extra-regional sales (intermediate, capital creation and household) reflects the degree of interregional dependency of each region, from the point of view of demand from the other regions. Thus, the values for the North (28.68%), Northeast (12.43%), and Center-South (3.73%) establish a hierarchy of interregional dependency within the country. However, when exports to other countries are considered, the Center-South reveals a greater orientation for its sales (Center-South, 6.95%; North, 5.36%; Northeast, 4.49%).

Figure 4.2 Sectoral Shares of Gross Output, by Region, 1985

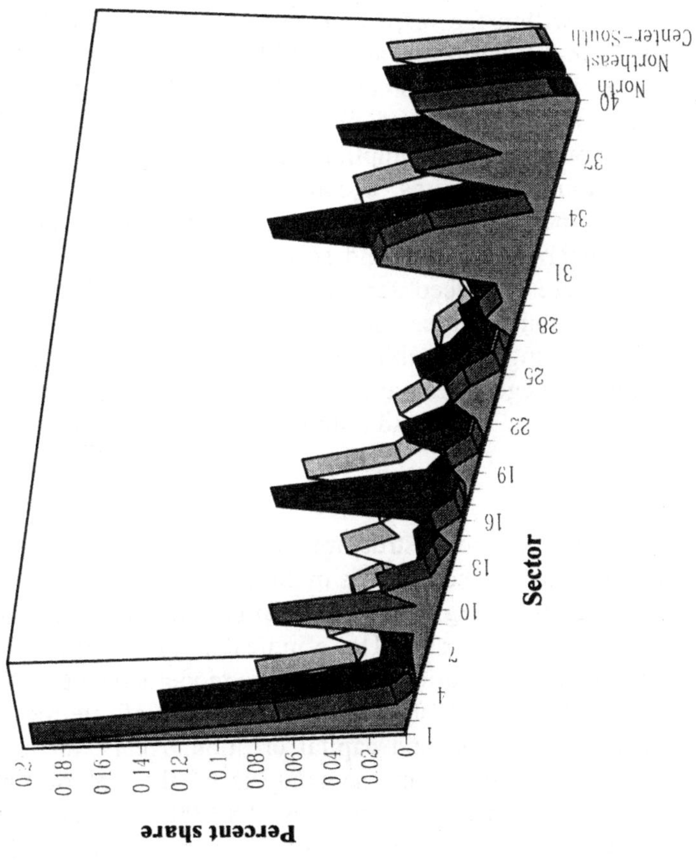

At the sectoral level, sales-orientation varies within the region. Extraregional markets for inputs such as rubber, transportation equipment, mining, and agriculture, from the North, account for a large share of these sectors' sales. Inputs produced by the Northeastern transportation equipment industry and the nonmetallic minerals industry in the Center-South also find a considerable share of their demand outside the respective producing regions. Capital creation within the region is the main user of regional construction. Destination of the regional construction output for capital creation within the respective regions account for 67.80% in the North, 91.05% in the Northeast, and 87.68% in the Center-South. The main destination of electronic equipment produced in the North is outside the region, being for purposes of production (16.85%), capital creation (26.85%) or household consumption (33.91%). Regarding the sales to households within the regions, a common pattern appears in that most goods for consumer's basic needs, such as clothing, dairy products, meat products, and pharmaceuticals, and services such as community services and real estate are produced for the consumption of local households. Export-oriented commodities in each region include mining, paper products and printing, vegetable oil mills, and footwear, in the North; sugar, processed vegetables, and steel, in the Northeast; and coffee, vegetable oil mills, footwear, and mining, in the Center-South.

Purchases Shares

The analysis of the cost structure of different industries and the consumption structure of households in the three regions is provided in this section, focusing on the regional sources of commodities (regional, rest of the country, rest of the world). These indicators are useful for the future analysis of regional substitution effects in the model's results.

Tables 4.2, 4.6, and 4.10 show the cost structure of intermediate inputs used in current production and capital creation. Again, an interregional dependency pattern appears in the analysis of the use of inputs from intraregional and extraregional sources. 88.63% of total intermediate inputs used by industries in the Center-South in current production are provided from regional industries, 3.60% come from the rest of the country, and 7.77% are imported. The situation changes completely for the North, whose industries consume only 54.10% of intermediate inputs from the region, and 40.61% and 5.29% from the rest of the country and from abroad, respectively. Even though the Northeast depends relatively less on foreign inputs (only 1.64% of expenditures on intermediate inputs), that region still has a considerable link with the rest of the country, from where

18.46% of the intermediate inputs are purchased. A similar situation appears in the case of the use of intermediate inputs for capital creation.

Some sectors in the North (steel, transportation equipment, plastics, construction, other chemicals, and other metal products) use more than 50% of their intermediate inputs from other parts of the country, while others (electrical equipment, petroleum refining, nonferrous metals, and electronic equipment) are heavily dependent on inputs from outside the country. In the Northeast, purchases by sectors such as electronic equipment, transportation equipment, pharmaceuticals and veterinary, machinery, footwear, and other metal products from the rest of the country represent more than 40% of sectors' total use of intermediate inputs in current production. The electronic equipment industry also depends heavily on foreign inputs. Finally, the results for the Center-South suggest that the regional production structure depends on primary inputs from outside the region for sectors like meat packing plants, and processed vegetables, on imported oil for the petroleum refining, and other chemicals sectors, as well as on foreign technological-intensive inputs for the transportation, and electronic equipment sectors.

Tables 4.3, 4.7, and 4.11 show the regional composition of the consumption bundle of households, in each region, by commodity. The aggregated results, at the bottom of the tables, reveal a similar pattern of consumption for families at the less developed regions of the North and Northeast, in which commodities from the rest of the country have a considerable weight (28.23%, in the North, and 21.87% in the Northeast). Almost 95% of the goods consumed by households in the Center-South are produced in the region. However, commodity composition varies across regions, revealing region-specific preferences and regional availability of certain goods. For services in general and agriculture, a common pattern is observed; for these commodities over 90% of supply are from within the regions. Electronic equipment produced in Manaus (North) has an important participation in the consumption of this commodity in the three regions; the same happens with transportation equipment, footwear, and pharmaceuticals and veterinary products produced in the Center-South. Foreign goods consumption does not reflect today's situation. In 1985, strong non-tariff barriers heavily restricted the consumption of imported commodities, such as transportation equipment and electronic equipment (it explains the respective low values in the data set). Therefore, the analysis of the results of the simulations should take this fact into account. This is of particular interest in the tariff-cut simulation, in which price-induced substitution between foreign and domestically produced goods is expected to occur.

The sales and purchases relations in the data base, described above, suggest a large asymmetry of changes derived from interregional linkages. The relatively weak intraindustry effects imply that agglomeration economies are likely to be smaller in the North and Northeast.

Other Structural Indicators

Three other indicators were selected from the relationships presented in the absorption matrix. The first one shows the share of capital and labor in total costs (excluding "other cost tickets") in each regional industry; the second specifies the capital-labor ratio in each sector; the third defines the destination of sectoral interregional exports (Tables 4.4, 4.8, and 4.12).

For the first indicator, there seems to be a technological pattern prevalent in the three regions: services sectors, such as community services, real estate, public administration, and financial institutions, present the highest value added share in total costs; agriculturally-based and mining-based industries are low value-added sectors. It is interesting to compare the classification based on value-added-cost shares, especially the top sectors in that hierarchy, to the respective sectoral capital-labor ratios; it gives a taste on the relative regional factor distribution of income, inherent to the model specification. Real estate is the most capital-intensive sector in the three regions. In the Center-South, it is followed by the coffee and vegetable oil mills sectors, which are also export-oriented sectors, as observed above (this relationship will be further discussed in the next chapter). The former is also relatively more capital-intensive in the North and in the Northeast. Also generalized is the high labor intensity in the public administration and community services sectors. The mining sector in the North is a high-value-added capital-intensive sector, and as was seen, export-oriented as well.

The average share of capital and labor in total costs is lower in the Center-South than in the other regions. In other words, the share of processed intermediate inputs in the Center-South is higher, which might also suggest a more integrated industrial development in the region. Regarding the regional capital-labor ratios, the lower value presented for the Northeast might be an indicator of the lower marginal productivity of labor in that region, suggesting more use of the abundant factor.

Finally, the distribution of the interregional exports from the less developed regions of the North and Northeast reveals the Center-South as the main destination. When exports from the Center-South are considered, the North receives roughly one third of the interregional exports, leaving the Northeast with the other two thirds.

Table 4.1 Sales Structure, by User and Destination: North

	COMMODITIES	Sales								
		Intermediate		Capital Creation		Household		Exports	Government	
		Regional	Rest of Brazil	Regional	Rest of Brazil	Regional	Rest of Brazil		Regional	Federal
S1	Agriculture	0.2864	0.4457	0.0324	0.0102	0.1034	0.0866	0.0353	0.0000	0.0000
S2	Mining	0.0948	0.5026	0.0000	0.0000	0.0000	0.0000	0.4026	0.0000	0.0000
S3	Nonmetallic Minerals	0.9049	0.0000	0.0000	0.0000	0.0951	0.0000	0.0000	0.0000	0.0000
S4	Steel	1.0000	0.0000	0.0000	0.0000	0.0000	0.0000	0.0000	0.0000	0.0000
S5	Nonferrous Metals	0.7704	0.1106	0.0000	0.0000	0.1187	0.0003	0.0000	0.0000	0.0000
S6	Other Metal Products	0.7441	0.0000	0.0393	0.0000	0.1981	0.0000	0.0185	0.0000	0.0000
S7	Machinery	0.7036	0.0600	0.1376	0.0941	0.0000	0.0009	0.0038	0.0000	0.0000
S8	Electrical Equipment	0.1592	0.3157	0.0433	0.0914	0.2155	0.1705	0.0045	0.0000	0.0000
S9	Electronic Equipment	0.1487	0.1685	0.0138	0.2685	0.0608	0.3391	0.0005	0.0000	0.0000
S10	Transportation Equipment	0.2069	0.5600	0.0446	0.0321	0.0709	0.0609	0.0245	0.0000	0.0000
S11	Wood Products and Furniture	0.2430	0.2208	0.0182	0.0728	0.0665	0.1988	0.1799	0.0000	0.0000
S12	Paper Products and Printing	0.2088	0.1669	0.0029	0.0005	0.2577	0.0343	0.3288	0.0000	0.0000
S13	Rubber	0.3648	0.5921	0.0000	0.0000	0.0359	0.0072	0.0000	0.0000	0.0000
S14	Chemicals	0.3920	0.0000	0.0000	0.0000	0.6080	0.0000	0.0000	0.0000	0.0000
S15	Petroleum Refining	0.7341	0.0000	0.0000	0.0000	0.2622	0.0000	0.0037	0.0000	0.0000
S16	Other Chemicals	0.8516	0.0000	0.0000	0.0000	0.0625	0.0000	0.0859	0.0000	0.0000
S17	Pharmaceuticals and Veterinary	0.0748	0.0000	0.0000	0.0000	0.9252	0.0000	0.0000	0.0000	0.0000
S18	Plastics	0.8777	0.0000	0.0000	0.0000	0.1223	0.0000	0.0000	0.0000	0.0000
S19	Textiles	0.4678	0.0040	0.0000	0.0000	0.5027	0.0047	0.0208	0.0000	0.0000
S20	Clothing	0.0000	0.0000	0.0000	0.0000	1.0000	0.0000	0.0000	0.0000	0.0000
S21	Footwear	0.1745	0.0000	0.0000	0.0000	0.6024	0.0000	0.2231	0.0000	0.0000
S22	Coffee	0.2628	0.0416	0.0000	0.0000	0.5801	0.0326	0.0829	0.0000	0.0000
S23	Processed Vegetables	0.1077	0.1031	0.0000	0.0000	0.4686	0.2730	0.0476	0.0000	0.0000
S24	Meat Packing Plants	0.1729	0.0045	0.0000	0.0000	0.7433	0.0092	0.0701	0.0000	0.0000
S25	Dairy Products	0.0100	0.0000	0.0000	0.0000	0.9900	0.0000	0.0000	0.0000	0.0000
S26	Sugar	0.1445	0.0000	0.0000	0.0000	0.8555	0.0000	0.0000	0.0000	0.0000
S27	Vegetable Oil Mills	0.2211	0.2763	0.0000	0.0000	0.2585	0.0000	0.2441	0.0000	0.0000
S28	Other Food Products	0.2683	0.0650	0.0000	0.0000	0.5203	0.0780	0.0684	0.0000	0.0000
S29	Other Manufacturing	0.2791	0.2804	0.0034	0.0196	0.2897	0.1153	0.0124	0.0000	0.0000
S30	Electric, Gas, and Sanitary Services	0.6591	0.0000	0.0000	0.0000	0.3409	0.0000	0.0000	0.0000	0.0000
S31	Construction	0.3220	0.0000	0.6780	0.0000	0.0000	0.0000	0.0000	0.0000	0.0000
S32	Trade	0.3873	0.1199	0.0361	0.0124	0.2450	0.1643	0.0350	0.0000	0.0000
S33	Transportation	0.4424	0.1362	0.0043	0.0018	0.2919	0.0707	0.0527	0.0000	0.0000
S34	Communication	0.6342	0.0000	0.0000	0.0000	0.3594	0.0000	0.0064	0.0000	0.0000
S35	Finanacial Institutions	0.6013	0.0000	0.0000	0.0000	0.3938	0.0000	0.0049	0.0000	0.0000
S36	Personal services	0.1051	0.0000	0.0000	0.0000	0.8949	0.0000	0.0000	0.0000	0.0000
S37	Business Services	0.8312	0.0000	0.1310	0.0000	0.0280	0.0000	0.0097	0.0000	0.0000
S38	Real Estate	0.1535	0.0000	0.0000	0.0000	0.8465	0.0000	0.0000	0.0000	0.0000
S39	Public Administration	0.0000	0.0000	0.0000	0.0000	0.0000	0.0000	0.0000	0.6941	0.3059
S40	Community Services	0.0000	0.0000	0.0000	0.0000	1.0000	0.0000	0.0000	0.0000	0.0000
	Total	0.2783	0.1796	0.0657	0.0297	0.2454	0.0775	0.0536	0.0487	0.0215

Table 4.2 Cost Structure, by User and Source: North

	SECTORS	Purchases					
		Intermediate			Capital Creation		
		Regional	Rest of Brazil	Rest of the World	Regional	Rest of Brazil	Rest of the World
S1	Agriculture	0.6530	0.3432	0.0038	0.7590	0.2056	0.0354
S2	Mining	0.7223	0.2777	0.0000	0.5674	0.3542	0.0784
S3	Nonmetallic Minerals	0.7843	0.1951	0.0206	0.5239	0.3951	0.0811
S4	Steel	0.1868	0.8132	0.0000	0.0437	0.7962	0.1601
S5	Nonferrous Metals	0.5753	0.1171	0.3076	0.0392	0.7958	0.1650
S6	Other Metal Products	0.4243	0.5407	0.0350	0.1640	0.6995	0.1364
S7	Machinery	0.4994	0.4355	0.0651	0.0734	0.7704	0.1567
S8	Electrical Equipment	0.1848	0.0902	0.7250	0.5650	0.3547	0.0802
S9	Electronic Equipment	0.3649	0.3785	0.2566	0.6808	0.2578	0.0615
S10	Transportation Equipment	0.4744	0.4684	0.0572	0.9912	0.0072	0.0016
S11	Wood Products and Furniture	0.9116	0.0848	0.0036	0.7707	0.1873	0.0421
S12	Paper Products and Printing	0.7431	0.2389	0.0180	0.8138	0.1507	0.0355
S13	Rubber	0.8964	0.0493	0.0544	0.4022	0.4839	0.1139
S14	Chemicals	0.9065	0.0768	0.0167	0.7082	0.2501	0.0413
S15	Petroleum Refining	0.0976	0.4039	0.4984	0.7083	0.2501	0.0415
S16	Other Chemicals	0.3902	0.5970	0.0128	0.0487	0.7897	0.1607
S17	Pharmaceuticals and Veterinary	0.4442	0.4592	0.0966	0.4866	0.4210	0.0924
S18	Plastics	0.2920	0.6539	0.0541	0.4329	0.4627	0.1044
S19	Textiles	0.7750	0.2015	0.0235	0.0650	0.7757	0.1593
S20	Clothing	0.7294	0.2550	0.0155	0.1962	0.6730	0.1310
S21	Footwear	0.7777	0.2044	0.0179	0.3124	0.5758	0.1118
S22	Coffee	0.9843	0.0157	0.0000	0.3944	0.5172	0.0885
S23	Processed Vegetables	0.7603	0.1119	0.1278	0.6558	0.2849	0.0593
S24	Meat Packing Plants	0.9929	0.0071	0.0000	0.6578	0.2792	0.0630
S25	Dairy Products	1.0000	0.0000	0.0000	0.2280	0.6493	0.1227
S26	Sugar	0.7427	0.2573	0.0000	0.7084	0.2504	0.0416
S27	Vegetable Oil Mills	1.0000	0.0000	0.0000	0.2383	0.6365	0.1252
S28	Other Food Products	0.7061	0.2857	0.0082	0.5076	0.4107	0.0817
S29	Other Manufacturing	0.5748	0.3297	0.0955	0.6154	0.3125	0.0721
S30	Electric, Gas, and Sanitary Services	0.5760	0.4202	0.0037	0.5041	0.4236	0.0723
S31	Construction	0.3471	0.6411	0.0118	0.3761	0.5171	0.1068
S32	Trade	0.7279	0.2652	0.0069	0.6776	0.2910	0.0314
S33	Transportation	0.3137	0.6603	0.0260	0.1323	0.7986	0.0692
S34	Communication	0.5469	0.4407	0.0124	0.2790	0.6086	0.1123
S35	Finanacial Institutions	0.8388	0.1612	0.0000	0.9774	0.0185	0.0041
S36	Personal services	0.6156	0.3612	0.0232	0.5844	0.3754	0.0401
S37	Business Services	0.6944	0.2545	0.0511	0.1283	0.7339	0.1380
S38	Real Estate	0.9562	0.0438	0.0000	0.1713	0.7405	0.0880
S39	Public Administration	0.7155	0.2713	0.0132	0.8591	0.1252	0.0157
S40	Community Services	0.6998	0.2806	0.0196	0.7083	0.2501	0.0415
	Total	0.5410	0.4061	0.0529	0.7177	0.2419	0.0404

Table 4.3 Household Consumption and Total Consumption of Commodities, by Source: North

	COMMODITIES	Purchases					
		Household			Total		
		Regional	Rest of Brazil	Rest of the World	Regional	Rest of Brazil	Rest of the World
S1	Agriculture	0.9155	0.0794	0.0052	0.9636	0.0232	0.0132
S2	Mining	0.0000	0.0000	0.0000	0.5904	0.2422	0.1674
S3	Nonmetallic Minerals	0.7374	0.1717	0.0909	0.1890	0.8007	0.0103
S4	Steel	0.0000	0.0000	0.0000	0.0784	0.8883	0.0334
S5	Nonferrous Metals	0.5379	0.2968	0.1653	0.5202	0.2717	0.2081
S6	Other Metal Products	0.3690	0.6103	0.0207	0.2368	0.7496	0.0136
S7	Machinery	0.0000	1.0000	0.0000	0.3104	0.6324	0.0572
S8	Electrical Equipment	0.4772	0.1449	0.3778	0.1613	0.5460	0.2928
S9	Electronic Equipment	0.8991	0.0020	0.0989	0.4252	0.3003	0.2744
S10	Transportation Equipment	0.1191	0.8550	0.0260	0.1447	0.7951	0.0602
S11	Wood Products and Furniture	0.4391	0.5586	0.0023	0.6859	0.3126	0.0015
S12	Paper Products and Printing	0.3973	0.5969	0.0059	0.4064	0.5881	0.0055
S13	Rubber	0.8000	0.0000	0.2000	0.4743	0.4684	0.0573
S14	Chemicals	0.4102	0.5898	0.0000	0.3222	0.6034	0.0745
S15	Petroleum Refining	0.4581	0.5419	0.0000	0.3199	0.6730	0.0071
S16	Other Chemicals	0.0699	0.9001	0.0300	0.0675	0.9274	0.0051
S17	Pharmaceuticals and Veterinary	0.2373	0.7520	0.0107	0.1554	0.8372	0.0074
S18	Plastics	0.4665	0.5007	0.0328	0.3369	0.6390	0.0241
S19	Textiles	0.7582	0.2245	0.0173	0.7620	0.2224	0.0156
S20	Clothing	0.0665	0.9198	0.0138	0.0663	0.9200	0.0137
S21	Footwear	0.0802	0.9079	0.0119	0.1010	0.8874	0.0116
S22	Coffee	1.0000	0.0000	0.0000	1.0000	0.0000	0.0000
S23	Processed Vegetables	0.7796	0.2204	0.0000	0.8051	0.1949	0.0000
S24	Meat Packing Plants	0.8966	0.1006	0.0028	0.9005	0.0973	0.0023
S25	Dairy Products	0.1992	0.7928	0.0080	0.1922	0.8001	0.0077
S26	Sugar	0.1881	0.8119	0.0000	0.1811	0.8189	0.0000
S27	Vegetable Oil Mills	0.0446	0.9554	0.0000	0.0570	0.9430	0.0000
S28	Other Food Products	0.6209	0.3686	0.0105	0.6694	0.3212	0.0094
S29	Other Manufacturing	0.6154	0.1082	0.2764	0.5667	0.2623	0.1710
S30	Electric, Gas, and Sanitary Services	0.6482	0.3518	0.0000	0.5893	0.4107	0.0000
S31	Construction	0.0000	0.0000	0.0000	1.0000	0.0000	0.0000
S32	Trade	0.9992	0.0008	0.0000	0.9868	0.0057	0.0075
S33	Transportation	0.9058	0.0000	0.0942	0.9194	0.0000	0.0806
S34	Communication	1.0000	0.0000	0.0000	0.9482	0.0503	0.0015
S35	Finanacial Institutions	0.9898	0.0000	0.0102	0.9919	0.0000	0.0081
S36	Personal services	0.8123	0.1868	0.0009	0.7992	0.2000	0.0008
S37	Business Services	0.9231	0.0641	0.0128	0.7725	0.2206	0.0069
S38	Real Estate	0.9826	0.0174	0.0000	0.9447	0.0553	0.0000
S39	Public Administration	0.0000	0.0000	0.0000	1.0000	0.0000	0.0000
S40	Community Services	1.0000	0.0000	0.0000	1.0000	0.0000	0.0000
	Total	0.6996	0.2823	0.0182	0.6474	0.3170	0.0356

Table 4.4 Selected Structural Indicators: North

	SECTORS	Capital+Labor/ Total Costs*	Capital-Labor Ratio	Output Share			Interregional Exports	
				Regional	National	Sectoral	Northeast	Center-South
S1	Agriculture	0.2876	0.7657	0.1946	0.0074	0.0914	0.0209	0.9791
S2	Mining	0.5953	1.5939	0.0686	0.0026	0.1148	0.0020	0.9980
S3	Nonmetallic Minerals	0.4496	0.5320	0.0084	0.0003	0.0225	0.0000	0.0000
S4	Steel	0.1777	0.6234	0.0005	0.0000	0.0006	0.0000	0.0000
S5	Nonferrous Metals	0.1044	0.7064	0.0027	0.0001	0.0088	0.0032	0.9968
S6	Other Metal Products	0.3345	0.2050	0.0059	0.0002	0.0102	0.0000	0.0000
S7	Machinery	0.2117	0.2597	0.0087	0.0003	0.0132	1.0000	0.0000
S8	Electrical Equipment	0.3291	0.1568	0.0097	0.0004	0.0308	0.0729	0.9271
S9	Electronic Equipment	0.2114	0.7118	0.0826	0.0031	0.2509	0.0074	0.9926
S10	Transportation Equipment	0.2251	0.8879	0.0121	0.0005	0.0140	0.0197	0.9803
S11	Wood Products and Furniture	0.4037	0.1122	0.0315	0.0012	0.0953	0.0573	0.9427
S12	Paper Products and Printing	0.3440	0.4249	0.0086	0.0003	0.0151	0.0637	0.9363
S13	Rubber	0.2530	1.8115	0.0061	0.0002	0.0307	0.0738	0.9262
S14	Chemicals	0.2507	0.1563	0.0022	0.0001	0.0064	0.0000	0.0000
S15	Petroleum Refining	0.1433	0.6684	0.0119	0.0004	0.0067	0.0000	0.0000
S16	Other Chemicals	0.1937	0.2578	0.0014	0.0001	0.0028	0.0000	0.0000
S17	Pharmaceuticals and Veterinary	0.2340	0.1652	0.0016	0.0001	0.0061	0.0000	0.0000
S18	Plastics	0.4284	0.9517	0.0037	0.0001	0.0160	0.0000	0.0000
S19	Textiles	0.2882	0.5156	0.0127	0.0005	0.0174	0.8751	0.1249
S20	Clothing	0.2914	0.3584	0.0012	0.0000	0.0031	0.0000	0.0000
S21	Footwear	0.2564	0.4662	0.0010	0.0000	0.0042	0.0000	0.0000
S22	Coffee	0.1058	1.6489	0.0068	0.0003	0.0229	0.0020	0.9980
S23	Processed Vegetables	0.1983	0.5411	0.0210	0.0008	0.0434	0.0125	0.9875
S24	Meat Packing Plants	0.1186	0.7575	0.0141	0.0005	0.0321	0.7835	0.2165
S25	Dairy Products	0.2418	0.4091	0.0011	0.0000	0.0055	0.0000	0.0000
S26	Sugar	0.1833	0.6121	0.0011	0.0000	0.0060	0.0000	0.0000
S27	Vegetable Oil Mills	0.4036	0.1620	0.0008	0.0000	0.0024	1.0000	0.0000
S28	Other Food Products	0.3028	0.3282	0.0159	0.0006	0.0320	0.0288	0.9712
S29	Other Manufacturing	0.2822	0.9625	0.0097	0.0004	0.0218	0.1040	0.8960
S30	Electric, Gas, and Sanitary Services	0.4315	0.8158	0.0151	0.0006	0.0267	0.0000	0.0000
S31	Construction	0.1560	0.2381	0.0719	0.0027	0.0367	0.0000	0.0000
S32	Trade	0.4445	0.1351	0.0703	0.0027	0.0369	0.0000	1.0000
S33	Transportation	0.3814	0.5321	0.0504	0.0019	0.0437	0.0143	0.9857
S34	Communication	0.6659	1.0934	0.0069	0.0003	0.0395	0.0000	0.0000
S35	Finanacial Institutions	0.7375	0.2792	0.0135	0.0005	0.0325	0.0000	0.0000
S36	Personal services	0.5483	0.3772	0.0650	0.0025	0.0440	0.0000	0.0000
S37	Business Services	0.3350	0.6701	0.0282	0.0011	0.0379	0.0000	0.0000
S38	Real Estate	0.9395	36.9059	0.0521	0.0020	0.0845	0.0000	0.0000
S39	Public Administration	0.7694	0.1629	0.0702	0.0027	0.0373	0.0000	0.0000
S40	Community Services	0.9457	0.1139	0.0105	0.0004	0.0787	0.0000	0.0000
	Total	0.4032	0.5827	1.0000	0.0378	0.0378	0.0249	0.9751

* Other cost tickets not included

Table 4.5 Sales Structure, by User and Destination: Northeast

	COMMODITIES	Sales								
		Intermediate		Capital Creation		Household		Exports	Government	
		Regional	Rest of Brazil	Regional	Rest of Brazil	Regional	Rest of Brazil		Regional	Federal
S1	Agriculture	0.6863	0.0356	0.0248	0.0017	0.2054	0.0166	0.0297	0.0000	0.0000
S2	Mining	0.6501	0.3279	0.0000	0.0000	0.0000	0.0000	0.0221	0.0000	0.0000
S3	Nonmetallic Minerals	0.9265	0.0173	0.0190	0.0000	0.0361	0.0000	0.0011	0.0000	0.0000
S4	Steel	0.4528	0.3143	0.0000	0.0000	0.0000	0.0000	0.2329	0.0000	0.0000
S5	Nonferrous Metals	0.7555	0.0467	0.0000	0.0000	0.1397	0.0010	0.0572	0.0000	0.0000
S6	Other Metal Products	0.3917	0.3186	0.0214	0.0074	0.2208	0.0376	0.0025	0.0000	0.0000
S7	Machinery	0.7321	0.0137	0.1726	0.0673	0.0086	0.0001	0.0057	0.0000	0.0000
S8	Electrical Equipment	0.3709	0.1521	0.0186	0.0487	0.3539	0.0427	0.0131	0.0000	0.0000
S9	Electronic Equipment	0.0318	0.0434	0.8469	0.0000	0.0779	0.0000	0.0000	0.0000	0.0000
S10	Transportation Equipment	0.3838	0.3892	0.0000	0.0443	0.1132	0.0523	0.0172	0.0000	0.0000
S11	Wood Products and Furniture	0.4416	0.0105	0.0000	0.0064	0.5187	0.0222	0.0006	0.0000	0.0000
S12	Paper Products and Printing	0.8483	0.0056	0.0000	0.0000	0.1420	0.0000	0.0041	0.0000	0.0000
S13	Rubber	0.6114	0.2042	0.0000	0.0000	0.1829	0.0016	0.0000	0.0000	0.0000
S14	Chemicals	0.3890	0.2418	0.0000	0.0000	0.3500	0.0000	0.0191	0.0000	0.0000
S15	Petroleum Refining	0.5005	0.2695	0.0000	0.0000	0.1209	0.0048	0.1043	0.0000	0.0000
S16	Other Chemicals	0.6311	0.1909	0.0000	0.0000	0.0368	0.0182	0.1231	0.0000	0.0000
S17	Pharmaceuticals and Veterinary	0.1432	0.0308	0.0000	0.0000	0.6980	0.1271	0.0008	0.0000	0.0000
S18	Plastics	0.5747	0.1959	0.0000	0.0000	0.1337	0.0232	0.0726	0.0000	0.0000
S19	Textiles	0.4692	0.2645	0.0000	0.0000	0.1518	0.0252	0.0892	0.0000	0.0000
S20	Clothing	0.0261	0.0003	0.0000	0.0000	0.9162	0.0541	0.0034	0.0000	0.0000
S21	Footwear	0.1911	0.0164	0.0000	0.0000	0.5368	0.1305	0.1251	0.0000	0.0000
S22	Coffee	0.2521	0.0000	0.0000	0.0000	0.7479	0.0000	0.0000	0.0000	0.0000
S23	Processed Vegetables	0.1143	0.0467	0.0000	0.0000	0.5466	0.0506	0.2419	0.0000	0.0000
S24	Meat Packing Plants	0.0850	0.0053	0.0000	0.0000	0.8997	0.0096	0.0004	0.0000	0.0000
S25	Dairy Products	0.1399	0.0634	0.0000	0.0000	0.6764	0.1202	0.0000	0.0000	0.0000
S26	Sugar	0.1895	0.0018	0.0000	0.0000	0.1561	0.0072	0.6455	0.0000	0.0000
S27	Vegetable Oil Mills	0.4495	0.1277	0.0000	0.0000	0.2126	0.0846	0.1256	0.0000	0.0000
S28	Other Food Products	0.2705	0.0163	0.0000	0.0000	0.6166	0.0400	0.0566	0.0000	0.0000
S29	Other Manufacturing	0.8538	0.0410	0.0000	0.0130	0.0666	0.0203	0.0052	0.0000	0.0000
S30	Electric, Gas, and Sanitary Services	0.7766	0.0000	0.0000	0.0000	0.2234	0.0000	0.0000	0.0000	0.0000
S31	Construction	0.0895	0.0000	0.9105	0.0000	0.0000	0.0000	0.0000	0.0000	0.0000
S32	Trade	0.3989	0.1383	0.0259	0.0167	0.1225	0.2494	0.0484	0.0000	0.0000
S33	Transportation	0.4163	0.0520	0.0070	0.0007	0.3680	0.1342	0.0218	0.0000	0.0000
S34	Communication	0.8094	0.0000	0.0000	0.0000	0.1906	0.0000	0.0000	0.0000	0.0000
S35	Finanacial Institutions	0.8298	0.0000	0.0000	0.0000	0.1702	0.0000	0.0000	0.0000	0.0000
S36	Personal services	0.1297	0.0348	0.0000	0.0000	0.7183	0.1173	0.0000	0.0000	0.0000
S37	Business Services	0.9690	0.0000	0.0000	0.0000	0.0310	0.0000	0.0000	0.0000	0.0000
S38	Real Estate	0.1186	0.0000	0.0000	0.0000	0.8814	0.0000	0.0000	0.0000	0.0000
S39	Public Administration	0.0000	0.0000	0.0000	0.0000	0.0000	0.0000	0.0000	0.6929	0.3071
S40	Community Services	0.0000	0.0000	0.0000	0.0000	1.0000	0.0000	0.0000	0.0000	0.0000
	Total	0.3756	0.0816	0.1134	0.0024	0.2640	0.0403	0.0449	0.0538	0.0239

Table 4.6 Cost Structure, by User and Source: Northeast

	SECTORS	Purchases					
		Intermediate			Capital Creation		
		Regional	Rest of Brazil	Rest of the World	Regional	Rest of Brazil	Rest of the World
S1	Agriculture	0.7996	0.1941	0.0064	0.9446	0.0530	0.0024
S2	Mining	0.8148	0.0749	0.1103	0.9695	0.0282	0.0023
S3	Nonmetallic Minerals	0.9034	0.0937	0.0029	0.9448	0.0523	0.0029
S4	Steel	0.7438	0.2293	0.0269	0.9695	0.0288	0.0017
S5	Nonferrous Metals	0.7812	0.1829	0.0359	0.9738	0.0245	0.0017
S6	Other Metal Products	0.5980	0.4004	0.0016	0.3951	0.5807	0.0242
S7	Machinery	0.4487	0.4724	0.0789	0.8223	0.1685	0.0092
S8	Electrical Equipment	0.7830	0.1799	0.0370	0.9724	0.0258	0.0018
S9	Electronic Equipment	0.1306	0.5976	0.2717	0.0322	0.9067	0.0612
S10	Transportation Equipment	0.4456	0.5324	0.0220	0.6274	0.3532	0.0195
S11	Wood Products and Furniture	0.7002	0.2998	0.0000	0.6643	0.3175	0.0182
S12	Paper Products and Printing	0.7544	0.2294	0.0162	0.4076	0.5594	0.0330
S13	Rubber	0.6752	0.2550	0.0698	0.6693	0.3055	0.0252
S14	Chemicals	0.7766	0.2144	0.0090	0.9545	0.0416	0.0040
S15	Petroleum Refining	0.8731	0.1039	0.0230	0.9402	0.0555	0.0043
S16	Other Chemicals	0.6535	0.2634	0.0832	0.9532	0.0442	0.0026
S17	Pharmaceuticals and Veterinary	0.4889	0.4814	0.0298	0.9238	0.0710	0.0052
S18	Plastics	0.8646	0.1222	0.0132	0.9744	0.0240	0.0017
S19	Textiles	0.8497	0.1496	0.0006	0.9032	0.0911	0.0057
S20	Clothing	0.6894	0.3106	0.0000	0.9075	0.0880	0.0045
S21	Footwear	0.5337	0.4615	0.0048	0.9221	0.0742	0.0038
S22	Coffee	0.7689	0.2311	0.0000	0.8295	0.1661	0.0044
S23	Processed Vegetables	0.6903	0.2050	0.1046	0.9120	0.0830	0.0051
S24	Meat Packing Plants	0.9621	0.0379	0.0000	0.9236	0.0728	0.0037
S25	Dairy Products	0.9182	0.0818	0.0000	0.8010	0.1903	0.0086
S26	Sugar	0.9719	0.0281	0.0000	0.9431	0.0540	0.0028
S27	Vegetable Oil Mills	0.7371	0.2601	0.0028	0.9486	0.0489	0.0025
S28	Other Food Products	0.8814	0.1042	0.0144	0.9080	0.0881	0.0039
S29	Other Manufacturing	0.9274	0.0726	0.0000	0.8586	0.1326	0.0088
S30	Electric, Gas, and Sanitary Services	0.9330	0.0640	0.0030	0.9559	0.0407	0.0035
S31	Construction	0.7067	0.2886	0.0047	0.9414	0.0555	0.0031
S32	Trade	0.6889	0.3109	0.0002	0.7884	0.2094	0.0022
S33	Transportation	0.6587	0.3387	0.0026	0.8307	0.1678	0.0015
S34	Communication	0.8042	0.1887	0.0071	0.8060	0.1781	0.0159
S35	Finanacial Institutions	0.9167	0.0833	0.0000	0.9912	0.0083	0.0005
S36	Personal services	0.6920	0.3060	0.0019	0.9520	0.0475	0.0005
S37	Business Services	0.8795	0.1202	0.0003	0.6418	0.3454	0.0129
S38	Real Estate	0.9933	0.0056	0.0011	0.9979	0.0021	0.0000
S39	Public Administration	0.8782	0.1204	0.0014	0.9826	0.0166	0.0008
S40	Community Services	0.8508	0.1448	0.0044	0.9367	0.0611	0.0022
	Total	0.7991	0.1846	0.0164	0.9375	0.0603	0.0022

Table 4.7 Household Consumption and Total Consumption of Commodities, by Source: Northeast

	COMMODITIES	Purchases					
		Household			Total		
		Regional	Rest of Brazil	Rest of the World	Regional	Rest of Brazil	Rest of the World
S1	Agriculture	0.9184	0.0810	0.0006	0.9095	0.0731	0.0174
S2	Mining	0.0000	0.0000	0.0000	0.9115	0.0239	0.0646
S3	Nonmetallic Minerals	0.3513	0.6380	0.0108	0.5728	0.4265	0.0006
S4	Steel	0.0000	0.0000	0.0000	0.5143	0.4829	0.0027
S5	Nonferrous Metals	1.0000	0.0000	0.0000	0.9974	0.0008	0.0018
S6	Other Metal Products	0.9821	0.0179	0.0000	0.6201	0.3647	0.0153
S7	Machinery	0.0781	0.3086	0.6134	0.5127	0.3995	0.0878
S8	Electrical Equipment	0.3876	0.4882	0.1242	0.4704	0.4255	0.1042
S9	Electronic Equipment	0.0282	0.9707	0.0010	0.2104	0.7694	0.0203
S10	Transportation Equipment	0.0357	0.9612	0.0032	0.0799	0.9130	0.0071
S11	Wood Products and Furniture	0.4458	0.5542	0.0000	0.5019	0.4981	0.0000
S12	Paper Products and Printing	0.5046	0.4954	0.0000	0.6881	0.3034	0.0086
S13	Rubber	0.5035	0.4965	0.0000	0.2659	0.7146	0.0196
S14	Chemicals	1.0000	0.0000	0.0000	0.7857	0.1674	0.0469
S15	Petroleum Refining	0.6595	0.3405	0.0000	0.7015	0.2912	0.0073
S16	Other Chemicals	0.4772	0.5228	0.0000	0.5292	0.4351	0.0357
S17	Pharmaceuticals and Veterinary	0.3363	0.6614	0.0023	0.2879	0.7069	0.0052
S18	Plastics	0.6427	0.3407	0.0166	0.5642	0.4317	0.0041
S19	Textiles	0.4500	0.5500	0.0000	0.6053	0.3939	0.0009
S20	Clothing	0.5793	0.4201	0.0006	0.5860	0.4134	0.0006
S21	Footwear	0.4524	0.5446	0.0030	0.5126	0.4849	0.0025
S22	Coffee	1.0000	0.0000	0.0000	0.9839	0.0161	0.0000
S23	Processed Vegetables	0.7580	0.2413	0.0007	0.7711	0.2282	0.0007
S24	Meat Packing Plants	0.7134	0.2864	0.0002	0.6790	0.3208	0.0001
S25	Dairy Products	0.6939	0.3061	0.0000	0.6976	0.3024	0.0000
S26	Sugar	1.0000	0.0000	0.0000	1.0000	0.0000	0.0000
S27	Vegetable Oil Mills	0.6660	0.3340	0.0000	0.6384	0.3559	0.0057
S28	Other Food Products	0.4921	0.4975	0.0104	0.5250	0.4643	0.0107
S29	Other Manufacturing	0.2186	0.7814	0.0000	0.6582	0.3418	0.0000
S30	Electric, Gas, and Sanitary Services	1.0000	0.0000	0.0000	1.0000	0.0000	0.0000
S31	Construction	0.0000	0.0000	0.0000	1.0000	0.0000	0.0000
S32	Trade	1.0000	0.0000	0.0000	1.0000	0.0000	0.0000
S33	Transportation	0.9767	0.0233	0.0000	0.9467	0.0533	0.0000
S34	Communication	1.0000	0.0000	0.0000	1.0000	0.0000	0.0000
S35	Finanacial Institutions	1.0000	0.0000	0.0000	1.0000	0.0000	0.0000
S36	Personal services	1.0000	0.0000	0.0000	0.9936	0.0064	0.0000
S37	Business Services	1.0000	0.0000	0.0000	0.9578	0.0422	0.0000
S38	Real Estate	1.0000	0.0000	0.0000	0.9951	0.0049	0.0000
S39	Public Administration	0.0000	0.0000	0.0000	1.0000	0.0000	0.0000
S40	Community Services	1.0000	0.0000	0.0000	1.0000	0.0000	0.0000
	Total	0.7768	0.2187	0.0044	0.8241	0.1667	0.0092

Table 4.8 Selected Structural Indicators: Northeast

	SECTORS	Capital+Labor/ Total Costs*	Capital-Labor Ratio	Output Share			Interregional Exports	
				Regional	National	Sectoral	North	Center-South
S1	Agriculture	0.3953	0.4354	0.1246	0.0161	0.1998	0.0171	0.9829
S2	Mining	0.5866	0.7361	0.0402	0.0052	0.2300	0.0033	0.9967
S3	Nonmetallic Minerals	0.3260	0.7690	0.0087	0.0011	0.0797	1.0000	0.0000
S4	Steel	0.1268	1.1395	0.0093	0.0012	0.0375	0.0958	0.9042
S5	Nonferrous Metals	0.0793	1.0161	0.0137	0.0018	0.1540	0.0744	0.9256
S6	Other Metal Products	0.2454	0.3183	0.0064	0.0008	0.0374	0.3496	0.6504
S7	Machinery	0.1977	0.2091	0.0079	0.0010	0.0410	1.0000	0.0000
S8	Electrical Equipment	0.2013	0.2913	0.0054	0.0007	0.0582	0.5019	0.4981
S9	Electronic Equipment	0.3280	0.6226	0.0011	0.0001	0.0116	1.0000	0.0000
S10	Transportation Equipment	0.3720	0.3994	0.0022	0.0003	0.0089	0.5107	0.4893
S11	Wood Products and Furniture	0.3032	0.2007	0.0053	0.0007	0.0542	1.0000	0.0000
S12	Paper Products and Printing	0.2475	1.1562	0.0086	0.0011	0.0512	1.0000	0.0000
S13	Rubber	0.1970	1.7408	0.0013	0.0002	0.0217	0.2666	0.7334
S14	Chemicals	0.1288	0.4802	0.0166	0.0021	0.1658	0.0010	0.9990
S15	Petroleum Refining	0.0836	0.9988	0.0871	0.0112	0.1664	0.0260	0.9740
S16	Other Chemicals	0.0921	0.5838	0.0100	0.0013	0.0677	0.1491	0.8509
S17	Pharmaceuticals and Veterinary	0.1159	0.2872	0.0040	0.0005	0.0521	0.6183	0.3817
S18	Plastics	0.3189	2.6927	0.0056	0.0007	0.0829	0.2476	0.7524
S19	Textiles	0.1625	0.9139	0.0295	0.0038	0.1385	0.0227	0.9773
S20	Clothing	0.3312	0.4716	0.0095	0.0012	0.0828	1.0000	0.0000
S21	Footwear	0.1855	0.7033	0.0045	0.0006	0.0663	0.6620	0.3380
S22	Coffee	0.0964	1.7484	0.0073	0.0009	0.0845	0.0000	0.0000
S23	Processed Vegetables	0.1490	0.9527	0.0309	0.0040	0.2185	0.0252	0.9748
S24	Meat Packing Plants	0.0272	3.2600	0.0150	0.0019	0.1168	0.0144	0.9856
S25	Dairy Products	0.1916	0.7358	0.0090	0.0012	0.1546	0.1790	0.8210
S26	Sugar	0.2200	0.4694	0.0150	0.0019	0.2925	1.0000	0.0000
S27	Vegetable Oil Mills	0.0981	1.5693	0.0054	0.0007	0.0569	0.2728	0.7272
S28	Other Food Products	0.2110	0.5036	0.0165	0.0021	0.1137	0.3888	0.6112
S29	Other Manufacturing	0.4894	2.6945	0.0100	0.0013	0.0765	0.1873	0.8127
S30	Electric, Gas, and Sanitary Services	0.4791	1.0110	0.0201	0.0026	0.1218	0.0000	0.0000
S31	Construction	0.4375	0.0744	0.1149	0.0148	0.2003	0.0000	0.0000
S32	Trade	0.6187	0.1191	0.0680	0.0088	0.1218	0.1014	0.8986
S33	Transportation	0.4813	0.4938	0.0301	0.0039	0.0891	0.3914	0.6086
S34	Communication	0.5398	1.1833	0.0043	0.0006	0.0844	0.0000	0.0000
S35	Finanacial Institutions	0.6474	0.3327	0.0118	0.0015	0.0972	0.0000	0.0000
S36	Personal services	0.4778	0.3960	0.0924	0.0119	0.2137	0.0292	0.9708
S37	Business Services	0.4945	0.5797	0.0245	0.0032	0.1123	0.0000	0.0000
S38	Real Estate	0.8478	80.9788	0.0361	0.0047	0.1997	0.0000	0.0000
S39	Public Administration	0.7681	0.1633	0.0769	0.0099	0.1395	0.0000	0.0000
S40	Community Services	0.9261	0.1166	0.0104	0.0013	0.2678	0.0000	0.0000
	Total	0.4132	0.4568	1.0000	0.1291	0.1291	0.1021	0.8979

* Other cost tickets not included

Table 4.9 Sales Structure, by User and Destination: Center-South

	COMMODITIES	Sales								
		Intermediate		Capital Creation		Household		Exports	Government	
		Regional	Rest of Brazil	Regional	Rest of Brazil	Regional	Rest of Brazil		Regional	Federal
S1	Agriculture	0.7683	0.0144	0.0176	0.0000	0.1733	0.0060	0.0205	0.0000	0.0000
S2	Mining	0.7708	0.0122	0.0000	0.0000	0.0000	0.0000	0.2169	0.0000	0.0000
S3	Nonmetallic Minerals	0.7612	0.1613	0.0000	0.0019	0.0465	0.0064	0.0226	0.0000	0.0000
S4	Steel	0.8289	0.0225	0.0000	0.0000	0.0000	0.0000	0.1486	0.0000	0.0000
S5	Nonferrous Metals	0.8182	0.0038	0.0000	0.0000	0.0015	0.0005	0.1759	0.0000	0.0000
S6	Other Metal Products	0.8425	0.0394	0.0146	0.0006	0.0660	0.0029	0.0341	0.0000	0.0000
S7	Machinery	0.5699	0.0227	0.2950	0.0250	0.0034	0.0015	0.0826	0.0000	0.0000
S8	Electrical Equipment	0.5179	0.0434	0.0978	0.0083	0.2407	0.0299	0.0620	0.0000	0.0000
S9	Electronic Equipment	0.1806	0.0572	0.2582	0.0071	0.3246	0.0415	0.1308	0.0000	0.0000
S10	Transportation Equipment	0.4608	0.0253	0.1081	0.0147	0.1933	0.0347	0.1631	0.0000	0.0000
S11	Wood Products and Furniture	0.4589	0.0038	0.0747	0.0193	0.3535	0.0487	0.0409	0.0000	0.0000
S12	Paper Products and Printing	0.7826	0.0205	0.0019	0.0001	0.1248	0.0138	0.0563	0.0000	0.0000
S13	Rubber	0.8736	0.0549	0.0000	0.0000	0.0052	0.0041	0.0622	0.0000	0.0000
S14	Chemicals	0.5784	0.0392	0.0000	0.0000	0.3246	0.0067	0.0510	0.0000	0.0000
S15	Petroleum Refining	0.6658	0.0524	0.0000	0.0000	0.1408	0.0149	0.1261	0.0000	0.0000
S16	Other Chemicals	0.8555	0.0703	0.0000	0.0000	0.0351	0.0048	0.0343	0.0000	0.0000
S17	Pharmaceuticals and Veterinary	0.1593	0.0531	0.0000	0.0000	0.6778	0.0907	0.0191	0.0000	0.0000
S18	Plastics	0.8063	0.0703	0.0000	0.0000	0.0836	0.0083	0.0316	0.0000	0.0000
S19	Textiles	0.7428	0.0382	0.0000	0.0000	0.1268	0.0327	0.0595	0.0000	0.0000
S20	Clothing	0.0247	0.0002	0.0000	0.0000	0.8540	0.1022	0.0189	0.0000	0.0000
S21	Footwear	0.2403	0.0031	0.0000	0.0000	0.4184	0.0701	0.2681	0.0000	0.0000
S22	Coffee	0.3079	0.0015	0.0000	0.0000	0.1988	0.0000	0.4917	0.0000	0.0000
S23	Processed Vegetables	0.2693	0.0067	0.0000	0.0000	0.5140	0.0584	0.1517	0.0000	0.0000
S24	Meat Packing Plants	0.2345	0.0147	0.0000	0.0000	0.5755	0.0524	0.1227	0.0000	0.0000
S25	Dairy Products	0.3224	0.0115	0.0000	0.0000	0.5908	0.0750	0.0004	0.0000	0.0000
S26	Sugar	0.6254	0.0063	0.0000	0.0000	0.3398	0.0285	0.0000	0.0000	0.0000
S27	Vegetable Oil Mills	0.4484	0.0208	0.0000	0.0000	0.1839	0.0172	0.3296	0.0000	0.0000
S28	Other Food Products	0.3219	0.0237	0.0000	0.0000	0.5301	0.0919	0.0324	0.0000	0.0000
S29	Other Manufacturing	0.6259	0.0203	0.0529	0.0035	0.2480	0.0209	0.0284	0.0000	0.0000
S30	Electric, Gas, and Sanitary Services	0.7232	0.0161	0.0000	0.0000	0.2550	0.0058	0.0000	0.0000	0.0000
S31	Construction	0.1229	0.0000	0.8768	0.0000	0.0000	0.0000	0.0003	0.0000	0.0000
S32	Trade	0.3956	0.0006	0.0374	0.0000	0.5415	0.0003	0.0245	0.0000	0.0000
S33	Transportation	0.5266	0.0042	0.0058	0.0000	0.2713	0.0041	0.1880	0.0000	0.0000
S34	Communication	0.5979	0.0024	0.0000	0.0000	0.3862	0.0000	0.0135	0.0000	0.0000
S35	Finanacial Institutions	0.4927	0.0000	0.0000	0.0000	0.5032	0.0000	0.0041	0.0000	0.0000
S36	Personal services	0.3112	0.0041	0.0000	0.0000	0.6737	0.0110	0.0000	0.0000	0.0000
S37	Business Services	0.8864	0.0175	0.0519	0.0008	0.0174	0.0001	0.0259	0.0000	0.0000
S38	Real Estate	0.2525	0.0065	0.0000	0.0000	0.7392	0.0018	0.0000	0.0000	0.0000
S39	Public Administration	0.0000	0.0000	0.0000	0.0000	0.0000	0.0000	0.0000	0.4558	0.5442
S40	Community Services	0.0000	0.0000	0.0000	0.0000	1.0000	0.0000	0.0000	0.0000	0.0000
	Total	0.4937	0.0203	0.0840	0.0018	0.2452	0.0152	0.0695	0.0320	0.0382

Table 4.10 Cost Structure, by User and Source: Center-South

	SECTORS	Purchases					
		Intermediate			Capital Creation		
		Regional	Rest of Brazil	Rest of the World	Regional	Rest of Brazil	Rest of the World
S1	Agriculture	0.9549	0.0372	0.0079	0.8979	0.0601	0.0421
S2	Mining	0.8977	0.0166	0.0858	0.9531	0.0110	0.0359
S3	Nonmetallic Minerals	0.9237	0.0565	0.0198	0.9426	0.0146	0.0428
S4	Steel	0.9096	0.0211	0.0693	0.9711	0.0007	0.0282
S5	Nonferrous Metals	0.8378	0.0553	0.1070	0.9712	0.0006	0.0282
S6	Other Metal Products	0.9608	0.0163	0.0229	0.8602	0.0318	0.1080
S7	Machinery	0.9466	0.0154	0.0379	0.9066	0.0110	0.0825
S8	Electrical Equipment	0.9255	0.0229	0.0517	0.9579	0.0124	0.0297
S9	Electronic Equipment	0.7636	0.0853	0.1511	0.7819	0.0888	0.1293
S10	Transportation Equipment	0.9271	0.0176	0.0552	0.8401	0.0485	0.1114
S11	Wood Products and Furniture	0.9335	0.0430	0.0235	0.8364	0.0572	0.1064
S12	Paper Products and Printing	0.9521	0.0191	0.0288	0.7984	0.0810	0.1207
S13	Rubber	0.8673	0.0480	0.0847	0.8294	0.0567	0.1138
S14	Chemicals	0.8845	0.0255	0.0900	0.9457	0.0008	0.0535
S15	Petroleum Refining	0.5126	0.0670	0.4205	0.9419	0.0011	0.0571
S16	Other Chemicals	0.7641	0.0589	0.1769	0.9551	0.0041	0.0408
S17	Pharmaceuticals and Veterinary	0.8558	0.0371	0.1072	0.9236	0.0146	0.0618
S18	Plastics	0.8834	0.0939	0.0227	0.9608	0.0106	0.0285
S19	Textiles	0.9049	0.0743	0.0208	0.9321	0.0020	0.0659
S20	Clothing	0.9743	0.0200	0.0057	0.9403	0.0016	0.0582
S21	Footwear	0.9272	0.0186	0.0542	0.9459	0.0014	0.0527
S22	Coffee	0.9965	0.0026	0.0009	0.9206	0.0215	0.0579
S23	Processed Vegetables	0.8832	0.0987	0.0181	0.9295	0.0081	0.0625
S24	Meat Packing Plants	0.8439	0.1438	0.0123	0.9130	0.0353	0.0517
S25	Dairy Products	0.9780	0.0165	0.0055	0.9164	0.0024	0.0812
S26	Sugar	0.9799	0.0060	0.0142	0.9552	0.0011	0.0437
S27	Vegetable Oil Mills	0.8997	0.0599	0.0404	0.9608	0.0010	0.0382
S28	Other Food Products	0.9173	0.0422	0.0405	0.9320	0.0150	0.0530
S29	Other Manufacturing	0.8462	0.0615	0.0923	0.8732	0.0460	0.0807
S30	Electric, Gas, and Sanitary Services	0.9806	0.0046	0.0147	0.9320	0.0176	0.0504
S31	Construction	0.9580	0.0217	0.0202	0.9411	0.0098	0.0492
S32	Trade	0.9755	0.0102	0.0143	0.9419	0.0176	0.0404
S33	Transportation	0.8241	0.0198	0.1560	0.9361	0.0044	0.0595
S34	Communication	0.9033	0.0257	0.0709	0.8538	0.0365	0.1097
S35	Finanacial Institutions	0.9692	0.0038	0.0269	0.9888	0.0010	0.0101
S36	Personal services	0.9398	0.0327	0.0275	0.9814	0.0042	0.0144
S37	Business Services	0.9654	0.0086	0.0260	0.8949	0.0090	0.0962
S38	Real Estate	0.9955	0.0008	0.0037	0.9985	0.0003	0.0012
S39	Public Administration	0.9546	0.0175	0.0279	0.9722	0.0107	0.0171
S40	Community Services	0.9758	0.0129	0.0113	0.9525	0.0123	0.0352
	Total	0.8863	0.0360	0.0777	0.9478	0.0164	0.0358

Table 4.11 Household Consumption and Total Consumption of Commodities, by Source: Center-South

	COMMODITIES	Purchases					
		Household			Total		
		Regional	Rest of Brazil	Rest of the World	Regional	Rest of Brazil	Rest of the World
S1	Agriculture	0.8981	0.0804	0.0214	0.9089	0.0790	0.0121
S2	Mining	0.0000	0.0000	0.0000	0.3707	0.0975	0.5318
S3	Nonmetallic Minerals	0.9906	0.0000	0.0094	0.9905	0.0000	0.0095
S4	Steel	0.0000	0.0000	0.0000	0.9743	0.0130	0.0127
S5	Nonferrous Metals	0.9838	0.0162	0.0000	0.9243	0.0105	0.0653
S6	Other Metal Products	0.9741	0.0103	0.0156	0.9804	0.0099	0.0097
S7	Machinery	1.0000	0.0000	0.0000	0.9125	0.0000	0.0875
S8	Electrical Equipment	0.7561	0.0241	0.2198	0.8323	0.0251	0.1426
S9	Electronic Equipment	0.7385	0.2615	0.0000	0.6635	0.2278	0.1086
S10	Transportation Equipment	0.9756	0.0049	0.0194	0.9150	0.0136	0.0714
S11	Wood Products and Furniture	0.9401	0.0581	0.0019	0.9391	0.0551	0.0059
S12	Paper Products and Printing	0.9381	0.0035	0.0584	0.9778	0.0033	0.0190
S13	Rubber	0.7614	0.0325	0.2060	0.9440	0.0230	0.0330
S14	Chemicals	1.0000	0.0000	0.0000	0.8384	0.0449	0.1167
S15	Petroleum Refining	0.9546	0.0055	0.0399	0.8816	0.0588	0.0596
S16	Other Chemicals	0.8855	0.0201	0.0944	0.9154	0.0133	0.0712
S17	Pharmaceuticals and Veterinary	0.9956	0.0041	0.0004	0.9518	0.0038	0.0444
S18	Plastics	0.9779	0.0189	0.0032	0.9649	0.0164	0.0187
S19	Textiles	0.9666	0.0263	0.0070	0.9413	0.0503	0.0083
S20	Clothing	0.9991	0.0000	0.0009	0.9991	0.0000	0.0009
S21	Footwear	0.9934	0.0056	0.0009	0.9594	0.0052	0.0354
S22	Coffee	0.9958	0.0042	0.0000	0.9963	0.0037	0.0000
S23	Processed Vegetables	0.8982	0.0526	0.0492	0.9033	0.0575	0.0392
S24	Meat Packing Plants	0.9870	0.0024	0.0106	0.9837	0.0026	0.0137
S25	Dairy Products	0.9562	0.0264	0.0174	0.9559	0.0290	0.0151
S26	Sugar	1.0000	0.0000	0.0000	1.0000	0.0000	0.0000
S27	Vegetable Oil Mills	0.9892	0.0108	0.0000	0.9610	0.0142	0.0248
S28	Other Food Products	0.9704	0.0101	0.0195	0.9653	0.0111	0.0236
S29	Other Manufacturing	0.9476	0.0153	0.0371	0.9404	0.0143	0.0453
S30	Electric, Gas, and Sanitary Services	1.0000	0.0000	0.0000	1.0000	0.0000	0.0000
S31	Construction	0.0000	0.0000	0.0000	1.0000	0.0000	0.0000
S32	Trade	0.0000	1.0000	0.0000	0.5911	0.2612	0.1477
S33	Transportation	0.9269	0.0070	0.0661	0.8749	0.0082	0.1169
S34	Communication	1.0000	0.0000	0.0000	0.9959	0.0000	0.0041
S35	Finanacial Institutions	0.9793	0.0000	0.0207	0.9804	0.0000	0.0196
S36	Personal services	0.9519	0.0461	0.0020	0.9568	0.0413	0.0020
S37	Business Services	0.9195	0.0000	0.0805	0.9381	0.0000	0.0619
S38	Real Estate	0.9976	0.0000	0.0024	0.9970	0.0000	0.0030
S39	Public Administration	0.0000	0.0000	0.0000	1.0000	0.0000	0.0000
S40	Community Services	1.0000	0.0000	0.0000	1.0000	0.0000	0.0000
	Total	0.9477	0.0329	0.0194	0.9160	0.0305	0.0535

Table 4.12 Selected Structural Indicators: Center-South

	SECTORS	Capital+Labor/ Total Costs*	Capital-Labor Ratio	Output Share			Interregional Exports	
				Regional	National	Sectoral	North	Northeast
S1	Agriculture	0.2938	0.4250	0.0685	0.0570	0.7088	0.0516	0.9484
S2	Mining	0.2911	0.5902	0.0177	0.0148	0.6551	0.5259	0.4741
S3	Nonmetallic Minerals	0.2749	0.9005	0.0152	0.0127	0.8978	0.6174	0.3826
S4	Steel	0.1367	0.9660	0.0371	0.0309	0.9619	0.2648	0.7352
S5	Nonferrous Metals	0.1458	0.4263	0.0115	0.0096	0.8372	0.9711	0.0289
S6	Other Metal Products	0.2837	0.1614	0.0252	0.0210	0.9524	0.6579	0.3421
S7	Machinery	0.3520	0.1519	0.0281	0.0234	0.9458	0.4163	0.5837
S8	Electrical Equipment	0.2144	0.1688	0.0130	0.0109	0.9110	0.4906	0.5094
S9	Electronic Equipment	0.2778	0.3911	0.0110	0.0092	0.7375	0.5007	0.4993
S10	Transportation Equipment	0.2575	0.6649	0.0382	0.0318	0.9771	0.3101	0.6899
S11	Wood Products and Furniture	0.2192	0.2352	0.0128	0.0106	0.8504	0.1983	0.8017
S12	Paper Products and Printing	0.2779	0.7894	0.0243	0.0202	0.9337	0.3098	0.6902
S13	Rubber	0.2742	0.9709	0.0086	0.0071	0.9476	0.1961	0.8039
S14	Chemicals	0.1482	0.3093	0.0129	0.0107	0.8278	0.3132	0.6868
S15	Petroleum Refining	0.0968	0.7545	0.0670	0.0558	0.8269	0.2290	0.7710
S16	Other Chemicals	0.1976	0.2107	0.0214	0.0178	0.9296	0.4679	0.5321
S17	Pharmaceuticals and Veterinary	0.2006	0.1697	0.0113	0.0094	0.9418	0.2059	0.7941
S18	Plastics	0.3382	1.3261	0.0094	0.0078	0.9011	0.3655	0.6345
S19	Textiles	0.2017	0.6624	0.0278	0.0232	0.8441	0.0674	0.9326
S20	Clothing	0.2413	0.5607	0.0163	0.0136	0.9141	0.4121	0.5879
S21	Footwear	0.2785	0.3782	0.0098	0.0082	0.9295	0.3292	0.6708
S22	Coffee	0.0948	1.8820	0.0119	0.0099	0.8925	0.0000	1.0000
S23	Processed Vegetables	0.1705	0.6584	0.0162	0.0135	0.7381	0.1149	0.8851
S24	Meat Packing Plants	0.1136	0.9981	0.0170	0.0141	0.8511	0.0551	0.9449
S25	Dairy Products	0.1204	1.0414	0.0076	0.0063	0.8399	0.2469	0.7531
S26	Sugar	0.1225	1.0513	0.0056	0.0047	0.7015	1.0000	0.0000
S27	Vegetable Oil Mills	0.0995	1.7254	0.0138	0.0115	0.9407	0.4313	0.5687
S28	Other Food Products	0.1897	0.4954	0.0192	0.0160	0.8542	0.0975	0.9025
S29	Other Manufacturing	0.3139	0.4638	0.0182	0.0152	0.9018	0.1165	0.8835
S30	Electric, Gas, and Sanitary Services	0.4326	1.1158	0.0218	0.0182	0.8515	1.0000	0.0000
S31	Construction	0.1595	0.1978	0.0678	0.0565	0.7631	0.0000	1.0000
S32	Trade	0.4257	0.1658	0.0727	0.0606	0.8413	1.0000	0.0000
S33	Transportation	0.3535	0.7268	0.0453	0.0377	0.8671	0.0000	1.0000
S34	Communication	0.7371	0.8066	0.0069	0.0058	0.8760	1.0000	0.0000
S35	Finanacial Institutions	0.6582	0.2253	0.0164	0.0136	0.8702	0.0000	0.0000
S36	Personal services	0.3256	0.5656	0.0497	0.0414	0.7423	0.8966	0.1034
S37	Business Services	0.6706	0.7272	0.0287	0.0239	0.8499	0.6840	0.3160
S38	Real Estate	0.8571	11.1759	0.0200	0.0167	0.7158	0.8348	0.1652
S39	Public Administration	0.6906	0.1847	0.0703	0.0585	0.8232	0.0000	0.0000
S40	Community Services	0.8736	0.1257	0.0039	0.0033	0.6536	0.0000	0.0000
	Total	0.3394	0.4604	1.0000	0.8332	0.8332	0.3299	0.6701

* Other cost tickets not included

Production Linkages

The indicators described above are based on interdependence ratios of the absorption matrix, which only measure the direct linkages among agents in the economy. In this section, a comparative analysis of regional economic structure is carried out. Production linkages between sectors are considered through the analysis of the intermediate inputs portion of the interregional input-output data base (BAS1). Both the direct and indirect production linkage effects of the economy are captured by the adoption of different methods based on the evaluation of the Leontief inverse matrix. The purpose remains the comparison of economic structures rather than an evaluation of the methods of analysis themselves.

Intraregional Linkages and Key Sectors

An attempt to identify key sectors in the regional economies of the North, Northeast and Center-South is made in this section. Familiar complementary approaches are used in order to reveal particular regional production features. They include: Rasmussen-Hirschman indices, input-output multiplier product matrix (MPM), field of influence, and pure linkage indices. The presentation of each of these techniques,[1] accompanied by the empirical results, follows.

Rasmussen-Hirschman Indices Rasmussen (1956) and Hirschman (1958) proposed the use of two indices to capture the effects of backward and forward linkages in an economy, through the use of input-output tables. Let b_{ij} be a typical element in the Leontief inverse, B. Define $b_{.j}$, $b_{i\cdot}$, and $b_{..}$ as the column, row, and total sums of B, respectively. Further, define $B^{*} = b_{..}/n^{2}$ as the average value of all elements in the same matrix. Then, the backward linkage index, U_j, and the forward linkage index, U_i, can be calculated by:

$$U_j = \frac{b_{.j}/n}{B^{*}} \tag{4.1}$$

$$U_i = \frac{b_{i}./n}{B^{*}} \tag{4.2}$$

[1] The presentation of the methodology draws on Haddad (1995) and Guilhoto *et al.* (1997).

where n is the number of sectors. In U_j, the numerator is the average value of the elements in column j, while in U_i, the numerator is the average value of the elements in row i. Thus, interpretation of both indices is straightforward: $U_j > 1$ indicates that a unit change in final demand of sector j creates an above-average increase in the economy, i.e., sector j generates above-average response in other sectors; $U_i > 1$ indicates that a unit change in all sector's final demand creates an above-average increase in sector i, i.e., sector i displays above-average dependence on the output of other sectors. Sectors that have both $U_j > 1$ and $U_i > 1$ are considered key sectors in the economy.

Backward and forward linkage indices were calculated for the 40-sector regional tables of the three regions (Table 4.13). Table 4.14 presents the classification of the sectors in the Brazilian regions based on the estimates of these indices. Key sectors for each region are shown at the upper right corner of the table. In Brazil's North, six key sectors were identified: nonferrous metals (5), machinery (7), textiles (19), meat packing plants (24), electric, gas, and sanitary services (30), and construction (31). Both the nonferrous metals and the textiles sectors were also identified in the Northeast and Center-South as key sectors. Other key sectors in the Northeast are steel (4), paper products and printing (12), and petroleum refining (15). In the Center-South, key sectors are heavily associated with the heavy industry: steel (4), nonferrous metals (5), other metal products (6), machinery (7).

In addition to the estimates of U_j and U_i, Table 4.13 also shows the coefficients of variation of these indices.[2] They reveal comparative features related to the internal integration of the economies considered. For most of the sectors, the coefficients of variation are smaller in the Center-South, emphasizing the fact that the economic structure is more integrated at that region. The values for the Northeast, when compared to those for the North, also reveal a relatively more integrated economy.

---

[2] The coefficients of variation show how the linkage effects spread over the other sectors and are defined by:

$$V_{\cdot j} = \frac{\sqrt{\frac{1}{n-1}\sum_i \left[b_{ij} - \left(b_{\cdot j}/n\right)\right]^2}}{b_{\cdot j}/n} \quad \text{and} \quad V_{i\cdot} = \frac{\sqrt{\frac{1}{n-1}\sum_j \left[b_{ij} - \left(b_{i\cdot}/n\right)\right]^2}}{b_{i\cdot}/n}$$

The lower the value of $V_{\cdot j}$, the larger the number of sectors related to the intermediate demand induced by j; and the lower the value of $V_{i\cdot}$, the more sectors are supplied by sector i, within the region.

Table 4.13 Rasmussen-Hirschman Backward and Forward Linkages

	SECTOR	North						Northeast						Center-South					
		BL	*Rank*	$V_{\cdot j}$	*FL*	*Rank*	$V_{i\cdot}$	*BL*	*Rank*	$V_{\cdot j}$	*FL*	*Rank*	$V_{i\cdot}$	*BL*	*Rank*	$V_{\cdot j}$	*FL*	*Rank*	$V_{i\cdot}$
S1	Agriculture	0.891	26	5.426	4.434	1	1.662	0.806	32	5.235	4.428	1	2.364	0.912	29	4.231	3.251	1	1.742
S2	Mining	0.737	38	5.875	1.064	6	4.170	0.678	37	5.564	1.421	7	2.746	0.850	31	3.835	1.088	12	2.979
S3	Nonmetallic Minerals	1.076	12	4.247	0.841	18	5.458	1.079	13	4.015	0.791	19	5.489	1.120	12	3.522	0.839	19	4.703
S4	Steel	0.822	32	5.244	0.706	35	6.108	1.242	4	4.506	1.030	10	5.435	1.415	1	4.337	2.029	3	3.123
S5	Nonferrous Metals	1.071	13	4.932	0.864	16	6.024	1.408	2	5.168	1.605	3	4.561	1.036	19	4.006	1.046	14	3.997
S6	Other Metal Products	0.876	29	5.008	0.838	19	5.243	0.837	31	4.551	0.729	23	5.221	1.192	8	3.212	1.255	9	2.770
S7	Machinery	1.062	14	4.458	1.055	8	4.467	1.014	19	4.307	0.975	11	4.456	1.110	13	3.321	1.262	8	2.831
S8	Electrical Equipment	0.766	36	5.640	0.707	34	6.110	1.019	17	4.073	0.765	21	5.284	1.174	9	3.001	0.711	25	4.904
S9	Electronic Equipment	0.877	28	5.666	0.813	23	6.117	0.627	40	6.056	0.603	37	6.298	0.913	28	3.833	0.593	36	5.951
S10	Transportation Equipment	1.031	18	4.929	0.819	22	6.204	0.869	27	4.414	0.627	35	6.142	1.291	4	3.398	0.925	16	4.707
S11	Wood Products and Furniture	1.111	9	4.255	0.837	20	5.521	0.906	25	4.404	0.676	31	5.920	1.069	18	3.500	0.692	27	5.426
S12	Paper Products and Printing	1.161	7	3.916	0.789	27	5.669	1.046	15	5.171	1.143	9	4.715	0.989	22	4.194	1.238	10	3.318
S13	Rubber	1.124	8	4.248	0.802	24	5.409	1.075	14	3.872	0.703	27	5.904	1.015	20	4.128	0.902	17	4.611
S14	Chemicals	1.182	5	4.039	0.735	30	5.866	0.968	21	4.071	0.891	15	4.283	1.076	17	3.077	0.804	20	3.893
S15	Petroleum Refining	0.710	40	6.152	1.037	11	4.182	1.167	6	4.492	2.246	2	2.409	0.789	33	4.597	2.346	2	1.544
S16	Other Chemicals	0.966	20	4.548	0.733	31	5.979	1.093	11	3.786	0.882	16	4.381	0.915	27	4.001	1.419	6	2.552
S17	Pharmaceuticals and Veterinary	0.936	22	4.607	0.685	36	6.303	1.011	20	3.819	0.617	36	6.248	0.944	24	3.395	0.539	37	5.995
S18	Plastics	0.805	34	5.356	0.801	25	5.375	1.088	12	3.782	0.680	30	5.543	0.946	23	3.674	0.803	21	4.073
S19	Textiles	1.053	15	5.604	1.365	5	4.620	1.230	5	4.314	1.264	8	4.204	1.086	15	4.398	1.394	7	3.714
S20	Clothing	1.168	6	4.167	0.682	38	6.325	0.936	23	4.120	0.601	38	6.241	1.094	14	3.398	0.506	38	6.136
S21	Footwear	1.366	4	3.581	0.708	33	6.301	1.108	10	3.967	0.699	28	6.240	1.085	16	3.557	0.634	33	6.139
S22	Coffee	1.621	1	3.934	0.868	15	6.255	1.130	9	4.340	0.755	22	6.276	1.368	3	3.587	0.680	29	6.182
S23	Processed Vegetables	0.926	24	4.802	0.776	28	5.701	1.018	18	4.024	0.716	25	5.387	1.141	11	3.137	0.651	31	4.995
S24	Meat Packing Plants	1.542	2	3.854	1.052	9	4.739	2.435	1	4.143	0.666	33	5.647	1.157	10	3.375	0.638	32	5.356
S25	Dairy Products	1.039	17	4.422	0.682	37	6.323	1.039	16	4.266	0.662	34	6.230	1.290	5	3.383	0.654	30	6.139
S26	Sugar	1.045	16	4.407	0.713	32	6.246	1.146	8	3.820	0.712	26	5.597	1.381	2	3.114	0.759	24	5.338
S27	Vegetable Oil Mills	1.108	10	4.068	0.746	29	5.797	1.252	3	3.671	0.834	17	5.372	1.284	6	3.229	0.795	22	4.825
S28	Other Food Products	1.079	11	4.192	0.790	26	5.666	1.166	7	3.417	0.722	24	5.383	1.225	7	2.727	0.705	26	4.640
S29	Other Manufacturing	0.891	25	5.108	0.898	13	5.074	0.644	39	5.856	0.966	12	3.893	0.668	35	4.707	0.999	15	3.106
S30	Electric, Gas, and Sanitary Services	1.003	19	5.058	1.064	7	4.754	0.967	22	4.990	1.471	6	3.261	0.941	25	4.758	1.232	11	3.596
S31	Construction	1.461	3	3.864	1.040	10	5.432	0.853	29	4.526	0.768	20	5.081	0.992	21	3.291	0.689	28	4.763
S32	Trade	0.939	21	4.707	1.908	2	2.264	0.744	34	5.247	1.584	4	2.398	0.799	32	3.971	1.522	4	2.016
S33	Transportation	0.848	30	5.153	1.470	4	2.934	0.844	30	4.542	0.945	13	4.004	0.889	30	3.807	1.463	5	2.214
S34	Communication	0.812	33	5.357	0.828	21	5.251	0.903	26	4.206	0.670	32	5.633	0.656	36	4.732	0.615	35	5.053
S35	Finanacial Institutions	0.745	37	5.892	0.953	12	4.582	0.687	36	5.691	0.792	18	4.924	0.605	40	5.205	0.787	23	3.952
S36	Personal services	0.842	31	5.162	0.853	17	5.096	0.853	28	4.481	0.938	14	4.080	0.941	26	3.362	0.869	18	3.612
S37	Business Services	0.932	23	5.159	1.782	3	2.636	0.931	24	4.661	1.551	5	2.736	0.625	38	5.087	1.051	13	2.969
S38	Real Estate	0.767	35	5.628	0.897	14	4.787	0.730	35	5.170	0.687	29	5.441	0.636	37	4.890	0.633	34	4.878
S39	Public Administration	0.885	27	4.860	0.682	39	6.325	0.792	33	4.714	0.592	39	6.325	0.774	34	3.989	0.490	39	6.325
S40	Community Services	0.725	39	5.944	0.682	40	6.325	0.659	38	5.669	0.592	40	6.325	0.608	39	5.070	0.490	40	6.325

Table 4.14 Sector Classification in the Brazilian Regions, 1985

	Backward-Linkage-Oriented Sectors	Key Sectors
North	3, 10, 11, 12, 13, 14, 20, 21, 22, 25, 26, 27, 28	5, 7, 19, 24, 30, 31
Northeast	3, 7, 8, 13, 16, 17, 18, 21, 22, 23, 24, 25, 26, 27, 28	4, 5, 12, 15, 19
Center-South	3, 8, 10, 11, 13, 14, 20, 21, 22, 23, 24, 25, 26, 27, 28	4, 5, 6, 7, 19
	Less Important Sectors	**Forward-Linkage-Oriented Sectors**
North	4, 6, 8, 9, 16, 17, 18, 23, 29, 34, 35, 36, 38, 39, 40	1, 2, 15, 32, 33, 37
Northeast	6, 9, 10, 11, 14, 20, 29, 31, 33, 34, 35, 36, 38, 39, 40	1, 2, 30, 32, 37
Center-South	9, 17, 18, 29, 31, 34, 35, 36, 38, 39, 40	1, 2, 12, 15, 16, 30, 32, 33, 37

Multiplier Product Matrix (MPM) The concept of the multiplier product matrix (MPM) was developed by Sonis *et al.* (1994) as an alternative approach to the Rasmussen-Hirschman indices. The definition of the MPM is as follows: given the Leontief inverse, B, let $b_{\cdot j}$ and $b_{i\cdot}$ be the column and row multipliers of the Leontief inverse, as above. Further, let $V = b_{\cdot\cdot}$ be the global intensity of the Leontief inverse. Then, the input-output MPM is defined as:

$$M = \frac{1}{V}\left\| b_{i\cdot} b_{\cdot j} \right\| = \frac{1}{V}\begin{pmatrix} b_{1\cdot} \\ b_{2\cdot} \\ \vdots \\ b_{n\cdot} \end{pmatrix} \begin{pmatrix} b_{\cdot 1} & b_{\cdot 2} & \dots & b_{\cdot n} \end{pmatrix} \tag{4.3}$$

It can be shown that the MPM has a cross structure; this cross structure can be exploited to reveal a hierarchy of transactions such that there exists a cross (one row and column) in which the elements of this row (column) are larger than the corresponding elements of every other row (column). If this cross is now excluded, another cross with the same properties can be identified and the procedure repeated until all the rows and columns have been arranged. This new arrangement will be conducted in such a way that the centers of subsequent crosses will appear on the main diagonal, thereby providing a descending economic landscape.

An attempt was made to compare the economic structure of the Brazilian regions, by considering the hierarchy of backward and forward linkages – related to the column and row multipliers, respectively – and their economic landscape associated with the cross structure of the MPM. The results, depicted in Figures 4.3 to 4.6, reveal the cross structure for the country and its three regions; the rows represent the hierarchy of forward linkages while the columns provide similar detail for the backward linkages. For purposes of comparison, the sectors in the regional economic landscapes were arranged in the same order as that for Brazil. Hence, the sectors with the higher backward linkages in the Brazilian economy as a whole are those that appear in the first columns of the matrix, while sectors with higher forward linkages occupy the first rows. If all the three regional economies had identical interindustry structures, then the regional economic landscapes would be as smooth as the one shown for Brazil. With the Brazilian sectoral hierarchy imposed on the regional economies, it can be seen that these economies do not have exactly the same linkage structure as the nation. However, for the Center-South, Figure 4.6 shows that there is a good fit between the imposed hierarchy of Brazil and the regional economy. A slight difference appears in that the sectoral connections are smoother in the country, suggesting that in the Center-South there are more dominant sectors than in the country as a whole. Sectoral dominance in the North and Northeast is even stronger, as it is apparent from the peaks in the respective landscapes. The visual impression obtained from these landscapes is that the regional economies appear to be rather more different in structure than the Rasmussen-Hirschman indices would lead one to suggest.

Figure 4.3 Brazil, 1985: Cross-Structure "Landscape" for First Order MPM

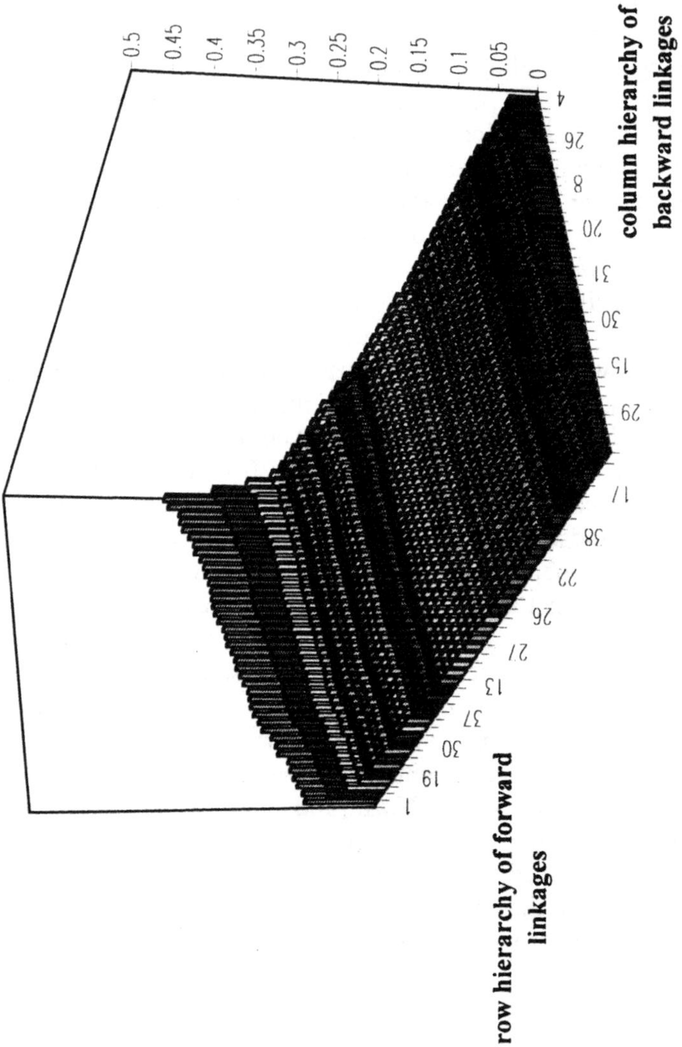

Figure 4.4 North, 1985: Cross-Structure "Landscape" Using Brazil Imposed Hierarchy

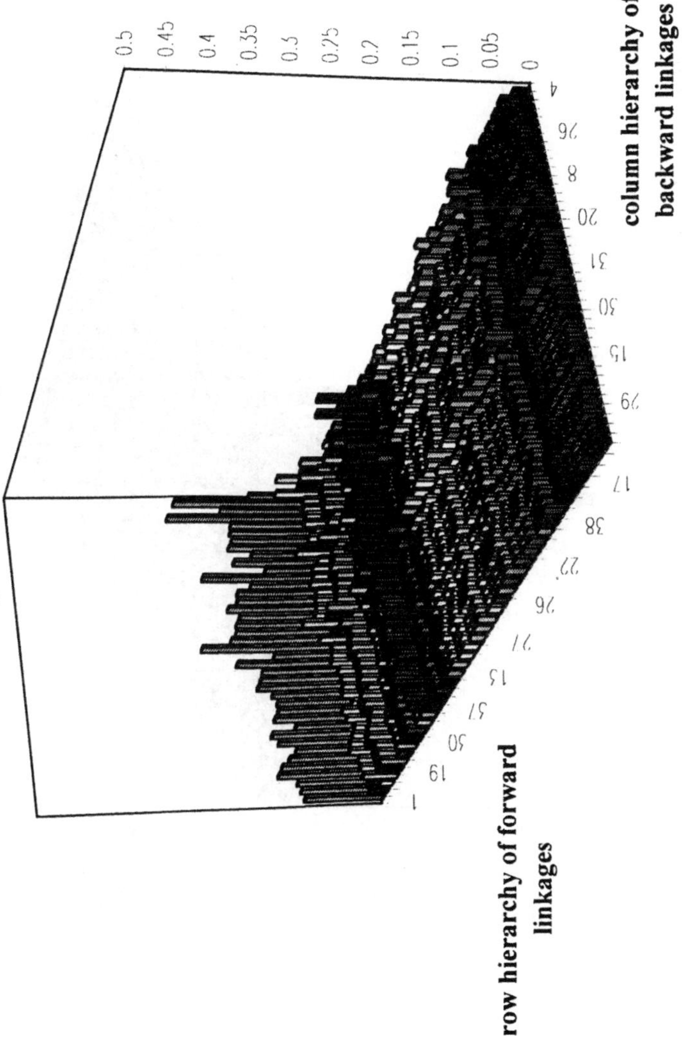

Figure 4.5 Northeast, 1985: Cross-Structure "Landscape" Using Brazil Imposed Hierarchy

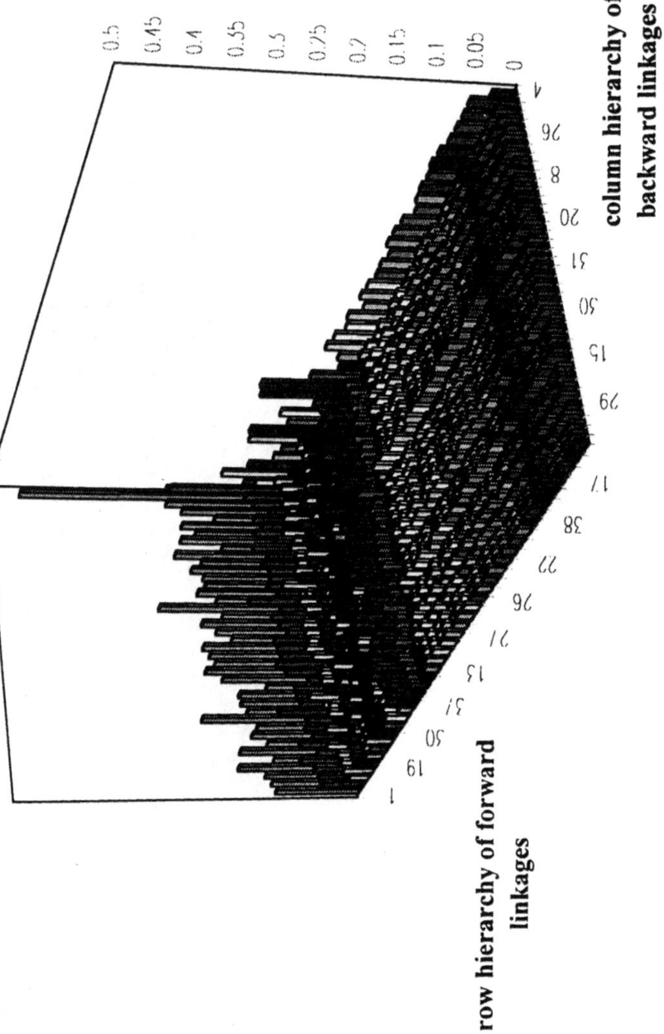

Figure 4.6 Center-South, 1985: Cross-Structure "Landscape" Using Brazil Imposed Hierarchy

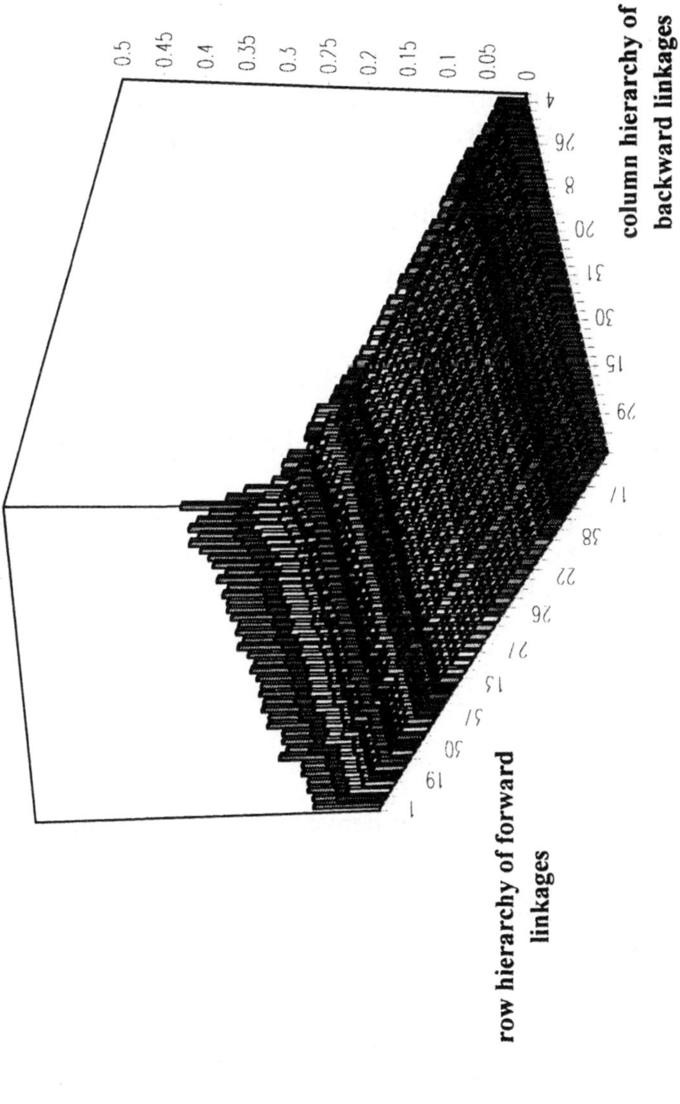

Field of Influence The concept of field of influence was introduced and elaborated by Sonis and Hewings (1989, 1993). It is mainly concerned with the problem of coefficient change, namely the influence of a change in one or more direct coefficients on the associated Leontief inverse. Since, given an economic system, some coefficients are more "influential" than others, the sector responsible for the greater changes in the economy can be determined. In the simplest case, i.e., the case in which a small enough change, ε, occurs in only one input parameter, a_{ij}, the basic solution of the coefficient change problem may be presented as follows. Define:

$A = \|a_{ij}\|$ is the matrix of direct input coefficients;

$E = \|\varepsilon_{ij}\|$ is the matrix of incremental changes in the direct input coefficients;

$B = (I - A)^{-1} = \|b_{ij}\|$ is the Leontief inverse before changes;

$B(\varepsilon) = (I - A - E)^{-1} = \|b_{ij}(\varepsilon)\|$ is the Leontief inverse after changes.

Using the notion of inverse-important input coefficients, which is based on the conception of the field of influence associated with the change in only one input coefficient, assume that this change occurs in location (i_1, j_1), that is,

$$\varepsilon_{ij} = \begin{cases} \varepsilon & i = i_1, j = j_1 \\ 0 & i \neq i_1, j \neq j_1 \end{cases} \tag{4.4}$$

The field of influence can be derived from the approximate relation:

$$F(\varepsilon_{ij}) \cong \frac{\left[B(\varepsilon_{ij}) - B\right]}{\varepsilon_{ij}} \tag{4.5}$$

where $F(\varepsilon_{ij})$ is the matrix of the field of influence of the change on the input coefficient, a_{ij}. For every coefficient, a_{ij}, there will be an associated field of influence matrix. In order to determine which coefficients have the greater field of influence, reference is made to the rank-size ordering of the elements, S_{ij}, from the largest to the smallest ones. Therefore, for every matrix $F(\varepsilon_{ij})$, there will be an associated value given by:

$$S_{ij} = \sum_{k=1}^{n}\sum_{l=1}^{n}\left[f_{kl}\left(\varepsilon_{ij}\right)\right] \tag{4.6}$$

Thus, from the values of S_{ij}, a hierarchy can be developed of the direct coefficients based on their field of influence, i.e., ranking sectoral relations in terms of their sensitivity to changes, in a sense that they will be responsible for more significant impacts on the economy.

The estimates of the field of influence for the Brazilian regions show that the sectors which have the greatest values are agriculture (1) and textiles (19), in the North; agriculture (1) and meat packing plants (24), in the Northeast; and agriculture (1) and steel (4), in the Center-South. Textiles, in the North, and steel, in the Center-South, are also characterized as key sectors in the Rasmussen-Hirschman approach; agriculture presented the greatest forward linkage in the three regions, and meat packing plants presented the greatest backward linkage in the Northeast. Again, the field of influence approach reinforces the notion of the North as an economy with a more limited structure; the concentration of coefficients with highest field of influence presents a less dispersed pattern (Figures 4.7, 4.8, and 4.9).

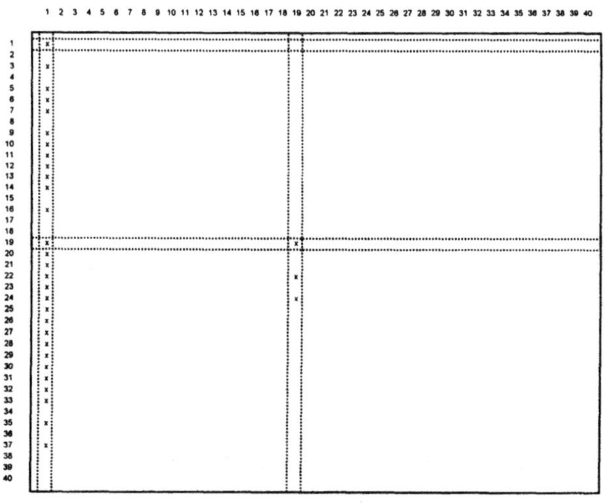

Figure 4.7 North, 1985: Coefficients with the Largest Field of Influence

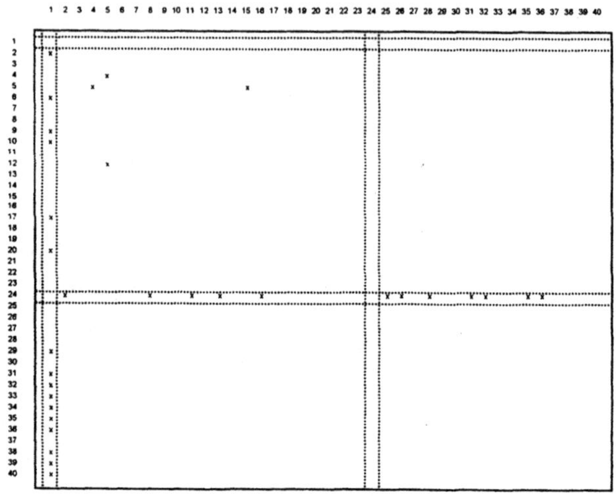

Figure 4.8 Northeast, 1985: Coefficients with the Largest Field of Influence

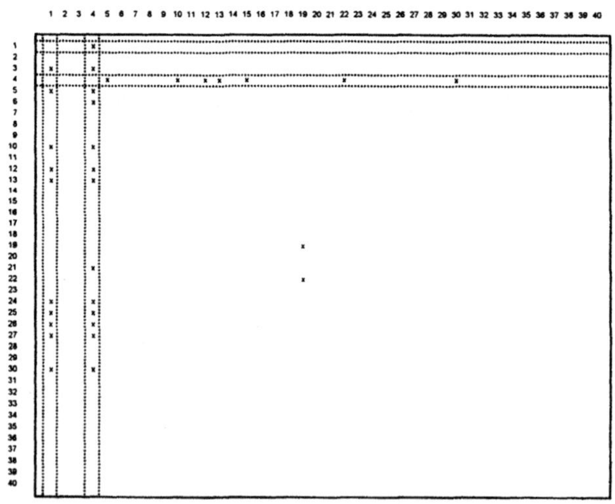

Figure 4.9 Center-South, 1985: Coefficients with the Largest Field of Influence

Pure Linkage Indices The pure linkage approach was introduced by Sonis et al. (1995) as a refinement of the work of Cella-Clements for backward and forward linkages.[3] In contrast to the Rasmussen-Hirschman, and to the field of influence approaches, it does take into consideration the level of production in each sector, complementing, in a sense, the analysis of key sector determination in an economy.

The pure linkage approach may be summarized as follows. Consider the direct input coefficient matrix, A:

$$A = \begin{bmatrix} A_{jj} & A_{jr} \\ A_{rj} & A_{rr} \end{bmatrix} \tag{4.7}$$

where A_{jj} and A_{rr} are square matrices of direct inputs, respectively, within sector j and within the rest of the economy (economy less sector j); A_{jr} and A_{rj} are rectangular matrices showing , respectively, the direct inputs purchased by sector j from the rest of the economy, and the direct inputs purchased by the rest of the economy from sector j. Define the Leontief inverse as

$$B = (I - A)^{-1}, \tag{4.8}$$

and the internal Leontief inverse for the rest of the economy as

$$\Delta_r = \left(I - A_{rr}\right)^{-1}. \tag{4.9}$$

The *pure backward linkage* (PBL) can be defined as

$$PBL = i'_{rr} \Delta_r A_{rj} q_j \tag{4.10}$$

where i'_{rr} is a unit row vector of the appropriate dimension, and q_j is the value of total production in sector j. The pure forward linkage can be defined as

$$PFL = A_{jr} \Delta_r q_r \tag{4.11}$$

[3] See Cella (1984) and Clements (1990) for a formal treatment of the subject, and Clements and Rossi (1990, 1992) for an application to the Brazilian economy.

where q_r is a column vector of total production in each sector in the rest of the economy.

The following interpretation of the indices may be provided: the PBL will give the pure impact on the economy of the value of the total production in sector j, i.e., the impact that is free from the demand of inputs that sector j makes from sector j, and the feedback from the economy to sector j, and vice-versa; the PFL will give the pure impact on sector j of the total production in the rest of the economy. Furthermore, the definition of *pure total linkage* (PTL) is given by the addition of the PBL to the PFL. Hence, in this approach, key sectors are considered as those with the largest values of PTL.

In the computation of pure linkage indices, the input coefficient matrix and the sectoral output vector for the respective economies were used. The output values are given in Cr$1 billion of 1985. Both the PBL and the PFL were estimated, which provided an estimate for the PTL (Table 4.15). From the values obtained for the PTL, a hierarchy of the sectors was established for each region, from which the key sectors were selected.

Agriculture (1) and construction (31) were selected for the three regions, while petroleum refining (15) was selected for both the Northeast and the Center-South. Other sectors with high PTL include trade (32), business services (37), and transportation (33), in the North; mining (2), personal services (36), and meat packing plants (24), in the Northeast; other metal products (6), personal services (36), and transportation (33), in the Center-South. Services sectors in general presented above-average PTL in the three regions. These are the dominant sectors in the sense that they contribute significantly to changes in the level of the GRP and other macro-level measures of the respective economies.

Interregional Linkages

In this section, interdependence among sectors in different regions is considered through the analysis of the complete intermediate input portion of the interregional input-output table.[4] The direct input coefficient matrix considered is of the form:

[4] Foreign inputs are disregarded.

Table 4.15 Pure Linkage Indices

	SECTOR	North			Northeast			Center-South		
		PBL	PFL	PTL	PBL	PFL	PTL	PBL	PFL	PTL
S1	Agriculture	2872.5	3907.5	6780.0	7900.3	26848.1	34748.5	68117.5	125836.3	193953.8
S2	Mining	467.9	907.0	1374.9	1686.3	14263.7	15950.0	22717.7	59576.9	82294.5
S3	Nonmetallic Minerals	374.6	932.4	1307.1	1546.5	2427.5	3974.0	24090.2	22926.8	47017.1
S4	Steel	9.6	72.5	82.1	1162.3	499.5	1661.8	33380.6	54721.5	88102.1
S5	Nonferrous Metals	73.3	210.1	283.5	947.5	1595.3	2542.8	13122.6	26920.0	40042.6
S6	Other Metal Products	139.8	565.5	705.2	765.9	1094.4	1860.3	58253.7	65621.0	123874.8
S7	Machinery	328.5	634.1	962.5	1134.8	2560.6	3695.4	52446.8	52454.9	104901.7
S8	Electrical Equipment	105.9	177.3	283.3	995.3	877.6	1872.8	29336.4	16523.7	45860.1
S9	Electronic Equipment	856.6	32.1	888.7	15.0	14.4	29.4	14012.5	2656.9	16669.3
S10	Transportation Equipment	309.9	37.3	347.2	297.4	258.3	555.7	66367.1	19887.8	86254.9
S11	Wood Products and Furniture	1497.1	687.8	2184.9	700.4	751.6	1452.0	20357.0	10321.2	30678.1
S12	Paper Products and Printing	501.5	197.1	698.6	584.1	2011.3	2595.4	24190.4	37792.1	61982.5
S13	Rubber	355.5	266.2	621.7	250.2	250.4	500.6	9191.8	18165.6	27357.4
S14	Chemicals	145.6	91.7	237.3	3062.7	2693.3	5756.1	29689.7	25638.6	55328.3
S15	Petroleum Refining	29.6	868.0	897.7	11783.5	8787.3	20570.8	50538.1	123360.5	173898.6
S16	Other Chemicals	50.1	142.0	192.1	2429.3	3275.3	5704.6	24647.4	65656.4	90303.7
S17	Pharmaceuticals and Veterinary	54.7	14.0	68.6	822.3	177.6	999.9	19160.8	3753.3	22914.1
S18	Plastics	60.2	400.5	460.7	1420.8	1202.3	2623.1	15254.2	21817.6	37071.8
S19	Textiles	146.4	259.0	405.4	4460.1	2029.3	6489.5	24179.5	28168.5	52348.0
S20	Clothing	79.0	0.0	79.0	1715.1	123.4	1838.5	40189.9	1337.8	41527.7
S21	Footwear	83.9	16.1	100.0	851.4	101.1	952.6	15065.4	1186.9	16252.3
S22	Coffee	546.8	30.9	577.6	1153.3	118.2	1271.5	25309.0	1466.4	26775.4
S23	Processed Vegetables	624.7	209.5	834.2	6494.1	1199.2	7693.3	39807.6	11654.3	51461.9
S24	Meat Packing Plants	1370.9	128.2	1499.2	14486.8	459.2	14945.9	38784.1	6595.6	45379.7
S25	Dairy Products	52.3	1.1	53.5	1661.1	158.4	1819.6	15659.9	1856.4	17516.3
S26	Sugar	46.4	14.6	61.0	3819.7	841.5	4661.2	12903.2	7227.3	20130.5
S27	Vegetable Oil Mills	43.4	17.4	60.8	1295.3	654.5	1949.8	30877.4	12926.0	43803.5
S28	Other Food Products	752.4	435.7	1188.2	4585.3	1973.9	6559.2	52315.2	19236.0	71551.2
S29	Other Manufacturing	206.4	294.8	501.2	242.7	4831.1	5073.8	12264.0	46012.1	58276.1
S30	Electric, Gas, and Sanitary Services	338.6	752.0	1090.6	1639.4	5241.9	6881.3	14072.6	32835.6	46908.2
S31	Construction	4143.7	630.9	4774.6	13923.9	2423.9	16347.8	124259.9	13569.6	137829.5
S32	Trade	467.4	3080.8	3548.1	2234.3	9880.1	12114.4	6839.7	95957.4	102797.1
S33	Transportation	389.8	2301.2	2691.0	1744.8	4238.0	5982.8	40193.0	75863.8	116056.8
S34	Communication	110.8	444.2	555.0	680.4	1238.7	1919.0	4551.3	11020.5	15571.8
S35	Finanacial Institutions	89.0	830.9	919.8	402.1	2892.7	3294.7	6961.2	25131.7	32092.9
S36	Personal services	1304.3	583.2	1887.5	11547.4	4079.6	15626.9	86193.3	34876.3	121069.7
S37	Business Services	571.1	2136.4	2707.5	2684.9	7828.2	10513.1	13995.3	55661.5	69656.9
S38	Real Estate	585.0	794.7	1379.7	2576.6	1800.7	4377.3	11870.6	11352.9	23223.6
S39	Public Administration	1896.7	0.0	1896.7	8070.9	0.0	8070.9	81593.9	0.0	81593.9
S40	Community Services	59.6	0.0	59.6	366.8	0.0	366.8	1907.6	0.0	1907.6
	Average	553.541	577.614	1131.155	3103.5	3042.6	6146.1	31866.7	31189.2	63055.9

$$A = \begin{bmatrix} A_{NN} & A_{NNE} & A_{NCS} \\ A_{NEN} & A_{NENE} & A_{NECS} \\ A_{CSN} & A_{CSNE} & A_{CSCS} \end{bmatrix} \tag{4.12}$$

where A_{NN}, A_{NENE}, and A_{CSCS} correspond to the intraregional (domestic) inputs in the North, Northeast and Center-South, respectively; and A_{NNE}, A_{NCS}, A_{NEN}, A_{NECS}, A_{CSN}, and A_{CSNE} capture the system of interregional inputs.

The Leontief inverse matrix, $B = (I - A)^{-1}$, based on the system (5.12), will be considered, and some summary interpretations of the structure of the economy derived from it will be provided.

Multiplier Analysis The column multipliers derived from *B* were computed (see Miller and Blair, 1985). An output multiplier is defined for each sector *j*, in each region *r*, as the total value of production in all sectors and in all regions of the economy that is necessary in order to satisfy a dollar's worth of final demand for sector *j*'s output. The multiplier effect can be decomposed into intraregional (internal multiplier) and interregional (external multiplier) effects, the former representing the impacts on the outputs of sectors within the region where the final demand change was generated, and the latter showing the impacts on the other regions of the system (interregional spillover effects).

Table 4.16 shows the direct and indirect effects of a unit change in final demand in each sector in each region net of the initial injection, i.e., the output multiplier effect net of the initial change. The entries are shown in percentage terms, providing insights into the degree of dependence of each sector in each region on the other regions. The Center-South is by far the most self-sufficient region; the flow-on effects from a unit change in sectoral final demand are always in excess of 85.0%. For the Northeast, there is a lower degree of intraregional self-sufficiency, and the dominant interregional flows generated by the region usually end up in the Center-South. In the North, the degree of regional self-sufficiency is much lower, and the intraregional flow-on effects, on the average, are lower than the total interregional effects. Again, the latter is largely directed to the Center-South, showing a large dependency of the North upon the more developed part of the country.

Table 4.16 Regional Percentage Distribution of Output Multiplier Effects Net of the Initial Injection: Brazil, 1985

	SECTOR	North			Northeast			Center-South		
		North	Northeast	Center-South	North	Northeast	Center-South	North	Northeast	Center-South
S1	Agriculture	52.3%	3.9%	43.8%	0.3%	68.8%	30.8%	2.1%	4.2%	93.7%
S2	Mining	55.0%	7.5%	37.5%	0.7%	71.8%	27.5%	1.1%	2.6%	96.2%
S3	Nonmetallic Minerals	61.5%	3.9%	34.7%	0.3%	78.8%	20.8%	3.1%	3.4%	93.5%
S4	Steel	10.2%	2.0%	87.8%	0.4%	60.2%	39.4%	1.0%	3.1%	95.9%
S5	Nonferrous Metals	67.9%	1.2%	30.9%	1.2%	71.0%	27.8%	3.3%	3.5%	93.2%
S6	Other Metal Products	31.5%	21.3%	47.2%	0.5%	48.9%	50.6%	1.0%	2.9%	96.1%
S7	Machinery	38.8%	6.8%	54.4%	2.5%	38.4%	59.1%	1.1%	2.6%	96.3%
S8	Electrical Equipment	49.4%	11.8%	38.8%	1.8%	67.7%	30.4%	1.4%	3.3%	95.2%
S9	Electronic Equipment	38.2%	3.9%	57.8%	4.0%	16.3%	79.8%	6.9%	2.7%	90.4%
S10	Transportation Equipment	32.2%	6.8%	61.0%	1.3%	35.8%	62.9%	1.4%	2.6%	96.0%
S11	Wood Products and Furniture	71.7%	3.6%	24.7%	2.5%	64.0%	33.5%	2.9%	4.1%	93.1%
S12	Paper Products and Printing	58.3%	2.2%	39.6%	0.3%	66.0%	33.7%	1.1%	3.0%	95.9%
S13	Rubber	76.5%	2.6%	20.9%	4.6%	64.1%	31.4%	1.5%	7.8%	90.7%
S14	Chemicals	71.8%	4.0%	24.2%	0.3%	68.6%	31.1%	1.7%	2.9%	95.3%
S15	Petroleum Refining	14.7%	1.8%	83.5%	0.2%	81.1%	18.7%	0.5%	11.8%	87.6%
S16	Other Chemicals	32.7%	7.6%	59.7%	0.3%	65.5%	34.2%	1.1%	8.7%	90.2%
S17	Pharmaceuticals and Veterinary	43.4%	3.4%	53.2%	0.8%	46.8%	52.4%	1.2%	5.5%	93.2%
S18	Plastics	22.5%	6.0%	71.5%	0.1%	80.0%	19.8%	0.4%	13.8%	85.7%
S19	Textiles	62.5%	6.5%	31.0%	0.2%	73.2%	26.6%	0.5%	11.8%	87.7%
S20	Clothing	58.5%	4.7%	36.8%	0.2%	60.6%	39.2%	0.4%	7.7%	91.9%
S21	Footwear	71.4%	2.2%	26.3%	2.8%	46.8%	50.4%	1.8%	4.3%	93.9%
S22	Coffee	82.7%	1.3%	16.0%	0.3%	66.6%	33.0%	1.0%	1.8%	97.2%
S23	Processed Vegetables	70.4%	2.1%	27.5%	0.8%	67.3%	31.9%	4.8%	4.6%	90.6%
S24	Meat Packing Plants	81.7%	1.4%	16.8%	1.2%	85.3%	13.5%	10.5%	2.2%	87.3%
S25	Dairy Products	81.7%	1.5%	16.8%	0.2%	78.3%	21.5%	1.0%	3.3%	95.8%
S26	Sugar	51.2%	1.9%	46.9%	0.2%	85.4%	14.4%	0.8%	2.4%	96.7%
S27	Vegetable Oil Mills	80.5%	1.5%	17.9%	2.0%	59.8%	38.2%	4.3%	3.1%	92.7%
S28	Other Food Products	53.9%	3.0%	43.2%	0.6%	76.1%	23.4%	2.3%	4.2%	93.4%
S29	Other Manufacturing	51.3%	2.6%	46.1%	0.4%	80.5%	19.1%	3.1%	4.6%	92.3%
S30	Electric, Gas, and Sanitary Services	41.7%	5.0%	53.2%	0.3%	81.9%	17.8%	0.4%	1.5%	98.1%
S31	Construction	25.1%	5.8%	69.1%	0.6%	59.8%	39.6%	1.6%	2.8%	95.6%
S32	Trade	54.5%	2.7%	42.8%	0.1%	64.9%	35.0%	0.6%	3.2%	96.2%
S33	Transportation	23.0%	6.3%	70.7%	0.5%	56.6%	42.8%	0.9%	5.0%	94.1%
S34	Communication	39.7%	3.4%	56.9%	0.5%	69.1%	30.4%	2.2%	2.3%	95.5%
S35	Finanacial Institutions	70.9%	2.1%	27.1%	0.2%	82.1%	17.7%	0.6%	1.3%	98.1%
S36	Personal services	47.1%	6.1%	46.9%	0.6%	57.6%	41.8%	2.0%	3.3%	94.7%
S37	Business Services	55.8%	2.6%	41.6%	0.3%	76.4%	23.3%	1.1%	1.6%	97.3%
S38	Real Estate	38.8%	4.7%	56.5%	0.3%	82.0%	17.7%	0.8%	1.5%	97.7%
S39	Public Administration	46.9%	3.3%	49.8%	0.3%	76.2%	23.5%	1.1%	2.8%	96.1%
S40	Community Services	56.3%	2.7%	41.0%	0.6%	75.1%	24.3%	2.0%	2.5%	95.5%
	Average	48.6%	4.4%	47.1%	1.0%	65.7%	33.3%	2.1%	4.2%	93.7%

Output Decomposition A complementary analysis to the multiplier approach is presented in this section. Sectoral output in each region is decomposed, by taking into account not only the multiplier structure, but also the structure of final demand in the three regions (Sonis et al., 1996).

In the interregional input-output model, output, X, is defined by $B \bullet f = X$, where f is the final demand vector. In the Brazilian table,

$$\begin{bmatrix} B_{NN} & B_{NNE} & B_{NCS} \\ B_{NEN} & B_{NENE} & B_{NECS} \\ B_{CSN} & B_{CSNE} & B_{CSCS} \end{bmatrix} \begin{bmatrix} f_N \\ f_{NE} \\ f_{CS} \end{bmatrix} = \begin{bmatrix} X_N \\ X_{NE} \\ X_{CS} \end{bmatrix} \tag{4.13}$$

which can be rewritten as

$$\underbrace{B_{iN} f_N}_{\alpha_i} + \underbrace{B_{iNE} f_{NE}}_{\beta_i} + \underbrace{B_{iCS} f_{CS}}_{\gamma_i} = \underbrace{X_i}_{x_i} \qquad i = N, NE, CS \tag{4.14}$$

Define:

$$\begin{aligned} p_i &= \frac{\alpha_i}{x_i} \\ q_i &= \frac{\beta_i}{x_i} \\ r_i &= \frac{\gamma_i}{x_i} \end{aligned} \tag{4.15}$$

Each of these three components, p_i, q_i and r_i, defines the contribution of final demand from the North, Northeast, and Center-South, respectively, to the actual level of output in region i. Notice that $p_i + q_i + r_i = 1$.

Output for all the sectors in the three regions was decomposed, and the components p_i, q_i and r_i were calculated. The results are presented in Table 4.17. On the average, the self-generated component of output in each region, i.e., the share of output generated by demand within the region, is lower in the North (78.32%) and higher in the Center-South (95.56%), reinforcing the previous conjecture of the higher dependency of the North upon the rest of the country (the value of the self-generated component for

Table 4.17 Components of Triple Decomposition of the Sectoral Gross Output

		North			Northeast			Center-South		
		p_i	q_i	r_i	p_i	q_i	r_i	p_i	q_i	r_i
S1	Agriculture	0.4807	0.0228	0.4965	0.0015	0.9171	0.0813	0.0039	0.0294	0.9667
S2	Mining	0.5242	0.0211	0.4548	0.0210	0.4667	0.5123	0.0294	0.0416	0.9290
S3	Nonmetallic Minerals	0.9959	0.0002	0.0039	0.0229	0.9630	0.0141	0.1368	0.0766	0.7866
S4	Steel	0.9452	0.0005	0.0543	0.0621	0.5368	0.4011	0.0325	0.0442	0.9233
S5	Nonferrous Metals	0.8487	0.0036	0.1477	0.0256	0.8442	0.1301	0.0261	0.0178	0.9561
S6	Other Metal Products	0.9214	0.0084	0.0702	0.1080	0.6427	0.2493	0.0387	0.0306	0.9307
S7	Machinery	0.7897	0.0607	0.1497	0.0233	0.8267	0.1500	0.0171	0.0328	0.9500
S8	Electrical Equipment	0.6865	0.0144	0.2991	0.0931	0.8078	0.0991	0.0408	0.0159	0.9433
S9	Electronic Equipment	0.8282	0.0030	0.1688	0.0369	0.9577	0.0054	0.0514	0.0081	0.9405
S10	Transportation Equipment	0.4103	0.0151	0.5746	0.1291	0.6029	0.2680	0.0148	0.0192	0.9660
S11	Wood Products and Furniture	0.7604	0.0021	0.2376	0.0111	0.9723	0.0166	0.0060	0.0037	0.9903
S12	Paper Products and Printing	0.8055	0.0126	0.1819	0.0128	0.9324	0.0548	0.0146	0.0326	0.9529
S13	Rubber	0.3752	0.0578	0.5671	0.0497	0.7412	0.2090	0.0222	0.0682	0.9096
S14	Chemicals	0.9347	0.0017	0.0636	0.0114	0.6937	0.2949	0.0183	0.0416	0.9401
S15	Petroleum Refining	0.8385	0.0066	0.1549	0.0184	0.6125	0.3691	0.0227	0.0525	0.9248
S16	Other Chemicals	0.5761	0.0160	0.4079	0.0211	0.7470	0.2319	0.0369	0.0599	0.9032
S17	Pharmaceuticals and Veterinary	0.9802	0.0005	0.0194	0.0134	0.9650	0.0216	0.0090	0.0394	0.9516
S18	Plastics	0.8931	0.0052	0.1017	0.0495	0.7824	0.1681	0.0358	0.0555	0.9087
S19	Textiles	0.9452	0.0055	0.0493	0.0056	0.6451	0.3493	0.0059	0.0524	0.9417
S20	Clothing	1.0000	0.0000	0.0000	0.0003	0.9994	0.0004	0.0005	0.0006	0.9989
S21	Footwear	0.9526	0.0014	0.0460	0.0001	0.9789	0.0209	0.0004	0.0043	0.9953
S22	Coffee	0.9461	0.0006	0.0533	0.0000	0.9986	0.0014	0.0003	0.0023	0.9974
S23	Processed Vegetables	0.8918	0.0030	0.1053	0.0005	0.9504	0.0490	0.0014	0.0119	0.9867
S24	Meat Packing Plants	0.9927	0.0037	0.0036	0.0003	0.9918	0.0079	0.0011	0.0164	0.9825
S25	Dairy Products	1.0000	0.0000	0.0000	0.0016	0.9294	0.0690	0.0019	0.0135	0.9846
S26	Sugar	0.9804	0.0006	0.0191	0.0025	0.9794	0.0181	0.0115	0.0123	0.9761
S27	Vegetable Oil Mills	0.7237	0.2383	0.0380	0.0081	0.8485	0.1434	0.0078	0.0265	0.9656
S28	Other Food Products	0.8279	0.0058	0.1663	0.0027	0.9667	0.0306	0.0034	0.0265	0.9701
S29	Other Manufacturing	0.6777	0.0400	0.2823	0.0195	0.6660	0.3145	0.0125	0.0340	0.9535
S30	Electric, Gas, and Sanitary Services	0.9411	0.0025	0.0563	0.0085	0.8857	0.1058	0.0320	0.0142	0.9539
S31	Construction	0.9969	0.0001	0.0030	0.0000	0.9992	0.0007	0.0007	0.0008	0.9985
S32	Trade	0.7912	0.0066	0.2022	0.0043	0.8382	0.1575	0.0049	0.0075	0.9876
S33	Transportation	0.7890	0.0080	0.2029	0.0026	0.9319	0.0655	0.0091	0.0172	0.9736
S34	Communication	0.9072	0.0033	0.0896	0.0012	0.9771	0.0217	0.0089	0.0089	0.9823
S35	Finanacial Institutions	0.9576	0.0017	0.0407	0.0002	0.9964	0.0034	0.0014	0.0019	0.9967
S36	Personal services	0.9766	0.0010	0.0224	0.0008	0.9601	0.0391	0.0046	0.0049	0.9905
S37	Business Services	0.8642	0.0061	0.1297	0.0065	0.9225	0.0711	0.0153	0.0134	0.9712
S38	Real Estate	0.9669	0.0014	0.0317	0.0002	0.9952	0.0046	0.0063	0.0044	0.9893
S39	Public Administration	1.0000	0.0000	0.0000	0.0000	1.0000	0.0000	0.0000	0.0000	1.0000
S40	Community Services	1.0000	0.0000	0.0000	0.0000	1.0000	0.0000	0.0000	0.0000	1.0000
	Average	0.7832	0.0095	0.2073	0.0074	0.8786	0.1140	0.0133	0.0210	0.9656

the Northeast was 87.86%). A sectoral pattern appears in which "local" goods, such as services (in general), clothing, dairy products, and other consumer goods present a higher share of the self-generated component, in the three regions. For the North, the leading sectors, like agriculture and mining, are heavily dependent on demands from the Center-South. The same phenomenon occurs in the Northeast, in the petroleum refining and textiles sectors, for instance.

The focus of attention in the analysis performed thus far has been on comparisons of internal and external structures. The understanding of the functioning of the Brazilian regional economies within an integrated system is one of the main goals of this book. By exploring different methods of comparative structure analysis, it is hoped that the complementarity among them might result in a better appreciation of the full dimensions of differences and similarities that exist among the three regions considered in this study.

The analysis provided for the North, Northeast, and Center-South suggests that there are some important differences in the internal structure of the regional economies and the external interactions among their different agents. As the absorption matrix used throughout the structural analysis will serve as the basis for the calibration of the CGE model, understanding of the relationships underlying it is fundamental for a better understanding of B-MARIA's results. In the last section of this chapter, a brief description of the data files used in the model calibration procedure is presented.

Additional Data Files

The complete set of data files used in the calibration of B-MARIA also includes estimates for various elasticities and some other variables in the satellite groups of equations. The elasticities files used in the model are borrowed from the literature. Existing estimates for Brazil, when available, are used; however, in some cases, the necessary estimates are not available for the Brazilian economy, and estimates for other countries had to be used as starting points for "best guess" evaluation. In these cases, sensitivity analysis is carried out to evaluate the impact of the choice of the parameters on the model results.

The remaining data necessary to calibrate the model are taken from published sources. For instance, data for the government finance block are taken from the publication of the municipal, state, and federal governments' accounts, and aggregated properly;[5] data on household disposable income come from household budget studies; estimates for demographic variables are taken from the interpolation of the population censuses of 1980 and 1991; other sources of data include sectoral studies and academic publications. Given small discrepancies among data from different sources, the input-output estimates were used as the benchmark for homogenization.

In the next chapter, B-MARIA is used to evaluate the regional and sectoral impacts of recent changes in the Brazilian economy. The role played by the parameters of the model, which are directly or indirectly derived from the data files described above, is crucial for the understanding of the model's results.

[5] See Dinsmoor and Haddad (1996).

5 The Regional Impacts of Macroeconomic, Structural and Sectoral Policies in the Brazilian Economy

As the process of global integration has reached the boundaries of developing countries, there has been concern about the role to be played by these nations in the new world economic order. In many parts of the developing world, efforts are being made to intensify economic activities so as to enhance their international competitiveness. Parallel to these efforts, market-oriented policies have been generally adopted based on the World Bank and IMF recommendations, supported by the recognition of the distorting effects of government intervention.

Distributional effects of such policies have been neglected on the grounds that greater efficiency would lead to rapid growth which would ultimately benefit the population in the lower income groups (Baer and Maloney, 1997). At the regional level, the desire to maximize economic growth, implied by the aim of increasing international competitiveness, is very likely to negatively impact the distribution of income among regions in developing countries (Baer *et al.*, 1998). As these countries present strong evidence of regional dualism, the more developed regions are those that concentrate the resources which can foster export-led national growth.

Brazil was late in its efforts towards integrating the country in the global economic network, as was the case for most Latin American countries.[1] In this chapter, the more open policies of the 1990s and related national strategies for increasing international competitiveness are examined. The model described in the previous chapters is used to analyze the regional effects of trade liberalization policies, represented by a tariff cut simulation; structural policies, represented by the simulation of the effects of an increase in the total factor productivity in the transportation

[1] Sachs and Warner (1995) provide a categorization of developing countries according to the timing of trade liberalization – defined by the absence of certain characteristic impediments to open trade – in which most Latin American countries present relative late opening, often not until the 1990s.

sector; and sectoral policies, represented by the analysis of the new investments in the automobile industry. The choice of these policies was made based on the relevance for the Brazilian case. They are part of a broader economic reform that is being carried out in the country and whose *regional* effects have yet to be considered in an integrated formal framework. The general equilibrium nature of economic interdependence and the fact that the policy impacts in various regional markets differ are considered in the original results presented below.

Trade Liberalization Policies

The effects of trade reforms have been extensively studied in the international trade literature. Trade liberalization processes are said to have long-run benefits derived from gains in both the production side (there is an overall increase in the foreign exchange revenue earned in export industries, or saved in import industries, per unit of labor and capital) and the consumption side (the same basket of products can be obtained at lower cost). However, the liberalization process also involves two kinds of short-run costs to the economy: distributional costs (protected sectors tend to lose); and balance of payments pressures due to the rapid increase in imports (Bruno, 1987). In a cross-country study, Sachs and Warner (1995) reach the general conclusion that economic reform, in which trade liberalization plays the major role, leads to economic growth. However, the short-term growth consequences of a trade reform will depend on the structure of the reforming economy. Evidence for trade liberalization and macroeconomic performance in developing countries is documented in Agénor and Montiel (1996). It is found that, contrary to general beliefs, there is no strong evidence suggesting that liberalization, in a broader sense, is associated with sharp reductions in employment and a short-run contraction in output. Another finding refers to the short-run improvement in the balance of payments, as the growth of exports outpaces the increase in imports, in developing countries where trade reforms were undertaken after World War II.[2]

At the regional level, the (computable) general equilibrium framework is considered to be more adequate as a theoretical tool for tariff-policy-type of analysis than partial equilibrium and traditional fixed-price general equilibrium models such as economic base and input-output models.

[2] In the successful cases, the adoption of more liberal commercial policies in the countries surveyed was accompanied by the depreciation of the real exchange rate.

Firstly, and more obviously, the latter do not accommodate, by definition, shocks in relative prices, and, therefore, fixed-price models do not represent a viable alternative. Secondly, Walrasian models provide an ideal framework for appraising the effects of trade and tax policy changes on resource allocation and for assessing who gains and loses, policy impacts not well covered by empirical partial equilibrium models (Shoven and Whalley, 1984). Moreover, at the sub-national level, many aspects of regional economies, which are taken as exogenous in partial equilibrium analysis, are endogeneized; this process captures feedback effects that occur throughout a regional economy that are ignored in partial equilibrium analysis, attempting to determine, more precisely, the regional impact of such macroeconomic policies.

Experiments on trade liberalization policies adopting the CGE approach are common for national models. In general, the question posed refers to the effects of changes in trade policy, and the results show that the welfare effects are relatively small compared to the effects of other kinds of policies, such as taxes – distortions that affect a relatively small portion of total activity can be expected to have small distorting effects (Shoven and Whalley, 1984). Studies that consider the regional impacts of trade policies are less common [Dixon *et al.* (1982) present a top-down regional disaggregation of the effects of tariff increases in Australia; Liew (1984) uses a bottom-up approach to compare the effects of a tariff increase in Australia with the results achieved in a top-down framework; Whalley and Trela (1986) report results from an interregional CGE model for the regional impacts of tariffs in Canada; Gazel (1994) developed an interregional CGE model to measure the regional effects of the Free Trade Agreement between the US and Canada].[3]

Modeling of changes of trade policy in Brazil has always neglected the regional dimension. At the national level, Guilhoto (1995) estimates the short-run effects (fixed capital stocks) of a uniform 25% increase in tariff rates showing a negative performance of the economy: employment decreases by -1.2%. A similar simulation carried out for the Australian economy using the ORANI model (Dixon *et al.*, 1982) shows that total employment in the Australian economy would fall by -0.2% with a 25% across-the-board tariff increase, suggesting greater flexibility of the Australian markets (CPI in Brazil would increase by 0.31%, while in Australia the rise in prices would reach approximately 2.1%). Other CGE models' results dealing with trade issues in Brazil are described in Guilhoto (1995). However, with the exception of Sousa (1987), who

[3] For more details about the models and results, see Chapter 2.

explored the effects of protectionism on the distribution of income between urban and rural areas, no attention has been directed to differential regional impacts.

Simulation Results

As an example of the type of results which can be generated for policy analysis using B-MARIA, a simulation of the effects of tariff-barriers decrease will be discussed in this section. Trade liberalization is an important element of the range of structural changes that the Brazilian economy has undergone in the last years, especially in the context of the creation of regional trade agreements (Mercosul). The rapid growth in the volume of trade among the Mercosul countries, recorded since the *Asuncion Treaty* was signed, benefited, to a great extent, from reductions in trade barriers. Although, in Brazil, most of the gains tend to be spatially concentrated in the South and Southeast regions, more remote regions, such as the Northeast, have also increased their exports to the Mercosul (Haddad, 1997). To explore the effects of such policies, B-MARIA is used to simulate the impacts of tariff changes in the Brazilian economy.

The model is applied to analyze the effects on the Brazilian economy of a uniform 25% decrease in all tariff rates. All exogenous variables were set equal to zero, except the changes in the power of tariffs, i.e., one plus the tariff rates, which were set such that the percentage change decrease in each tariff rate was 25%. Results of the simulation computed via a four-step Euler procedure, under short-run and long-run closures, are presented in Tables 5.2-5.5.; they show the percentage deviation from the base case (which is the situation without policy changes). The analysis is concentrated on the effects on industrial activity levels, and on some general macro and regional variables.[4]

Because of the nature of the data base, it should be pointed out that the model deals with changes in the *real* tariff rates (the ratio of import tax collected over the volume of imports), as opposed to *nominal* tariff rates, which are much higher. Moreover, the model does not consider non-tariff barriers. Braga *et al.* (1988) discuss this issue in detail, showing the extent to which preferential imports face reductions in the nominal tariff rates as

[4] The volume of information that the model produces in each simulation is overwhelming. To interpret the results, we tried to focus the analysis on a few interesting issues associated with the respective simulations, in order to rationalize particular results in terms of the model's theoretical framework and its underlying data base. This process, apart from giving insights into a particular economic phenomenon, serves to act as an informal verification of the simulations' results.

well as tax exemptions. Thus, the real tariff rate in 1985 (benchmark year) was close to 5% as compared to the average nominal rate of over 25%.

Short-Run To better understand the sector results of the model, a thorough analysis of the structure of the economy is needed. A close inspection on the benchmark data base is necessary, conducted not only on the relationships in the input-output data base, but also on the other relevant parameters of the model. Some of the main structural features of the economy in the base-year were revealed in Chapter 4.

Industry activity results show that, in general, export sectors benefit most from the tariff cut, while import-competing sectors are the main losers. Explanations for specific sector results should consider structural and parametric aspects of the data base. Sectors that present higher increases in their output tend to have high share of imports in their cost structure, and greater export demand elasticity (in the case of traditional exports). On the other hand, sectors with high import substitution elasticities, high import shares in their domestic markets, and high percentage changes in their tariff rates are more likely to be harmed by the policy change.

The tariff reduction stimulates the export sectors in different ways. These sectors benefit, to a great extent, from reductions in the cost of production. Imported intermediate inputs, which have import duties levied upon them, experience a relatively sharp reduction in their cost (see Table 5.2). As was noted elsewhere (Agénor and Montiel, 1996), imported intermediate goods play a prominent role in the economic activity in the developing world, and so is the case of Brazil, especially in the Center-South. In addition, the general price level decreases with the tariff cut, and through indexation mechanisms, the cost of primary factors of production also decreases.

The mining sector in the North and in the Center-South (0.162% and 0.222%, respectively), the coffee sector in the Center-South (0.187%), and the sugar sector in the Northeast (0.282%) are examples of traditional export sectors that gain from the increased competitiveness in the international markets. On the other hand, import-competing industries are adversely affected by the substitution away from regionally produced goods towards imports. The sectoral production of chemicals and chemical-based products, for instance, faces a relative high competition from foreign products (Table 5.1). Moreover, their base case tariff rates are relatively high, which also contributes to their weak performance in the simulation. When interregional feedback effects are considered, the electric-electronic industries of the North, which also face relative high international competition, can reverse the adverse situation by increasing their sales to the markets in the other regions, especially to household consumption in the Center-South. However, substitution towards imported products in the latter region are underestimated by the model; the import coefficients in the benchmark year reflect the protectionist policies towards the *Zona Franca de Manaus* (North region), showing negligible consumption of imported electronic equipment by households. Moreover, these sectors face small elasticities of substitution of the Armington type.[5]

In general, the group of industries including nonmetallic minerals and the chemical complex (chemicals, petroleum refining, pharmaceuticals), because of the greater change in their exposure to international competition due to prevailing higher protection levels, reveals weak performance in the simulation. In the case of the mining sector, which faces the strongest competition, the tariff rate is close to zero and hence, direct substitution effects from changes in tariff-based market distortions are negligible. Trade and transportation face zero tariff rates. For these two margin commodities, performance is closely related to the economy-wide performance.

Table 5.1 Brazil: Market-Share of Selected Commodities, by Source, 1985 (in %)

Commodity	Source			
	North	Northeast	Center-South	Foreign
Mining	4.4	14.6	33.2	47.8
Electrical Equipment	2.8	5.2	77.0	15.0
Electronic Equipment	24.3	1.1	62.1	12.5
Trade	4.9	40.8	43.4	10.9
Transportation	2.8	7.4	79.1	10.8
Chemicals	0.6	15.2	73.6	10.6

Source: Interregional Input-Output Table, 1985

[5] The Armington assumption suggests that similar commodities produced in different regions or countries should be treated as different goods in the estimation process, thus facilitating evaluation of substitution by region/country of origin.

Table 5.2 B-MARIA Projected Percentage Effects of a 25% Across-the-board Tariff Rate Reduction: Short-Run

		Employment by Industry			Activity by Industry			Basic price of Commodities			
		North	Northeast	Center-South	North	Northeast	Center-South	North	Northeast	Center-South	Imported
S1	Agriculture	0.287	0.159	0.250	0.162	0.111	0.176	-0.058	-0.065	-0.100	-0.398
S2	Mining	0.420	0.097	0.354	0.162	0.056	0.222	-0.019	-0.054	-0.054	-0.008
S3	Nonmetallic Minerals	-0.165	-0.078	-0.041	-0.108	-0.044	-0.022	-0.161	-0.105	-0.131	-4.559
S4	Steel	0.157	0.935	0.709	0.097	0.435	0.360	0.028	0.116	0.061	-1.895
S5	Nonferrous Metals	0.276	0.305	0.322	0.162	0.151	0.225	-0.412	-0.123	-0.148	-1.171
S6	Other Metal Products	0.061	0.048	0.160	0.050	0.037	0.138	-0.091	-0.049	-0.061	-2.811
S7	Machinery	0.049	0.075	0.071	0.039	0.062	0.061	-0.224	-0.363	-0.121	-2.756
S8	Electrical Equipment	0.263	-0.084	0.053	0.228	-0.065	0.045	-0.657	-0.123	-0.189	-2.084
S9	Electronic Equipment	0.146	-0.142	-0.012	0.085	-0.088	-0.008	-0.836	-0.466	-0.530	-4.642
S10	Transportation Equipment	0.438	0.295	0.565	0.232	0.210	0.339	0.017	-0.055	0.034	-0.582
S11	Wood Products and Furniture	0.270	0.042	0.169	0.243	0.035	0.137	-0.057	-0.071	-0.094	-0.352
S12	Paper Products and Printing	0.546	0.091	0.282	0.382	0.042	0.157	-0.010	-0.064	-0.054	-1.058
S13	Rubber	-0.564	-0.017	0.209	-0.201	-0.006	0.106	-0.219	-0.262	-0.239	-2.366
S14	Chemicals	-0.484	-0.640	-0.239	-0.419	-0.433	-0.183	-0.119	-0.121	-0.275	-2.668
S15	Petroleum Refining	-0.046	0.008	-0.011	-0.028	0.004	-0.006	-0.088	-0.108	-0.119	-2.896
S16	Other Chemicals	-0.669	-0.182	-0.098	-0.533	-0.115	-0.081	-0.221	-0.269	-0.419	-2.539
S17	Pharmaceuticals and Veterinary	-0.983	-0.858	-0.321	-0.845	-0.668	-0.274	-0.235	-0.245	-0.358	-4.628
S18	Plastics	-0.072	0.036	0.039	-0.037	0.010	0.017	-0.221	-0.100	-0.123	-5.412
S19	Textiles	0.030	0.169	0.262	0.020	0.088	0.158	-0.105	-0.053	-0.079	-1.959
S20	Clothing	0.221	0.077	0.202	0.162	0.052	0.130	-0.073	-0.054	-0.053	-0.610
S21	Footwear	0.634	0.544	0.632	0.432	0.319	0.458	-0.033	-0.016	0.001	-0.052
S22	Coffee	0.266	0.128	0.541	0.100	0.047	0.187	-0.022	-0.055	-0.009	0.000
S23	Processed Vegetables	0.190	0.558	0.262	0.123	0.285	0.158	-0.078	-0.030	-0.054	-0.823
S24	Meat Packing Plants	0.204	0.286	0.456	0.116	0.067	0.228	-0.036	-0.049	-0.040	-0.588
S25	Dairy Products	0.037	0.047	0.171	0.026	0.027	0.084	-0.069	-0.059	-0.066	-0.275
S26	Sugar	-0.211	0.415	-0.007	-0.131	0.282	-0.004	-0.098	-0.018	-0.120	0.000
S27	Vegetable Oil Mills	0.572	0.591	1.060	0.492	0.229	0.386	-0.017	0.030	0.061	-0.939
S28	Other Food Products	-0.240	-0.294	-0.193	-0.181	-0.196	-0.129	-0.114	-0.129	-0.154	-3.602
S29	Other Manufacturing	-0.021	0.189	0.154	-0.011	0.051	0.105	-0.170	-0.043	-0.133	-2.849
S30	Electric, Gas, and Sanitary Services	0.162	0.059	0.221	0.089	0.029	0.104	0.010	-0.053	0.034	0.000
S31	Construction	0.002	0.001	0.006	0.002	0.001	0.005	-0.263	-0.078	-0.123	0.000
S32	Trade	0.146	0.137	0.132	0.129	0.123	0.113	-0.047	-0.065	-0.059	0.000
S33	Transportation	0.207	0.110	0.523	0.135	0.074	0.302	-0.027	-0.048	0.013	0.000
S34	Communication	0.183	0.083	0.226	0.087	0.038	0.125	-0.007	-0.048	0.016	0.000
S35	Finanacial Institutions	0.135	0.054	0.211	0.105	0.041	0.172	-0.040	-0.054	-0.046	0.000
S36	Personal services	0.107	0.095	0.261	0.078	0.068	0.167	-0.066	-0.048	-0.065	0.000
S37	Business Services	0.142	0.058	0.209	0.085	0.036	0.121	-0.023	-0.042	-0.019	0.000
S38	Real Estate	0.206	0.219	0.288	0.005	0.003	0.024	0.307	0.311	0.409	0.000
S39	Public Administration	0.000	0.000	0.000	0.000	0.000	0.000	-0.088	-0.078	-0.079	0.000
S40	Community Services	0.081	0.079	0.207	0.073	0.071	0.184	-0.062	-0.061	-0.027	0.000

Finally, the non-traditional export industries reveal results that distinct from each other; the explanation lies in the diverse nature of each sector's demand and cost structure. For instance, the footwear industry, in each region, increases its output far above the regional average: 0.432% (North), 0.319% (Northeast), and 0.458% (Center-South). As a consumption good, it is affected by the increase in real household expenditure; it also benefits from prevailing low tariff rates and its already established international competitiveness (even facing insignificant tariff rates, the market-share of foreign footwear accounts for only 3.0% in the base year). Output in the steel industry in the Center-South and in the Northeast also increases significantly (0.360% and 0.435%, respectively), reflecting the sales orientation of the sector towards international markets. In general, sectors with already established higher share of sales to other countries benefit from tariff reduction, as do sectors producing consumption goods.

According to the model, industry employment levels expand/contract in the same direction as activity levels. However, the expansion of these changes are more intense for employment, in both directions. The absolute value of the percentage changes in employment by industry is higher than the absolute value of percentage changes in activity by industry, for all industries in all regions. The explanation for the more intense changes in the level of employment lies in the nature of the closure adopted in the simulation. It reflects the combined effects of fixed capital stocks and the general reduction in the price of *hiring* labor, which captures movements in the nominal wage paid to workers relative to movements in the producers' product price.

Figures 5.1-5.3 show the percentage changes in employment, for each sector in each region. Given the nature of the closure, which allows for producers to respond to exogenous shocks through changes in the employment level only, the figures reveal the short-run supply responses from the model, for a tariff decrease. With a few exceptions, the changes are similar in sign, across the three regions, although the percentage changes do vary with negative changes of greater intensity in the North and Northeast and somewhat greater positive changes in the Center-South.

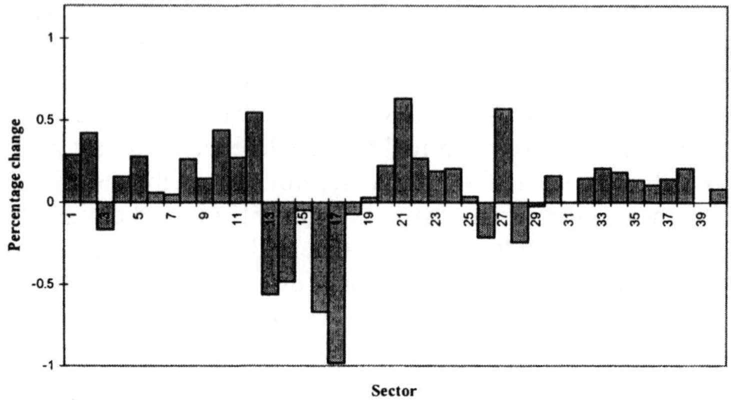

Figure 5.1 B-MARIA Projected Short-Run Employment Effects of a Uniform 25% Tariff Reduction: North

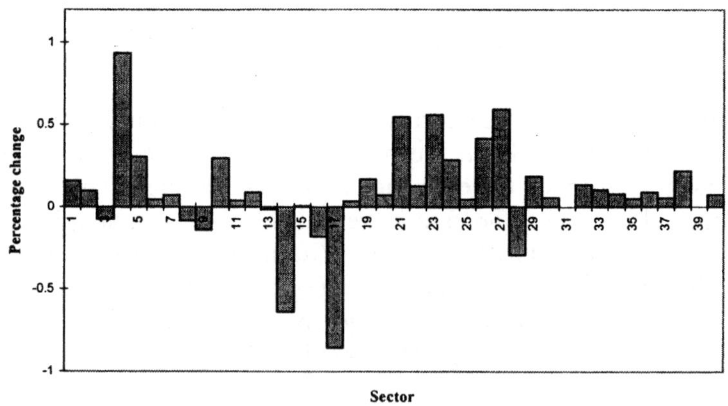

Figure 5.2 B-MARIA Projected Short-Run Employment Effects of a Uniform 25% Tariff Reduction: Northeast

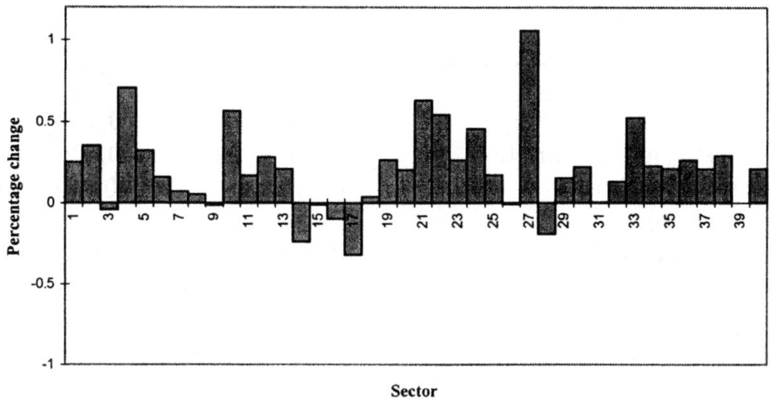

Figure 5.3 B-MARIA Projected Short-Run Employment Effects of a Uniform 25% Tariff Reduction: Center-South

Table 5.3 summarizes the simulation results on some macro variables. The real GDP of Brazil is shown to increase by 0.120 % with all the regions positively affected, with real GRP increases ranging from 0.057% (Northeast) to 0.132% (Center-South). Regarding the regional distribution of income, the tariff reduction worsens the Northeast's relative position in the country, even though that is a Pareto-improvement situation (outcome of tariff policy is said to be Pareto superior to outcome without tariff change, as GRP improves in all the regions). Another indication of the potential regional concentration effects of the reduction in tariffs is the result achieved for the regional/national consumption rate, which shows the Center-South increasing its share in national consumption at the expense of the other two regions.

In B-MARIA, household consumption in each region is assumed to be a function of household disposable income, in a Keynesian specification. Real household consumption in all the regions experiences an increase: North (0.051%), Northeast (0.049%), Center-South (0.126%). Since real wages are assumed fixed (nominal wages are indexed to the national CPI), this effect results directly from the increase in the activity level (employment effect). An examination of regional unemployment rates (which fall – see Table 5.3) confirms this result. Moreover, differential movements in the regional CPI also contribute to the consumption pattern verified.

Table 5.3 Brazil: Short-Run Effects on Selected Regional and Macro Variables

	N	NE	C-S	Brazil
Real GDP/GRP	0.118	0.057	0.132	0.120
Real Household Consumption	0.051	0.049	0.126	0.110
Unemployment Rate (% point change)	-0.102	-0.061	-0.151	-0.124
Consumer Price Index	-0.080	-0.57	-0.82	-0.078
Regional/National Consumption Rate	-0.058	-0.061	0.016	--
Employment: Persons	0.105	0.063	0.156	0.129
Export Volume	0.719	1.096	1.061	1.054
Import Volume	1.199	1.705	1.106	1.124
Balance of Trade (ordinary change)	2.9	106.9	504.5	614.3

One final comment on the short-run impacts refers to the results achieved for the balance of trade. In every region, the percentage change in the import volume is greater than the export volume. However, because of trade surpluses presented in the benchmark year, this movement of imports is not enough to produce a deficit in the balance of trade in the short-run. Even though a trend towards the reduction of trade surplus is suggested by the results, the model does not project balance of trade problems in the short-run.

Long-Run The results described above refer to the short-run effects of the tariff reduction, which are important for macroeconomic management. As trade reform aims at improving the allocation of resources in the long-run, a simulation was carried out adopting the long-run closure, described in Chapter 3. In this exercise, the assumptions on interregional mobility of capital and labor are relaxed and a steady-state-type of solution is achieved, in which regional natural unemployment rates and regional aggregate rates of return are reestablished. Attention will be focused on the interregional flows of capital and labor and their effects on regional and macro variables.

Table 5.4 shows the long-run results of the simulation for selected regional and national variables. As the aggregate level of employment is now assumed exogenously determined by demographic variables, the national real wage is allowed to change to keep national employment in the base case level. Supply-side effects are restricted to the distribution of labor across sectors and regions, and to capital movements. At the national level, the increase in GDP by 0.166% above the base case level is possible through the increase in the capital stock of the economy (0.320%) induced by the fall in the aggregate rental price of capital. Imported commodities are important inputs for capital creation and the fall in the prices of imports reduces the cost of producing capital. Contributing to the increase in GDP is also an increase in the productivity of the labor force as measured by the percentage change in employment using wage-bill weights; with the number of people employed fixed, the impact of the tariff cut has been to increase the output produced per worker by 0.109%.

Regional unemployment and wage differentials are assumed constant in the simulation. B-MARIA accommodates the labor market assumptions by allowing population movements between regions so that labor supply is increased in regions experiencing employment expansion, and vice-versa. The impact of the trade liberalization policy favors employment in the North (0.131%) and Center-South (0.217%) at the expense of the Northeast (-0.521%), with a consequent transfer of population from the latter. The estimates of regional wage differentials considered in the benchmark data base show the average wage in the Center-South as 119.8% of the national average wage, with the North and Northeast presenting average wages which are, respectively, 81.5% and 53.0% of the national average. Because labor is paid the value of its marginal product, the value of the marginal product of labor in the Northeast is, on the average, smaller than in the other regions. Hence, as labor moves towards the North and Center-South, the economy experiences an increase in the productivity of labor (assuming the level of national employment constant).

The overall increase in the national supply is met by movements in the demand aggregates. Investment in each regional industry is assumed to deviate from the base case line together with deviations in the industry capital stock; as capital moves away from the regional industries in the Northeast, that region is harmed by lower levels of investment (-0.493%), while the recipient regions benefit from the positive flows of capital. An increase in capital stocks also provides a rise in the household income derived from capital earnings; in combination with the rising wage income from higher levels of employment and higher real wages, household disposable income in the North and Center-South goes up, inducing an increase in the real household consumption (led by an increase in the rate of household formation). In the Northeast, an opposite movement appears. This finding is also reflected in the declining share of the Northeast in national consumption, as shown by the estimates of the regional/national consumption rate. Again, the Center-South is the region that increases most its share in national consumption.

Table 5.4 Brazil: Long-Run Effects on Selected Regional and Macro Variables

	N	NE	C-S	Brazil
Real GDP/GRP	0.210	-0.579	0.299	0.166
Real Household Consumption	0.260	-0.468	0.379	0.233
Real Investment	0.396	-0.493	0.451	0.295
Capital Stock	0.386	-0.499	0.456	0.320
Regional Government Consumption	0.260	-0.468	0.379	0.208
Federal Government Consumption	0.233	0.233	0.233	0.233
Consumer Price Index	-0.039	0.107	-0.015	0.004
Regional/National Consumption Rate	0.027	-0.699	0.145	--
Employment: Persons Weights	0.131	-0.521	0.217	--
Employment: Wage-Bill Weights	0.131	-0.521	0.217	0.109
Interregional Export Volume	0.316	-0.339	-0.126	--
Interregional Import Volume	0.210	-0.313	-0.067	--
International Export Volume	-0.231	-1.598	0.509	0.306
International Import Volume	1.480	1.026	1.269	1.268
Balance of Trade (ordinary change)	-50.4	-246.8	-431.3	-728.5
Nominal Wage	0.333	0.333	0.333	0.333
GDP/GRP Deflator	-0.069	0.212	0.005	0.032
Population	0.131	-0.521	0.217	--

Regional government consumption of public goods is assumed to move with regional household consumption. In the case of federal public goods, a compensatory rule is imposed in which its consumption follows the national household consumption level. As the latter is a weighted average of the regional results, federal government redistributes resources towards the less favored regions.

B-MARIA projects balance of trade problems in the long-run generated by tariff reductions. Even though this result seems to go against the general goals of trade liberalization, it has to be kept in mind that the simulation only takes into account the reduction in tariff rates, which, as noted above, is only part of a successful trade liberalization program. Moreover, the results for the export volumes from the Center-South signal a potential increase in international competitiveness in the region.

In the long-run, producers are able to reevaluate their investment decisions, which was not possible in the short-run. The long-run movements in the rental values of capital and cost of capital define differential rates of returns in each sector, providing indicators of more profitable investment opportunities. As was mentioned before, current rates of return are defined by the ratio of the rental values of a unit of capital (that depends on the productivity of the current capital stock in each industry) and the cost of a unit of capital, based on its cost structure. B-MARIA assumes that if the percentage change in the rate of return in a regional industry grows faster than the national average rate of return, capital stocks in that industry will increase at a higher rate than the average national stock. For industries with lower-than-average increase in their rates of return to fixed capital, capital stocks increase at a lower-than-average rate, i.e., capital is attracted to higher return industries. Figures 5.4-5.6 depict the *short-run* movements of the industry-specific rates of return and the *long-run* investment in capital creation. Differential rates of return in the short-run play a major role in explaining investments in the model. The demand stimulus of lower prices for imported commodities may increase rates of return in regional industries, initially, drawing capital to those industries exhibiting above-average increases until the point that rates of return are driven back to their initial levels. Because the Northeast economy is relatively closed to international markets, the cost of capital in the region is relatively less affected by the tariff cut, influencing long-term investment decisions.[6]

Regarding the rental value of capital (and abstracting from the temporal dichotomy presented by the closures), changes might be thought to be related also to short-term changes in unemployment; as capital stocks are fixed, changes in the employment level determine changes in capital productivity by altering the industry capital-labor ratio. It was shown that, on the average, sectors in the Northeast had a smaller change in the unemployment rate (Table 5.3). The combined effects of higher costs to capital creation and lower productivity of capital, reinforced by internal multiplier effects, determine the generalized outflow of capital in the Northeast. This discussion is important to show how the short-run and long-run results are connected in the model. When capital is allowed to

---

[6] As it is shown in Tables 4.2, 4.6 and 4.10, the average share of imports used in capital creation is only 0.22% in the Northeast, compared to 3.58% in the Center-South and 4.04% in the North.

move, short-run rates of return represent a crude indicator of its future direction.

Table 5.5 shows the long-run results for employment, activity level, and capital creation, by industry. Producers are not restricted anymore to respond to production decisions through labor changes, as was the case in the short-run. Employment changes are less strong, in the sense that the changes in employment are no longer necessarily greater than the changes in activity in absolute terms. The generalized flow of capital away from the Northeast towards the North and Center-South is induced, as suggested above, by differential industry rates of return in the first round, and multiplier effects, derived from the increasing demand for investments in the recipient regions and decreasing demand for investment in the Northeast. The effects of the simulation on the industrial activity are depicted in Figures 5.7-5.9 below. As a general result, the industries that become exposed to higher levels of foreign competition, more precisely those of the chemical complex, are adversely affected in the three regions. The activity in these sectors is hampered by a switch of expenditure in favor of foreign produced goods (import volume changes for these commodities are among the highest).

Primary factors movements play a major role in the results achieved for the long-run. The Northeast is the most harmed region (all the sectors reveal output results below the base case level). As capital moves away from the region, multiplier effects operate, further deteriorating the regional economy. The increase in the demand for investment in the other regions operates in the opposite direction. The increasing demand for capital goods generates a round of expenditures in these regions (North and Center-South). The capital goods industries are characterized by using a great amount of regional commodities (especially construction) and facing lower elasticity of substitution of the Armington type (both for substitution between foreign and the domestic composite, and between goods from different regions in the country). In combination, these effects contribute to the generation of higher internal multipliers in the regions. Labor migration to these regions is another source of stimuli to the regional economies. By increasing the demand for consumption goods, which are to a great extent provided by regional sources, the new migrants induce the expansion of those sectors, which sell predominantly to domestic markets and face little foreign import competition. Finally, the higher level of domestic absorption allows higher activity levels in the non-tradable-commodity sectors, such as services.

Table 5.5 B-MARIA Projected Percentage Effects of a 25% Across-the-board Tariff Rate Reduction: Long-Run

		Employment by Industry				Activity by Industry				Capital Creation by Industry		
		North	Northeast	Center-South	Brazil	North	Northeast	Center-South	Brazil	North	Northeast	Center-South
S1	Agriculture	0.074	-0.846	0.133	-0.068	0.208	-0.765	0.224	0.024	0.383	-0.580	0.440
S2	Mining	0.122	-0.867	-0.025	-0.212	0.306	-0.749	0.124	-0.070	0.422	-0.588	0.379
S3	Nonmetallic Minerals	-0.149	-0.888	0.097	-0.001	0.012	-0.765	0.252	0.159	0.317	-0.604	0.425
S4	Steel	0.007	-0.801	0.157	0.125	0.177	-0.683	0.293	0.258	0.452	-0.579	0.435
S5	Nonferrous Metals	0.416	-0.626	0.112	0.059	0.510	-0.562	0.202	0.127	0.642	-0.499	0.415
S6	Other Metal Products	0.193	-0.284	0.255	0.246	0.248	-0.288	0.294	0.283	0.515	-0.299	0.537
S7	Machinery	-0.099	-0.600	0.153	0.131	0.003	-0.578	0.195	0.171	0.397	-0.475	0.472
S8	Electrical Equipment	0.462	-0.453	0.207	0.194	0.477	-0.447	0.243	0.226	0.570	-0.426	0.462
S9	Electronic Equipment	0.293	-0.646	-0.009	0.038	0.373	-0.560	0.118	0.163	0.484	-0.421	0.442
S10	Transportation Equipment	0.145	-0.240	0.262	0.253	0.245	-0.257	0.371	0.361	0.358	-0.300	0.535
S11	Wood Products and Furniture	-0.063	-0.513	0.284	0.178	-0.026	-0.497	0.335	0.231	0.307	-0.414	0.557
S12	Paper Products and Printing	-0.492	-0.772	0.096	0.046	-0.301	-0.632	0.264	0.211	0.151	-0.510	0.478
S13	Rubber	-0.915	-1.168	-0.101	-0.128	-0.317	-0.870	0.141	0.113	0.016	-0.698	0.391
S14	Chemicals	-0.505	-1.207	-0.205	-0.314	-0.419	-1.054	-0.084	-0.201	0.134	-0.733	0.308
S15	Petroleum Refining	-0.160	-1.087	-0.195	-0.318	0.014	-0.884	0.024	-0.117	0.277	-0.681	0.315
S16	Other Chemicals	-0.994	-1.195	-0.139	-0.168	-0.783	-1.023	-0.058	-0.092	0.043	-0.726	0.328
S17	Pharmaceuticals and Veterinary	-0.885	-1.571	-0.225	-0.272	-0.762	-1.426	-0.150	-0.199	-0.009	-0.918	0.293
S18	Plastics	-0.147	-0.952	-0.093	-0.131	0.090	-0.711	0.157	0.099	0.340	-0.621	0.347
S19	Textiles	-0.104	-1.052	0.135	0.005	0.067	-0.867	0.262	0.123	0.399	-0.664	0.455
S20	Clothing	0.077	-0.846	0.249	0.143	0.176	-0.761	0.337	0.236	0.451	-0.582	0.494
S21	Footwear	-0.012	-0.609	0.343	0.305	0.118	-0.558	0.394	0.348	0.398	-0.487	0.528
S22	Coffee	-0.111	-0.554	-0.022	-0.067	0.165	-0.494	0.240	0.183	0.334	-0.460	0.381
S23	Processed Vegetables	0.095	-0.940	0.069	-0.081	0.200	-0.786	0.210	0.038	0.395	-0.623	0.425
S24	Meat Packing Plants	-0.119	-1.012	0.201	0.142	0.066	-0.739	0.338	0.247	0.313	-0.655	0.476
S25	Dairy Products	0.142	-0.838	0.186	-0.026	0.238	-0.726	0.336	0.143	0.471	-0.573	0.481
S26	Sugar	-0.217	-1.779	-0.024	-0.854	-0.040	-1.525	0.179	-0.489	0.250	-0.977	0.372
S27	Vegetable Oil Mills	-1.098	-1.283	0.043	-0.060	-0.952	-0.970	0.268	0.184	-0.042	-0.769	0.398
S28	Other Food Products	-0.421	-1.354	-0.154	-0.298	-0.268	-1.168	0.004	-0.136	0.201	-0.796	0.326
S29	Other Manufacturing	-0.170	-0.948	0.096	0.072	0.067	-0.697	0.209	0.167	0.314	-0.603	0.455
S30	Electric, Gas, and Sanitary Services	-0.046	-0.684	0.129	0.015	0.134	-0.599	0.295	0.177	0.356	-0.515	0.444
S31	Construction	0.351	-0.494	0.415	0.036	0.387	-0.490	0.438	0.076	0.537	-0.442	0.555
S32	Trade	0.128	-0.474	0.278	0.154	0.158	-0.469	0.308	0.184	0.382	-0.429	0.488
S33	Transportation	-0.023	-0.664	0.239	0.113	0.100	-0.612	0.334	0.219	0.331	-0.508	0.464
S34	Communication	0.000	-0.477	0.173	0.131	0.213	-0.443	0.317	0.263	0.408	-0.415	0.497
S35	Finanacial Institutions	0.170	-0.450	0.303	0.243	0.214	-0.444	0.336	0.270	0.373	-0.427	0.485
S36	Personal services	0.164	-0.461	0.376	0.112	0.230	-0.453	0.426	0.171	0.405	-0.430	0.516
S37	Business Services	0.061	-0.662	0.183	0.056	0.213	-0.600	0.309	0.183	0.441	-0.492	0.482
S38	Real Estate	0.033	-0.585	0.204	0.168	0.368	-0.484	0.418	0.238	0.377	-0.483	0.437
S39	Public Administration	0.227	-0.238	0.268	0.194	0.252	-0.252	0.300	0.220	0.407	-0.340	0.473
S40	Community Services	0.142	-0.521	0.294	0.052	0.168	-0.514	0.317	0.072	0.401	-0.451	0.498

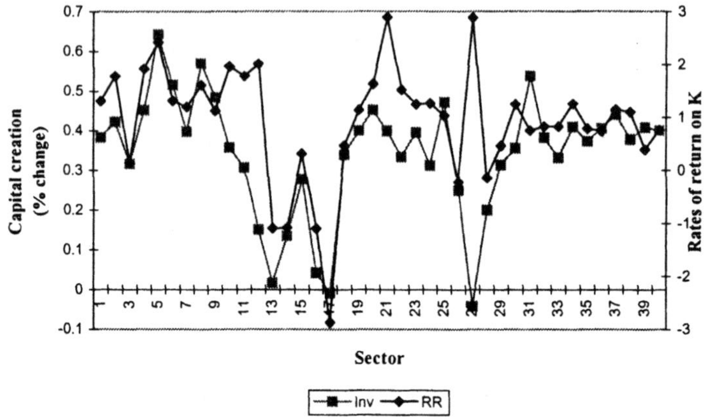

Figure 5.4 Short-Run Movements in Current Rates of Return on Capital and Long-Run Movements in Capital Creation: North

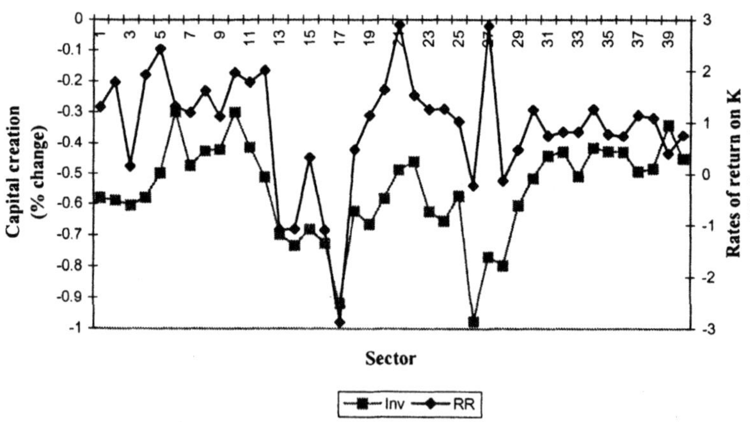

Figure 5.5 Short-Run Movements in Current Rates of Return on Capital and Long-Run Movements in Capital Creation: Northeast

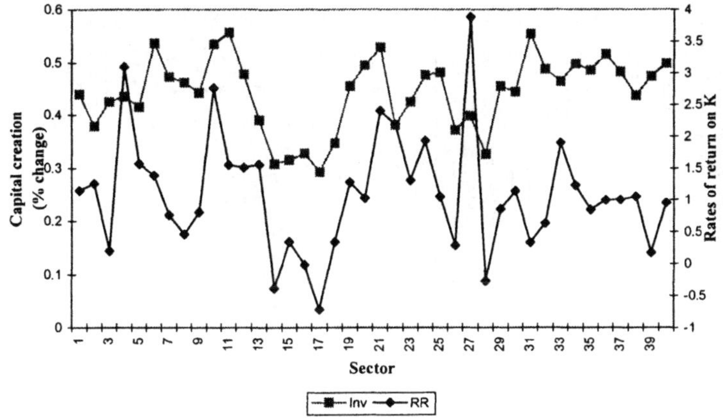

Figure 5.6 Short-Run Movements in Current Rates of Return on Capital and Long-Run Movements in Capital Creation: Center-South

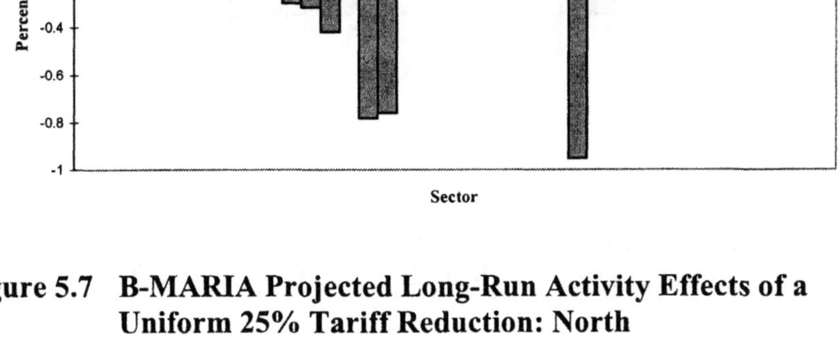

Figure 5.7 B-MARIA Projected Long-Run Activity Effects of a Uniform 25% Tariff Reduction: North

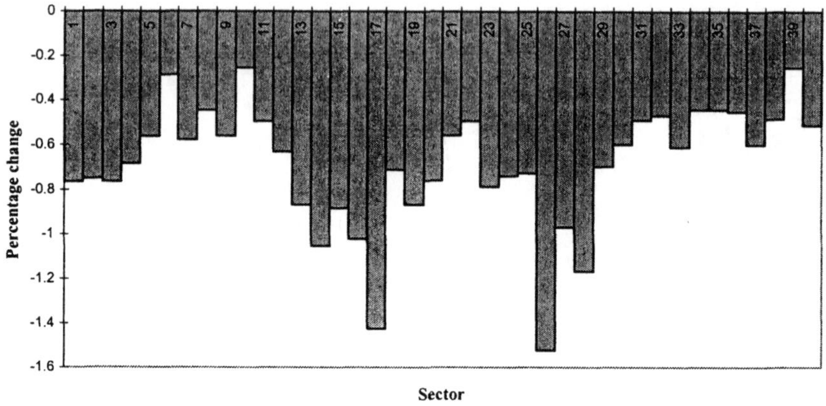

Figure 5.8 B-MARIA Projected Long-Run Activity Effects of a Uniform 25% Tariff Reduction: Northeast

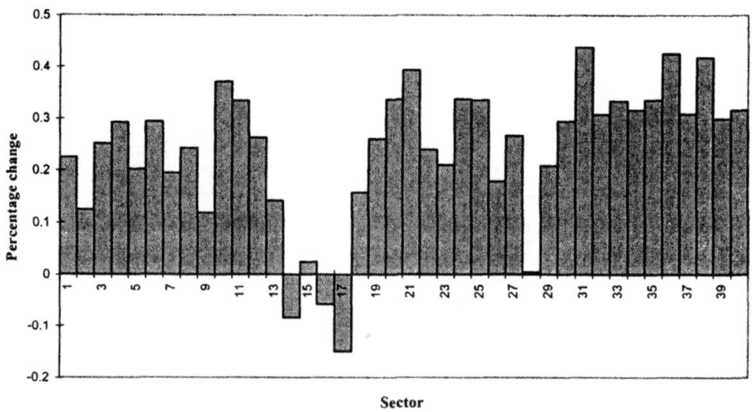

Figure 5.9 B-MARIA Projected Long-Run Activity Effects of a Uniform 25% Tariff Reduction: Center-South

These facts are reflected in the sectoral activity results; the weak performance of industries in the Northeast is shown dramatically in Figure 5.8. In the North (Figure 5.7), capital-goods industries lead growth in the region, with sectors producing consumer goods and services also achieving positive outcomes. The expansion of the mining sector is mainly induced by the increase in its exports (0.377%), the only regional sector with a favorable record in the international arena. Finally, the Center-South (Figure 5.9) presents the best performance overall. With the exception of the chemical complex industries and the other food products sector (which faces one of the highest tariff rates and includes typically luxury goods), all the sectors are positively affected. Because of the higher internal multipliers in the region, the relative performance of the non-capital-goods-producing sectors is better than in the North. Moreover, the region also benefits from increased international competitiveness, as suggested by the rise in its exports: mining, 0.103%; coffee, 0.184%; sugar, 0.560%, and non-traditional exports, 0.625% on average.

The changes in the basic price of commodities can be explained in three different ways, for each region (Figure 5.10). These price deviations from the base case levels influence the results for the GRP deflator presented above, in which the values for each region differ both quantitatively and qualitatively (North, -0.069%; Northeast, 0.212%; Center-South, 0.005%). The high value for the Northeast is the result of strong supply shortages. With lower levels of primary factors, the regional industries, given Leontief technology, decrease their demand for intermediate inputs. However, the supply restrictions that arise from the outflow of capital and labor are stronger than the fall in demand (most of the inputs for current production are from regional sources). Therefore, the relative excess demand (or, more precisely, supply shortage) in most sectors induces prices to increase so that market-clearing conditions are reached. The initial cost reduction due to the lowering of tariffs on imported inputs is counterbalanced by the price-increasing mechanism, generating higher production costs in the region. In the case of the Center-South, prices of intermediate inputs are forced to rise because of the increased demand generated by capital and labor appropriation in the regional industries. However, in many industries, the rising supply is more than enough to offset the increased demand for intermediate inputs, and prices fall. This is especially the case in most of the tradable-goods sectors that also benefit from the fall in the price of intermediate foreign inputs. In the non-tradable-goods sectors (mainly services), a rise in prices is verified; since they do not face international competition, the tariff effect on intermediate inputs is not observed. Finally, the North, led by the performance of the electronic equipment sector, presents an overall fall in prices of basic commodities.

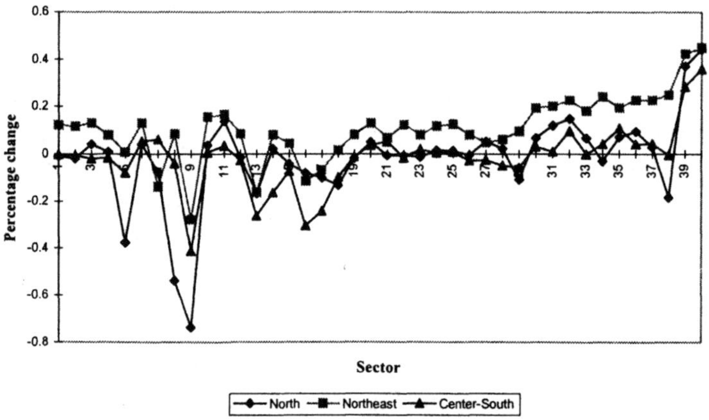

Figure 5.10 B-MARIA Projected Long-Run Effects of Tariff Cut on the Basic Prices of Commodities

In summary, the results achieved by the model when there is a tariff reduction show that there is a potential concentration of economic activities in the more competitive sectors of the Center-South. In the short-run, an increase in economic activity is observed in all regions; however, the less developed region (Northeast) experiences lower levels of economic growth. In the long-run, regional imbalance is reinforced as a result of the Northeast negative performance compared to the other regions.

The positive performance of the North should be taken with caution. The results for the region are heavily determined by the sectoral results of the electrical and electronic equipment industries of Manaus; these sectors are positively affected by their sales increases to the Center-South (the volume of the North's interregional exports to the Center-South increased by 0.340%). It is well known that the electric-electronic complex of the *Zona Franca de Manaus* benefited for a long time from non-tariff barriers as well (Diniz and Santos, 1996). Included in the trade liberalization is the removal of such barriers; hence, it is very likely that the region will be hampered by these policies. By facing cheaper, better-quality foreign products, not available before, consumers in the Center-South will tend to substitute away from the goods produced in the North. As was mentioned before, import coefficients for household consumption of electronic equipment, because of restrictions imposed by the federal government, are negligible in the year for which the model is calibrated. In addition, the model's data base overestimates the weight of import tax in the region; uniform tariff rates are assumed across sectors, and in the case of the industries in the *Zona Franca de Manaus*, some exemptions on imported inputs are not considered. Thus, the model's results overestimate the sectoral performance by neglecting substitution effects between the regional and foreign electronic products for internal consumption, and by overestimating the cost reduction in the production of regional industries.

Sensitivity Analysis

The analysis of the effects of tariff reduction described above revealed that substitution effects play a major role in the final results. As tariff rates go down, imported commodities become relatively cheaper and domestic agents tend to substitute away from the domestic goods: for instance, producers tend to use more imported inputs and consumers tend to purchase the cheaper imported goods. The strength of these substitution effects is captured in the model by a set of parameters usually called "Armington elasticities". In B-MARIA, there are six groups of such parameters for each commodity; these are divided into two subgroups defining elasticities of substitution between commodities from different domestic sources (interregional Armington elasticities), and defining substitution between imported commodities and a domestic composite (international Armington elasticities). As there are no econometric estimates for these parameters for the Brazilian economy, the model is calibrated by assuming that the value of the parameter for domestic/foreign products is equal to 0.5 for capital goods (sectors 1, 6-12, 29, 31), 4.0 for consumer goods (sectors 18-28), and 2.0 for the remaining sectors (basically, services). The values specified for the interregional elasticites are two times as large as those for the international elasticities (1.0 for capital goods, 8.0 for consumer goods, and 4.0 for the remaining sectors). The arbitrary choice of the values is based on the international literature that addresses the estimation of this type of elasticity but it also carries some personal judgment. It is implicitly assumed that consumer goods are more easily substitutable than capital goods, in the sense that, for instance, if the prices of imported shoes become cheaper it is more likely that consumers will buy more imported shoes; however if the price of a machine declines, given technological restrictions, the strength of substitution is smaller. Moreover, it assumed that substitution between goods from different regions inside the country is stronger than substitution between domestic and imported commodities.

In order to evaluate how these parameters affect the results of the model, the values of the international Armington elasticities were set equal to 2.0 to all commodities, and the interregional Armington elasticities were set to be, again, twice as high. Figures 5.11-513 indicate the intensity of changes by comparing industrial activity levels in the three regions for the results of the original and the new sets of Armington elasticities. The change in the parameters' values is felt more strongly by the industries in the North, which show a downward shift in their activity level. Capital goods facing relatively stronger substitution effects (the parameter affecting these commodities are four times higher) are deeply harmed, with the results reversing qualitatively in these industries. Since the increased demand for capital goods in the North had led the regional growth in the original simulation, the region now experiences a decrease in total GRP, as shown in Figure 5.14.[7] The results for the Northeast go in the opposite direction, led by better performance of the consumer goods industries that now face relatively weaker competition, as measured by the Armington elasticities. Finally, the Center-South also presents a qualitative reversal in the results for the capital goods industries. However, the consumer goods industries improve slightly, together with the traditional exports sectors. Overall, the results show stronger differential effects in the North (negative) and Northeast (positive), with the positive results for the Center-South counterbalancing the negative ones.

[7] It was previously shown that the electric-electronic complex in Manaus compensates the adverse effects of high international competition in the region by increasing its sales to capital creation in domestic markets.

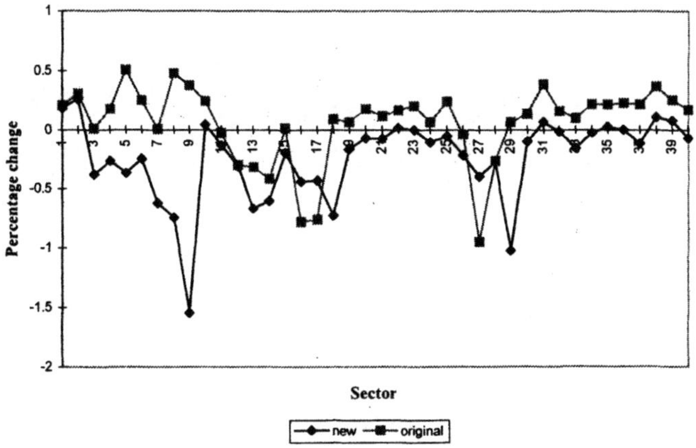

Figure 5.11 Long-Run Activity Effects of the Tariff Simulation Using Different Sets of Armington Elasticities: North

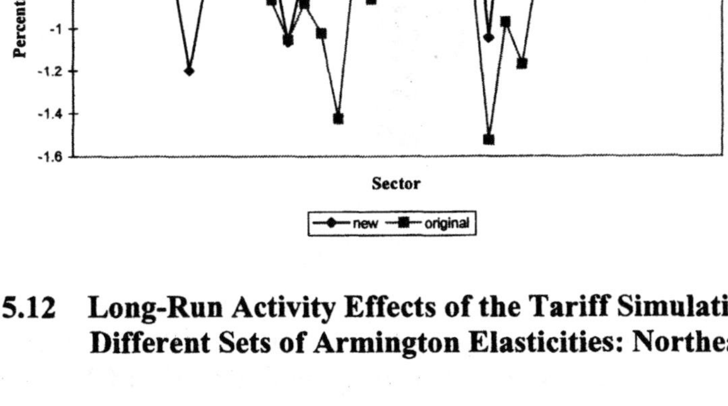

Figure 5.12 Long-Run Activity Effects of the Tariff Simulation Using Different Sets of Armington Elasticities: Northeast

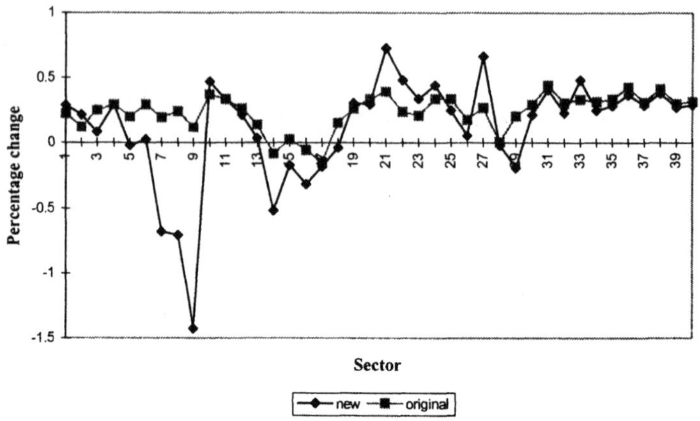

Figure 5.13 Long-Run Activity Effects of the Tariff Simulation Using Different Sets of Armington Elasticities: Center-South

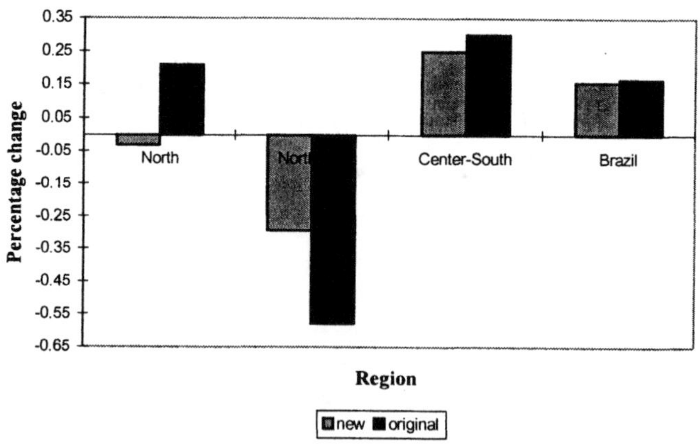

Figure 5.14 Long-Run Output Effects of the Tariff Simulation Using Different Sets of Armington Elasticities: GRP/GDP

Transportation Infrastructure Policies and the *Custo Brasil*

One of the main obstacles to economic development in Brazil is the so called *Custo Brasil*, the extra costs of doing business in the country. Enterprises are faced with a heavy burden that competing firms in other countries do not confront, hampering competitiveness. It includes different components that represent distortions in the relation between the public and the private sectors, reflecting inadequate legislation and deficient provision of public goods. Ongoing debate centers on the contribution of different sectors to the *Custo Brasil*: labor costs; transportation infrastructure; the tax system; and the regulatory system.[8]

A recent study by the World Bank (1996) provides a comprehensive examination of the diverse components of the *Custo Brasil* and an exploration of their implications for total firm costs. Regarding land transport costs, which are often viewed as a significant component of the *Custo Brasil*, the available evidence collected for the report suggests that the costs of providing rail and trucking services are high in Brazil. Nevertheless, because of overcapacity and significant competition in trucking, these costs are not passed on to shippers; transport rates per ton-kilometer are low by international standards. The principal problem with land transportation, from the point of view of shippers, is not the unit costs of different modes of transportation, but rather excessive reliance on trucking. Railroad and barge transport over long distances are far cheaper than trucking, particularly for bulk commodities. Inefficiencies and low productivity in the railroad sector have meant that the percentage of total cargo carried by trucks in Brazil is approximately twice as large as the share in Australia and the United States. Increased reliance on rail-based shipping could reduce freight costs along principal corridors by as much as 20 percent.

Brazilian transport infrastructure is deteriorating fast from lack of investment and maintenance. Decay in the transportation system curtails economic growth as well as international competitiveness. Deterioration of Brazil's transportation network in the last years contributed to high operational costs, obstructing the competitive integration of the country. A study developed by AERI/CNT (1996) shows that one of the main consequences of the impact of the Mercosul on the Brazilian highway network is the increase in the number of critical points, or bottlenecks, in most of the corridors, under the assumption that no investment in the expansion of the system takes place. The study analyzes the impact of

[8] See, for instance, CNI (1995) and World Bank (1996).

Mercosul on the transportation systems from a regional perspective, where the trade characteristics of each area are investigated in connection with the available transportation infrastructure. The expansion of multimodal systems is advocated, by enhancing participation of the railroad and inland waterway systems in the Brazilian transportation matrix, in order to increase productivity in the sector. Other measures including regulatory reform, acceleration of the privatization process to highways and railroads, and capacity expansion in some highway segments are also recommended in order to improve the Brazilian transportation system, and, hence, lead to gains in competitiveness both in the internal and external markets.

In this section, the issue related to the role of the transportation system in determining regional competitiveness is addressed. The ICGE model is used to measure the regional and sectoral impacts of the improvement of the transportation infrastructure component of the *Custo Brasil*.

Simulation Results

The modeling approach adopted here specifies the growth in total factor productivity of the transportation sector, in each region, which defines proportional direct effects on the respective regional output. The share in GRP of payments to factors of production of the transportation sector equals 3.50% (0.14% of GDP) in the North, 2.95% (0.45% of GDP) in the Northeast, and 3.81% (3.08% of GDP) in the Center-South. Thus, a 20.00% improvement in total factor productivity in the Center-South has a direct impact on GRP of approximately 0.76%; to get a similar direct effect in the other regions' output, a 21.77% increase is needed in the North, and 25.88% in the Northeast. Using these estimates, a simulation was carried out in which a regional-output-equivalent shock in total factor productivity was considered.

B-MARIA models explicitly transportation services and the costs of moving products based on origin-destination pairs. Thus, the model is calibrated taking into account the specific transportation structure cost of each commodity flow, providing spatial price differentiation.[9] The modeling specification is based on a mark-up structure which assumes that margins on goods used by industry, capital creators, regional households

[9] The lack of regional input-output tables for the Australian economy and the lack of regional margins data (Peter *et al.*, 1996a) make this feature unique in B-MARIA, as differential interregional costs are considered. Buckley (1992) provides an intermediary framework, in which the costs of *regional-composed* goods are based on origin-destination pairs.

and governments are produced at the point of consumption, and margins on exports are produced at the point of production. As the price paid for commodity *i* from source *s* by each user in region *q* equals the sum of its basic value and the costs of the relevant taxes and margins (transportation and trade), the growth in total factor productivity in a margin industry will have a direct impact on every user. Figure 5.15 shows the extent to which transportation costs are relevant in the total costs of industrial production, in each region. On the average, transportation costs have a relative higher weight in the North (1.20%) and Center-South (1.03%); the average share in the Northeastern industries is only 0.72%. Service sectors have a low transportation content, while some sectors such as nonmetallic minerals, wood products and furniture, and construction are transportation-intensive sectors. Regional specific contents refer to the relative high weight of transportation costs in some sectors in the North (e.g. other chemicals), in the Northeast (e.g. rubber) and in the Center-South (e.g. mining).

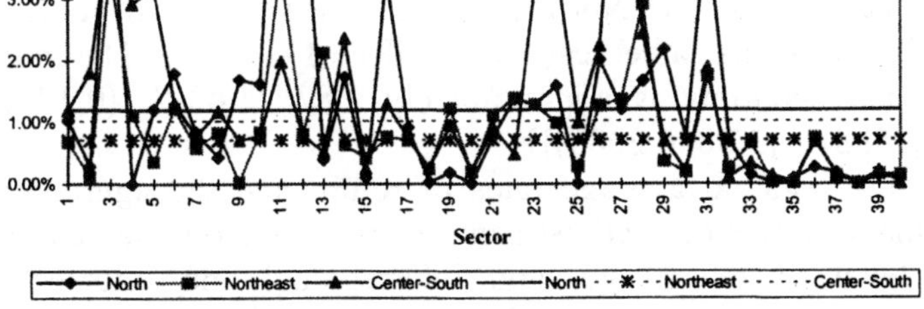

Figure 5.15 Brazil: Transportation Share in Total Costs, by Regional Industry

Higher efficiency in the transportation sector in the Center-South is reflected in the lower cost per unit flow, shown in Table 5.6; the North presents the less efficient transportation system. In the case of the relative low value of transportation costs from the North to the Northeast, it reflects the trade relations within the Carajás region, and the lower costs of waterways and railways available in the area, that account for a considerable part of interregional trade. As for the imported commodities, the Northeast presents much higher transportation costs in the benchmark data base.

Table 5.6 Brazil: Average Transportation Cost per Interregional Dollar-Flow[10]

		to		
		North	Northeast	Center-South
	North	0.035	0.022	0.042
from	Northeast	0.000*	0.020	0.005
	Center-South	0.000*	0.011	0.017
	Foreign	0.014	0.041	0.014

* Information disregarded in the published sources

The results of the simulation (Tables 5.7-5.9) using a long-run closure show again a concentration of economic activities in the Center-South portion of the country. It should be clear that the figures presented in each of the following tables refer to the percentage changes in the variables from the levels they would have reached in the benchmark year in the absence of the exogenous shock. Thus, the Center-South benefits from the total factor productivity growth with an increase in GRP of 2.009% above the base case, while the North presents relatively small gains (0.367%), and the Northeast has a decrease in its GRP of -1.464%. The multiplier for the national economy is approximately 1.87 {1.43 / [(0.14*0.2177) + (0.45*0.2588) + (3.08*0.2000)]}.

With the regional average rates of return and the aggregate level of employment exogenous, adjustments occur via industrial capital stocks, overall level of real wage, and interregional and intersectoral labor movements. The growth in total factor productivity reduces the cost of production of the transportation sector in each region and also, as a margin industry, reduces the unit cost of other industries through their transportation cost component, as the transportation sector becomes more efficient. This initial cost reduction increases the marginal productivity of primary factors, making it profitable to hire labor and capital at the initial

[10] One way to correct for the lack of information is to consider the transportation cost of the interregional purchases from the North to be symmetric to their respective sales flows, i.e., the average transportation cost per dollar would be $0.022 for purchases from the Northeast, and $0.042 from purchases from the Center-South.

levels of real wage and capital rental prices. The increased demand for capital and labor increases the real prices of hiring primary factors. However, as the productivity gains in the industries in the Center-South are relatively higher, capital and labor tend to move towards that region.[11] The net regional effects of factor movements are shown in the estimates for increases in capital stocks and employment – persons weights – for each region. It is clear that the net supply effects benefit heavily the Center-South, with negative results in the Northeast; even though there is a net increase in the capital stock of the North, the net effect in labor movements is negative in the region. The Northeast, again, suffers from lower levels of labor productivity. Thus, the productivity of the domestic labor force increases, as shown by the result for national employment using wage-bill weights.

From the demand side, real household consumption in the North and Center-South grows faster than GRP as a result, in the case of the Center-South, of the combined effects of higher real wages and increases in employment; in the North, the wage effect and the increase in capital income overcome the reduction in the employment level. In the Northeast, the wage effect is not strong enough to offset the fall in employment. Regional government expenditures follow the path of household consumption, showing a positive net effect in the country as a whole. Federal expenditures increase in the three regions at the same rate, suggesting the compensatory policies assumed in the model. The last component of domestic absorption reflects the differential attractiveness of investment opportunities in the regions, as explained above.

The initial reduction in the cost of production of the transportation commodity stimulates regional exports. However, the growth in domestic absorption generated through the increase in the factor income imposes demand pressures on the economy and the domestic prices go up, pushed also by the increase in nominal wages, which is due to the competition for labor in an environment of fixed employment level. Thus, exporters face two countervailing forces that affect their position in international markets. The net effects in the regions are perceived differently: in the North and Northeast, the domestic-demand-driven price effect is strong enough to harm the regions' competitiveness, decreasing their international exports; in the Center-South, the cost reduction prevails, showing net increments in the regional exports to foreigners. Imports are benefited by both the lower

[11] Wage differentials are set exogenously, and the capital-labor ratios in the transportation sector (North, 0.5321; Northeast, 0.4938; Center-South 0.7268) point to a higher increase in the capital productivity in the Center-South.

transportation margins and the increase in the activity levels in the North and Center-South; in the Northeast, the intensity of changes in economic activity is sufficiently detrimental to completely offset the positive effects of cheaper imports. Nevertheless, the results for regional exports (-13.457%) and imports (-1.321%) suggest strong substitution effects towards imported commodities, in the Northeast. As an aggregate result for the balance of trade, the deficits observed in the North and Northeast are compensated by an international trade surplus in the Center-South, revealing a total national surplus.

Table 5.7 Brazil: Long-Run Effects on Selected Regional and Macro Variables

	N	NE	C-S	Brazil
Real GDP/GRP	0.367	-1.464	2.009	1.430
Real Household Consumption	0.498	-0.993	2.305	1.675
Real Investment	0.370	-2.664	1.035	0.409
Capital Stock	0.024	-1.584	1.309	0.842
Regional Government Consumption	0.498	-0.993	2.305	1.570
Federal Government Consumption	1.675	1.675	1.675	1.675
Consumer Price Index	0.973	0.736	0.793	0.793
Regional/National Consumption Rate	-1.157	-2.624	0.620	--
Employment: Persons Weights	-0.630	-2.182	1.012	--
Employment: Wage-Bill Weights	-0.630	-2.182	1.012	0.494
Interregional Export Volume	1.188	1.475	-1.244	--
Interregional Import Volume	0.396	-2.078	1.464	--
Interregional BT (ordinary change)	113.0	1443.8	-1556.8	--
International Export Volume	-4.413	-13.457	3.910	2.170
International Import Volume	0.997	-1.321	2.541	2.395
Balance of Trade (ordinary change)	-239.6	-1826.5	3253.7	1187.6
Nominal Wage	2.359	2.359	2.359	2.359
GDP/GRP Deflator	1.151	1.149	1.010	1.032
Population	-0.630	-2.182	1.012	--

The last component of GRP, from the expenditure side, reflects the interregional trade linkages in the Brazilian economy. Interregional backward linkages from the Center-South are important to attenuate the adverse effects in the Northeast, as suggested by the increased volume of purchases by the former region from the latter, and the positive effects of the interregional trade balance presented in the Northeast. Table 5.8 also reveals the spread effects of the more developed region on the North, which, given its relative dependency on interregional linkages, faces trade increases in both directions.

Table 5.8 Brazil: Long-Run Effects on Interregional Trade Flows

		to		
		North	Northeast	Center-South
	North	0.912	-1.713	1.270
from	Northeast	-0.117	-1.449	1.602
	Center-South	0.449	-2.083	1.918

Sectoral results are presented in Table 5.9 and Figures 5.16-5.18. The only sectors in the Northeast that present a positive performance, besides the transportation sector, are transportation equipment and rubber, which have a large share of their sales to the transportation sector (36.4% and 29.3%, respectively), and the clothing sector, which benefits from labor productivity increase and its interregional sales.

Traditional exports such as mining (North), sugar (Northeast), and coffee (Center-South) are harmed. As these sectors present relatively low transportation content, the benefits arising from the initial cost reduction due to productivity gains are not strong enough to offset the price hike due to domestic demand pressures. In addition, interregional substitution effects operate, resulting in declining shares in domestic markets for the regional commodities. In the mining sector of the Center-South, the detrimental effect of increasing production costs is not sufficient to offset the direct effects of technological change, and the industry increases its shares in international markets.

Table 5.9 B-MARIA Projected Percentage Long-Run Effects of an Increase in Total Factor Productivity in the Transportation Sector

		Employment by Industry				Activity by Industry				Capital Creation by Industry		
		North	Northeast	Center-South	Brazil	North	Northeast	Center-South	Brazil	North	Northeast	Center-South
S1	Agriculture	0.788	-2.297	0.870	0.224	0.741	-2.064	1.055	0.407	0.680	-1.525	1.491
S2	Mining	-6.627	-1.765	8.634	5.455	-3.967	-1.590	6.973	4.110	-2.220	-1.352	4.272
S3	Nonmetallic Minerals	1.764	-2.239	0.854	0.624	1.526	-1.929	1.152	0.911	1.080	-1.522	1.486
S4	Steel	0.758	-5.636	1.858	1.609	0.741	-4.305	1.905	1.684	0.714	-3.106	1.953
S5	Nonferrous Metals	2.091	-3.443	1.875	1.483	1.766	-2.759	1.901	1.430	1.310	-2.075	1.963
S6	Other Metal Products	1.302	-0.380	1.688	1.652	1.247	-0.447	1.715	1.672	0.979	-0.650	1.884
S7	Machinery	0.373	-1.745	1.920	1.806	0.401	-1.671	1.920	1.802	0.509	-1.313	1.918
S8	Electrical Equipment	1.759	-0.613	1.646	1.575	1.669	-0.666	1.670	1.585	1.100	-0.846	1.818
S9	Electronic Equipment	2.310	-0.870	1.856	1.913	1.901	-0.895	1.862	1.847	1.324	-0.934	1.875
S10	Transportation Equipment	2.346	0.419	1.007	1.013	1.893	0.193	1.216	1.212	1.387	-0.369	1.533
S11	Wood Products and Furniture	2.011	-1.034	1.754	1.651	1.944	-1.017	1.784	1.661	1.353	-0.935	1.912
S12	Paper Products and Printing	2.648	-1.445	1.893	1.791	2.255	-1.318	1.871	1.737	1.341	-1.208	1.843
S13	Rubber	2.117	1.446	2.216	2.205	1.567	0.551	2.133	2.093	1.267	0.044	2.047
S14	Chemicals	1.855	-1.130	1.871	1.556	1.749	-1.120	1.869	1.518	1.076	-1.100	1.865
S15	Petroleum Refining	1.580	-3.169	2.416	1.640	1.338	-2.541	2.277	1.533	0.978	-1.905	2.093
S16	Other Chemicals	3.569	-3.419	1.193	1.082	3.189	-2.903	1.266	1.134	1.741	-2.005	1.615
S17	Pharmaceuticals and Veterinary	-0.330	-1.759	1.508	1.393	-0.250	-1.657	1.548	1.426	0.235	-1.302	1.785
S18	Plastics	1.406	-1.645	1.647	1.503	1.141	-1.398	1.716	1.502	0.864	-1.305	1.768
S19	Textiles	0.597	-1.213	1.527	1.218	0.593	-1.162	1.616	1.263	0.585	-1.106	1.750
S20	Clothing	-0.169	0.474	1.733	1.603	-0.052	0.182	1.771	1.618	0.276	-0.431	1.839
S21	Footwear	5.008	-0.834	2.024	1.926	4.138	-0.883	2.005	1.879	2.319	-0.953	1.955
S22	Coffee	-0.216	-1.207	-5.602	-5.094	0.096	-1.131	-2.820	-2.606	0.286	-1.088	-1.275
S23	Processed Vegetables	1.479	-4.991	1.320	0.377	1.299	-3.879	1.460	0.542	0.968	-2.683	1.673
S24	Meat Packing Plants	1.189	-0.863	1.838	1.710	1.048	-0.933	1.862	1.620	0.862	-0.954	1.886
S25	Dairy Products	5.526	-0.914	1.693	1.188	4.650	-0.936	1.764	1.292	2.570	-0.967	1.833
S26	Sugar	2.814	-8.841	1.176	-3.548	2.314	-7.466	1.402	-2.037	1.506	-4.376	1.617
S27	Vegetable Oil Mills	-1.418	-4.957	2.157	1.648	-1.255	-3.573	2.075	1.717	-0.238	-2.669	2.028
S28	Other Food Products	1.057	-0.670	0.788	0.642	0.994	-0.738	1.010	0.816	0.803	-0.873	1.460
S29	Other Manufacturing	1.919	-2.565	1.734	1.663	1.463	-1.897	1.743	1.580	0.994	-1.646	1.762
S30	Electric, Gas, and Sanitary Services	0.510	-1.584	1.988	1.465	0.536	-1.411	1.970	1.498	0.568	-1.242	1.954
S31	Construction	0.776	-2.490	1.449	-0.225	0.754	-2.430	1.493	-0.078	0.664	-1.624	1.716
S32	Trade	1.114	-1.068	1.837	1.352	1.080	-1.064	1.849	1.377	0.827	-1.034	1.920
S33	Transportation	-23.819	-29.525	-20.972	-22.186	2.402	0.666	4.537	4.015	-11.295	-15.356	-9.086
S34	Communication	0.920	-0.571	2.184	1.992	0.784	-0.741	2.077	1.845	0.661	-0.885	1.944
S35	Finanacial Institutions	0.921	-0.685	2.558	2.283	0.883	-0.734	2.492	2.198	0.747	-0.880	2.195
S36	Personal services	0.649	-0.160	2.708	1.722	0.648	-0.303	2.549	1.648	0.644	-0.662	2.269
S37	Business Services	1.349	-1.367	2.090	1.566	1.134	-1.304	2.020	1.548	0.814	-1.195	1.923
S38	Real Estate	0.569	-0.972	2.263	2.079	0.628	-0.996	2.094	1.362	0.629	-0.996	2.079
S39	Public Administration	0.881	-0.095	1.966	1.628	0.858	-0.174	1.962	1.617	0.713	-0.654	1.941
S40	Community Services	0.422	-0.994	2.280	1.204	0.435	-0.995	2.257	1.197	0.541	-1.001	2.078

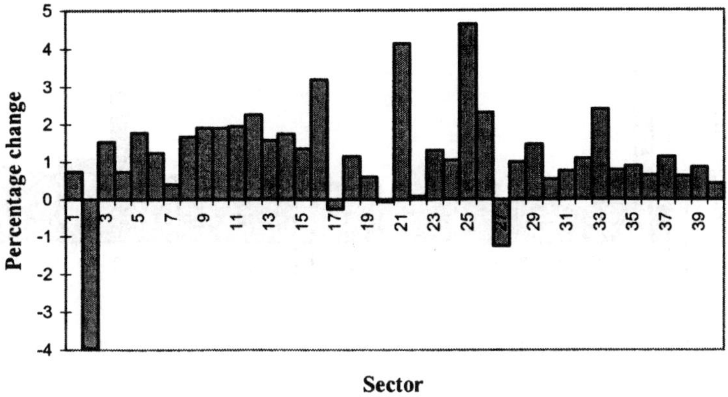

Figure 5.16 B-MARIA Projected Long-Run Activity Effects of an Increase in Total Factor Productivity in the Transportation Sector: North

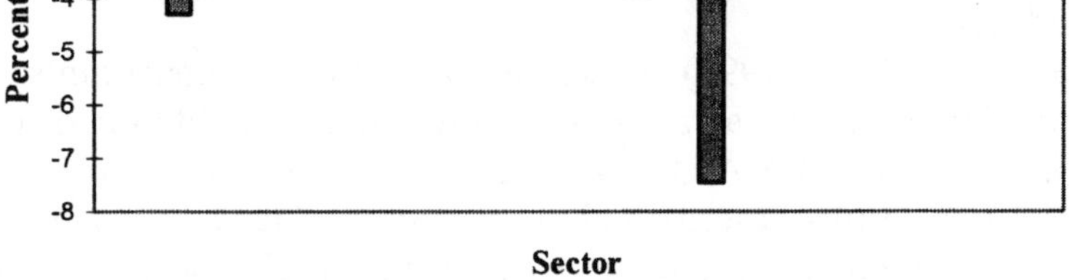

Figure 5.17 B-MARIA Projected Long-Run Activity Effects of an Increase in Total Factor Productivity in the Transportation Sector: Northeast

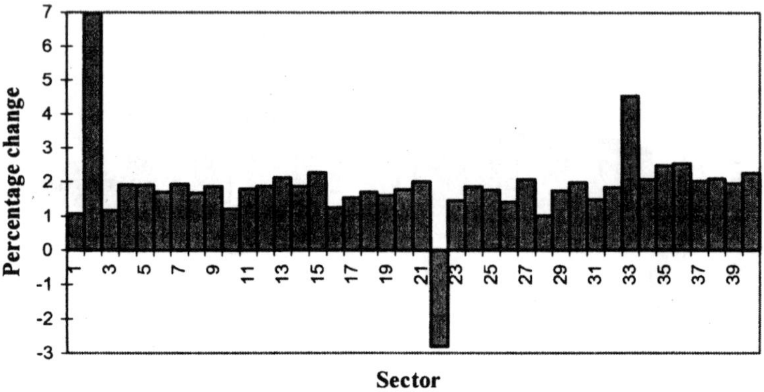

Figure 5.18 B-MARIA Projected Long-Run Activity Effects of an Increase in Total Factor Productivity in the Transportation Sector: Center-South

The productivity gains in the transportation sector free primary factors that are absorbed by other industries. Capital and labor movements benefit the sectors in the Center-South and North. Through multiplier effects driven by the increase in the investment and consumption components of domestic absorption in those regions, capital goods and consumer goods industries, in general, are positively affected; capital formation is an intensive user of local inputs in the Center-South, driving the overall positive results in the region. Internal multipliers generate increasing demand for capital goods, which also are favored by relatively low substitution effects. The few drawbacks in sectoral activity verified in the North are heavily influenced by substitution effects against the regional commodities.

As the AERI/CNT (1996) study shows, physical constraints in the transportation network play an important role in the facilitation of flows of goods and services. B-MARIA does not consider this issue explicitly, and the simulation results described above reflect productivity growth derived from the initial existing capacity. As a general result, the Center-South is the main beneficiary, suggesting that the interplay of the countervailing forces of backwash and spread effects, as implied by the intraregional and interregional linkage structure, favors the more developed region. In our simulation, the increase in the total factor productivity in the regional transportation sectors reduces transportation costs for commodity flows in both directions: *from* and *to* each of the regions. As the change occurs, production-cost oriented firms take new decisions concerning output, and through the operation of internal and external multipliers, asymmetric results in terms of regional development arise. The asymmetry of results of seemingly symmetric improvements in the transportation sector are very important and should be taken into account in the design of transportation and regional development policies.

The Automobile Industry

The automobile industry is considered to be a critical sector in the development process. Its effects are not only felt by neighboring sectors but also in the build-up of supporting infrastructure – the rise of a motor car industry entails not only the sale of cars, but also investments in road construction and traffic regulation, and in service and repair networks (Malecki, 1991). The backward and forward linkages of the sector help to foster development in the region in which production takes place. However, the intensity of the internal multiplier effects will depend on the degree of self-sufficiency of the producing region.

After the slowdown of the 1980s, the automobile industry is in a period of great transition in Brazil. Since 1991, the industry output has almost doubled, even though the level of employment in the sector fell significantly.[12] New investments attracted by policies implemented by the Brazilian government, which has been playing an active role in negotiations for foreign investments in the country, are being sought by the regions. State governments have engaged in strong competition for the incoming capital through fiscal incentives.

One of the main issues that concern labor unions refers to the production technology embodied in the new investments in the sector. It has been claimed that the new investments in the automobile industry are accompanied by sharp reductions in the employment levels, the reason being the higher capital intensity of the investments.[13] Recent estimates for the automobile industry show that employment has fallen, even though the sectoral output has been increasing (Table 5.10). Using alternative

---

[12] See "A Indústria Automobilística no Brasil a Mil Por Hora" (1997).

[13] The argument in favor of more capital intensive technology refers to the fact that, in an open economy, it is important to use more up-to-date technology to compete in the international markets.

measures of productivity for the sector, Peebles (1995) shows that productivity has increased dramatically in recent years, due, to a large extent to restructuring of operations, rather than simply scale economies.

In order to address this issue, B-MARIA is applied to evaluate the impacts of the new investments in the automobile sector under the assumption of technological upgrade in the industry, i.e., that labor-saving technology is embodied in the incoming capital. Technically, the modeling trick is to induce capital-labor substitution by imposing changes in the current capital stocks of the industry. As capital becomes relatively cheaper in the transportation equipment sector, producers will tend to substitute away from labor. The imposed changes in the capital stocks are set proportionally to the regional distribution of the new investments, so that for each dollar increase in the capital stock of the transportation equipment sector in the Northeast, there is a ten dollar increase in the sector in the Center-South.[14] A 5% increase in the capital stock of the transportation equipment sector in the Center-South, and a 55% increase in the Northeast are assumed. These estimates are based on the relation between the figures presented in Table 5.11 and the estimates for the sectoral current capital stocks in the benchmark data base. As the main interest here is to evaluate the impacts on the levels of employment which affect union negotiations, the short-run closure is adopted. A key parameter in this simulation is the elasticity of substitution between capital and labor in the transportation equipment sector. It can now be interpreted as the parameter that defines the degree of labor-saving in the technology embodied in the new investments: higher values imply higher degrees of labor saving (an increase in the stock of capital in the industry induces stronger substitution away from labor), and lower values imply smaller switch away from labor.

The automobile industry is part of the transportation equipment sector of the model (hereafter, both denominations will be used interchangeably). The transportation equipment sector is characterized in the benchmark data base, in the Northeast and in Center-South regions, as follows.

[14] This 10:1 ratio roughly represents the distribution of the planned investments, simplifying our exposition.

Table 5.10 Automobile Industry – Vehicles: Production and Employment (1990-1996)

	Production in Units	Employees
1990	914,466	117,396
1991	960,219	109,428
1992	1,073,861	105,664
1993	1,391,435	106,738
1994	1,581,389	107,134
1995	1,629,008	104,614
1996	1,804,328	101,857

Source: National Association of Automakers (ANFAVEA)

Table 5.11 Automobile Industry Projects to be Started: Brazil, 1997

Region	Project	Product	Investment (US$1,000)
Center-South:			6,508,000
Rio Grande do Sul	General Motors	cars	600,000
Santa Catarina	General Motors	engines	500,000
Paraná	Renault, Volkswagen, Chrysler	cars and pick-ups	2,065,000
São Paulo	Volkswagen, Toyota, Honda, General Motors	cars, engines, parts	1,100,000
Rio de Janeiro	Volkswagen	trucks	300,000
Minas Gerais	Fiat, Mercedes-Benz	cars, engines, trucks	1,793,000
Goiás	Mitsubishi	pick-ups	150,000
Northeast:			1,005,000
Bahia	Hyundai, Asia	cars	1,005,000

Source: National Association of Automakers (ANFAVEA) - Ministério da Indústria, comércio e Turismo (MICT)

Northeast. The sector, whose share in the regional output is less than 0.5%, is characterized by strong linkages with the rest of the country. From its total sales, 48.58% go to other regions of the country (38.92% for intermediate production, 4.43% for capital creation, and 5.23% for household consumption). The share of sales to buyers within the region accounts for 49.30% (38.38% for intermediate production, and 11.32% for household consumption); 1.72% are exported. The transportation equipment sector in the Northeast purchases 53.24% of its inputs for current production from the rest of the country; for capital creation, inputs from other national sources represent 35.32% of the total. Linkages with the rest of the world are weak. The sector faces strong competition from the Center-South, which is responsible for the provision of 91.30% of the total transportation equipment consumed in the Northeast region (the market share in the household market is even higher, reaching over 96%). Compared to the regional averages, the sector is relatively labor intensive and the share of value added in total costs is also relatively lower.

Center-South. The importance of the transportation equipment sector in the region is much greater than in the Northeast. With a share in regional output of 3.82% (3.18% of the national output), the industry is concentrated in the region (97.71% of the sectoral production take place in the Center-South). Its sales orientation is spread across users: 48.61% go to intermediate production within (46.08%) and outside (2.53%) the region; 12.28% to capital creation (10.81% within and 1.47% outside the region); 19.33% to regional consumers and 3.47% to consumers in the rest of the country; and 16.31% are exported to international markets. Even though most of the sector's suppliers of intermediate inputs for current production and capital creation are regional suppliers (92.71% and 84.01%, respectively), international sources are also important (5.52% for current production, and 11.14% for capital creation); direct interregional linkages are less important. Due to its supremacy in the national production and to strong restrictions on imports (in the benchmark year), the goods produced in the region face small competition from both interregional and international markets; market share of the Center-South is 91.50% in the country (97.56% in the household market). The sector is more capital intensive than in the Northeast and the value added share in total costs, compared to the regional average, is low.

The analysis is carried out in four steps: 1) the short-run results are analyzed focusing on the effects on employment and some regional and national aggregates; 2) the results are decomposed into the effects of investments in the Center-South and investments in the Northeast, determining the multiplier effects of the new technology; 3) the short-run output multiplier is decomposed in its intraregional and interregional components; and 4) sensitivity analysis is carried out using different values for the labor-saving-technology parameter.

Simulation Results

Short-run results A four-step Euler procedure is adopted in the solution of the model, and the results are reported as percentage deviations from the base case (except otherwise stated). Table 5.12 presents the industry results for employment, activity level, and basic prices of commodities; Figures 5.19-5.21 show the short-run employment effects of the increase in the current capital stocks in the transportation equipment sector. In the figures, the effect of the labor-saving technology becomes clear, as employment is freed from the sector. In the Center-South, because of the higher capital-labor ratio of the sector, relatively more labor is released. The decrease in employment in the transportation sector in the North, which does not receive any new investment, is due to interregional substitution effects, as its products become relatively more expensive than in the other regions of the country.

The increased demand generated by new investments in the transportation equipment sector affects the economy positively. The labor resources released in the sector are absorbed by other industries (recall that in the short-run, the supply responses are via changes in the employment level). The positive impact on the main suppliers of the automobile industry, such as steel, electronic equipment, rubber, and plastics, is also evident. The effects in the Northeast are relatively smaller because of the strong interregional linkages of the automobile industry; spillover effects benefit the other parts of the country. Sectors in the Center-South receive stronger impact; the stronger intraregional linkages generate higher internal multipliers in the region. The results achieved for the rubber sector in the North deserve to be mentioned. The sector sells 59.21% of its output for current production use in the rest of the country (92.62% of its interregional exports are directed to the Center-South), and therefore, interregional feedback effects operate to its benefit. Similar feedback effects operate in favor of the electronic equipment sector in the region, which has a much higher weight in the regional economic structure.

Industries producing goods for consumer use gain from the increased consumption originated by the increase in the employment level in sectors directly benefited from backward linkages of the automobile industry.

Table 5.12 B-MARIA Projected Percentage Effects of an Increase in the Production Capacity in the Transportation Equipment Sector: Short-Run

		Employment by Industry			Output by Industry			Basic price of Commodities			
		North	Northeast	Center-South	North	Northeast	Center-South	North	Northeast	Center-South	Imported
S1	Agriculture	0.144	0.015	0.120	0.081	0.011	0.084	0.095	0.056	0.089	0.000
S2	Mining	-0.251	0.065	-0.157	-0.097	0.038	-0.099	0.032	0.061	0.057	0.000
S3	Nonmetallic Minerals	0.238	0.258	0.178	0.155	0.146	0.094	0.132	0.138	0.147	0.000
S4	Steel	0.314	0.489	1.054	0.193	0.228	0.533	0.290	0.205	0.350	0.000
S5	Nonferrous Metals	0.276	0.079	0.702	0.162	0.039	0.491	0.067	0.079	0.138	0.000
S6	Other Metal Products	0.117	0.240	0.317	0.097	0.182	0.273	0.099	0.104	0.180	0.000
S7	Machinery	0.320	0.081	0.409	0.254	0.067	0.355	-0.032	0.118	0.116	0.000
S8	Electrical Equipment	0.216	0.129	0.244	0.187	0.100	0.209	0.065	0.071	0.129	0.000
S9	Electronic Equipment	0.381	0.219	0.458	0.222	0.135	0.329	0.123	0.087	0.153	0.000
S10	Transportation Equipment	-1.076	-6.692	-2.106	-0.573	5.515	0.614	-1.071	-7.986	-1.881	0.000
S11	Wood Products and Furniture	0.050	0.117	0.175	0.045	0.098	0.142	0.055	0.071	0.106	0.000
S12	Paper Products and Printing	-0.007	0.125	0.368	-0.005	0.058	0.205	0.053	0.108	0.177	0.000
S13	Rubber	0.748	0.791	0.662	0.265	0.287	0.335	0.259	0.289	0.297	0.000
S14	Chemicals	0.171	0.132	0.249	0.148	0.089	0.190	0.084	0.066	0.097	0.000
S15	Petroleum Refining	0.208	-0.032	0.508	0.124	-0.016	0.289	0.066	0.057	0.082	0.000
S16	Other Chemicals	0.156	-0.086	0.190	0.124	-0.054	0.157	0.078	0.054	0.083	0.000
S17	Pharmaceuticals and Veterinary	0.149	0.062	0.102	0.128	0.048	0.087	0.090	0.097	0.098	0.000
S18	Plastics	0.361	0.365	0.428	0.185	0.099	0.184	0.201	0.189	0.243	0.000
S19	Textiles	0.217	0.232	0.298	0.143	0.121	0.179	0.111	0.108	0.142	0.000
S20	Clothing	0.200	0.207	0.159	0.147	0.141	0.102	0.120	0.106	0.129	0.000
S21	Footwear	0.483	0.201	0.569	0.329	0.118	0.412	0.144	0.147	0.205	0.000
S22	Coffee	-0.158	0.080	-0.484	-0.060	0.029	-0.169	0.059	0.070	0.009	0.000
S23	Processed Vegetables	0.274	-0.193	0.293	0.178	-0.099	0.177	0.085	0.030	0.128	0.000
S24	Meat Packing Plants	0.137	0.455	0.450	0.078	0.106	0.225	0.098	0.122	0.141	0.000
S25	Dairy Products	0.381	0.226	0.112	0.270	0.130	0.055	0.105	0.085	0.107	0.000
S26	Sugar	0.312	-0.339	0.158	0.194	-0.231	0.077	0.102	0.016	0.117	0.000
S27	Vegetable Oil Mills	0.792	0.599	1.335	0.681	0.232	0.486	0.139	0.197	0.291	0.000
S28	Other Food Products	0.136	0.176	0.095	0.103	0.117	0.063	0.102	0.083	0.127	0.000
S29	Other Manufacturing	0.235	0.181	0.325	0.120	0.049	0.222	0.103	0.063	0.094	0.000
S30	Electric, Gas, and Sanitary Services	0.220	0.105	0.292	0.121	0.052	0.138	0.208	0.120	0.250	0.000
S31	Construction	0.002	0.098	0.031	0.001	0.091	0.026	0.193	0.082	0.104	0.000
S32	Trade	0.053	0.079	0.172	0.046	0.070	0.148	0.060	0.062	0.104	0.000
S33	Transportation	0.097	0.175	0.443	0.063	0.117	0.256	-0.220	-0.095	0.066	0.000
S34	Communication	0.144	0.089	0.266	0.069	0.041	0.147	0.154	0.119	0.220	0.000
S35	Finanacial Institutions	0.107	0.063	0.226	0.084	0.047	0.184	0.103	0.060	0.094	0.000
S36	Personal services	0.153	0.089	0.291	0.111	0.063	0.185	0.016	0.023	-0.007	0.000
S37	Business Services	0.105	0.107	0.233	0.063	0.068	0.135	0.103	0.104	0.141	0.000
S38	Real Estate	0.235	0.178	0.272	0.006	0.002	0.022	0.512	0.380	0.529	0.000
S39	Public Administration	0.000	0.000	0.000	0.000	0.000	0.000	0.075	0.058	0.065	0.000
S40	Community Services	0.131	0.061	0.180	0.117	0.055	0.160	0.084	0.073	0.109	0.000

These industries respond by creating jobs and inducing a second round of expenditures in their goods.

Traditional export sectors (especially mining, coffee and sugar) are the main losers. Initially positively affected by the increase in the domestic demand, their cost of production rises, driven by internal demand pressures and also increases in the input prices. By facing negatively sloped demand curves in the international markets, their exports go down, contributing to their poor performance. Exports from the mining sector decrease by -0.615% in the North, and -1.184% in the Center-South; exports of sugar from the Northeast fall by -0.365%; and exports of coffee from the Center-South decrease by -0.310%. Given the generalized demand-driven price hike, exports in all the sectors in the North and Northeast fall. However, in the Center-South, nontraditional exports growth is led by the performance of the transportation equipment sector, whose products become more competitive in the international markets.

The results calculated for some regional and national variables are presented in Table 5.13. The introduction of labor-saving technology in the automobile industry produces positive net employment effects in the country (0.105%) and in each region, individually. These results reflect directly in the GDP/GRP levels. Regarding the regional distribution of income, the Center-South is the region that achieves higher growth (0.159%, in the Center-South, as opposed to 0.068% in the North, and 0.050% in the Northeast). In money terms, this corresponds to an increment in the Center-South close to 17.5 times greater than the one in the Northeast. If the initial change is taken into consideration, which reflects a 10:1 ratio of investments in the Center-South and in the Northeast, the results show a striking difference in regional performance. The results also show the North growing faster than the Northeast; even though the region does not receive any new direct investment, the nature of its linkages with the other two regions contributes to this result. From the model's projections shown below, it is clear that interregional exports lead the performance in the region.

Considering the components of domestic absorption, with investments and government expenditures set fixed exogenously, household consumption is the only component allowed to move; it shows increases in real household consumption driven by the employment effect. As another indicator of the worsening of regional imbalances, the estimates for the regional/national consumption rate indicate a decrease in the regional shares of the North and Northeast in favor of the Center-South.

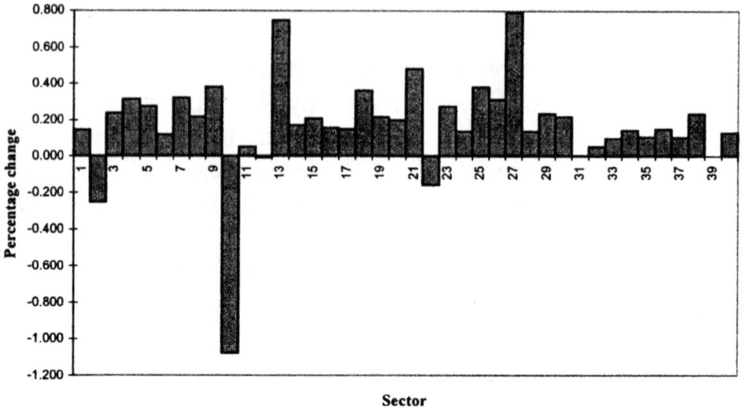

Figure 5.19 B-MARIA Projected Short-Run Employment Effects of Increased Production Capacity in the Transportation Equipment Sector: North

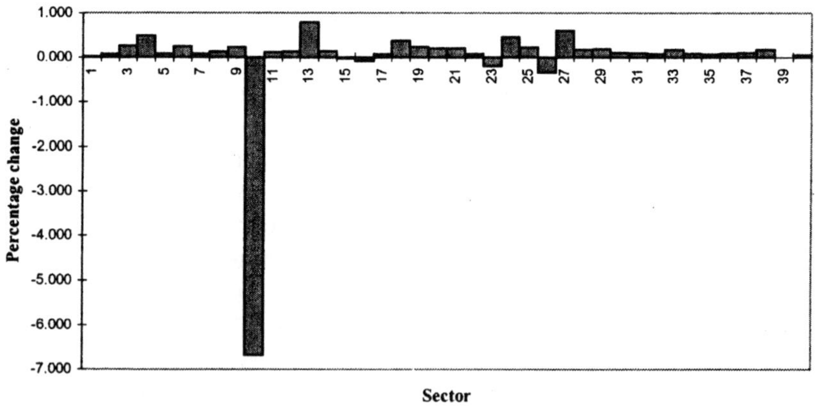

Figure 5.20 B-MARIA Projected Short-Run Employment Effects of Increased Production Capacity in the Transportation Equipment Sector: Northeast

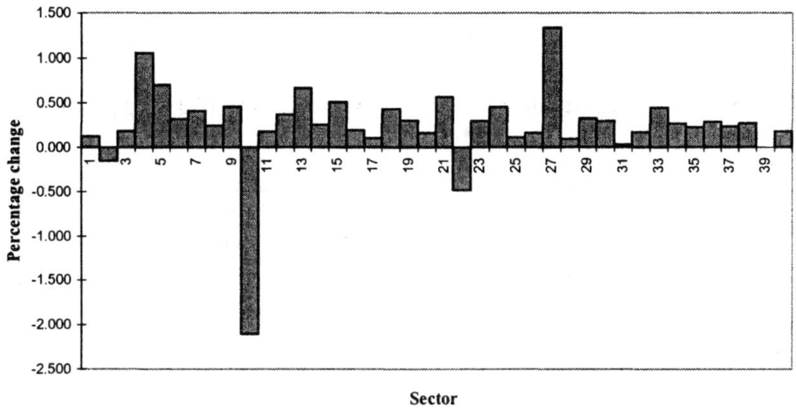

Figure 5.21 B-MARIA Projected Short-Run Employment Effects of Increased Production Capacity in the Transportation Equipment Sector: Center-South

As noted above, the results for the interregional trade balance of Brazil's North are relevant to understanding the regional performance. The weight of interregional trade in the region is very high when compared to the weight of international trade. In the benchmark data base, the ratio of the volume of interregional trade to the volume of international trade equals 6.20 in the North, 4.91 in the Northeast, and 0.52 in the Center-South. Thus, the weak performance in the international markets does not have a strong impact in the regional economy of the North, as it would have been the case if the changes had occurred in the *interregional* trade components. As was pointed out in the analysis of the sectoral results, international exports are harmed in the North and Northeast by the increase in the cost of production; however, the transportation equipment sector leads the exports in the Center-South, achieving overall positive results at the regional level. Finally, given the combined effects of demand-driven domestic prices increase and unchanged import prices, there is an increase in the volume of imports.

With the model calibrated with the interregional input-output table for 1985, it is important to emphasize that the import coefficients are underestimated. In the case of the transportation equipment sector, the opening of the market for imports in the 1990's led to their gradual increase in market share. With higher import coefficients for both foreign inputs to production and consumption of foreign products, B-MARIA overestimates the employment effects by neglecting part of the substitution effects between domestic and foreign commodities and by overestimating the weight of domestic demand.

Table 5.13 Brazil: Short-Run Effects on Selected Regional and Macro Variables

	N	NE	C-S	Brazil
Real GDP/GRP	0.068	0.050	0.159	0.140
Real Household Consumption	0.090	0.048	0.121	0.107
Unemployment Rate (% point change)	-0.074	-0.044	-0.126	-0.102
Consumer Price Index	0.070	0.044	0.056	0.055
Regional/National Consumption Rate	-0.018	-0.060	0.014	--
Employment: Persons	0.077	0.045	0.131	0.105
Interregional Export Volume	0.216	0.324	-0.025	--
Interregional Import Volume	0.041	-0.025	0.266	--
Interregional BT (ordinary change)	65.1	132.7	-197.8	--
International Export Volume	-0.678	-0.999	0.758	0.565
International Import Volume	0.111	0.119	0.328	0.316
Balance of Trade (ordinary change)	-35.7	-140.8	781.6	605.1

Decomposition of the Results In this sub-section, the results reported above are decomposed into the effects of the investments introducing labor-saving technology in the transportation equipment sector in the Center-South and in the Northeast. B-MARIA is solved twice: once for the shock in the Center-South holding capital stocks in the Northeast constant, and again for the shock in the Northeast, with the capital stock in the Center-South fixed. Two sets of results are produced giving the separate impacts of each regional component of investment. The one-step Johansen procedure is adopted so that the total impact is the sum of the two simulations. However, because of linearization errors, the results are only accurate to the first order. Table 5.14 shows the decomposition of the short-run effects on some selected regional and macro variables using the Johansen procedure. A comparison with the results provided in Table 5.13 shows the extent to the linearization errors.

By looking at the columns referring to the national aggregates, it is clear that the effects derived from the new investments in the Center-South are much stronger. Even though the output effect of increased investments in the Center-South is smaller in the Northeast, than it would be the case of investments increases departing from the Northeast region, because of the labor-saving character of the new investments the employment effect is stronger, generating higher levels of household consumption in the region. Figures 5.22-5.24 reveal the extent to which employment effects are decomposed at the industry level.

The results presented in Table 5.15 abstract from the level differences in investments; it is assumed that there is a 1:1 increase in the current capital stocks in the transportation equipment sector in both regions (the shock in the Center-South is ten times smaller). The idea is to compare the differential multiplier effects of investments in the two regions. The effects on the national economy as a whole are still slightly stronger when investments are carried out in the Center-South (led by the performance of the export sector). However, because of the relatively lower interregional backward linkages of the Center-South, a dollar's worth of investment in transportation equipment in the Northeast is more beneficial to the improvement of regional imbalances in the country. While new labor-saving investments in the Northeast improve the GRP of the region by 0.060% and that of the North by 0.039%, with a small increase in the Center-South (0.004%), when these investments are undertaken in the Center-South, the performance of GRP changes to 0.001% in the Northeast, 0.005% in the North, and 0.017% in the Center-South.

Interregional Multiplier As already mentioned, the decomposition of results presented above was based on one-step Johansen simulations which enabled the total impact of increased capacity in the transportation sector to be decomposed into the separate impacts of each regional component of investment. However, as noted, the results are not accurate because of linearization errors. In order to get more accurate results for the output multiplier effects, the impact for the investment originating in each region is calculated individually, adopting a four-step Euler procedure in each simulation to eliminate linearization errors. The analysis focuses on the short-run output multiplier. A 1:1 relationship between the increase in the current capital stock in each region is assumed.

Table 5.14 Decomposition of the Short-Run Effects Using the Johansen Procedure: Increased Production Capacity in the Automobile Industry (55% increase in the Northeast and 5% in the Center-South)

	North			Northeast			Center-South			Brazil		
	CS	NE	CS+NE	CS	NE	CS+NE	CS	NE	CS+NE	CS	NE	CS+NE
Real GDP/GRP	0.048	0.039	0.087	0.010	0.060	0.070	0.170	0.004	0.174	0.141	0.013	0.154
Real Household Consumption	0.059	0.057	0.116	0.028	0.031	0.059	0.128	0.005	0.133	0.108	0.012	0.120
Unemployment Rate (% point change)	-0.047	-0.050	-0.097	-0.019	-0.037	-0.056	-0.135	-0.004	-0.139	-0.099	-0.015	-0.114
Consumer Price Index	0.074	0.000	0.074	0.043	0.001	0.044	0.058	0.002	0.060	0.057	0.001	0.058
Regional/National Consumption Rate	-0.049	0.045	-0.004	-0.080	0.020	-0.060	0.020	-0.007	0.013	--	--	--
Employment: Persons	0.048	0.052	0.100	0.019	0.038	0.057	0.140	0.004	0.144	0.103	0.015	0.118
Interregional Export Volume	0.209	0.029	0.238	0.274	0.123	0.397	-0.060	0.027	-0.033	--	--	--
Interregional Import Volume	0.013	0.045	0.058	-0.091	0.062	-0.029	0.258	0.048	0.306	--	--	--
International Export Volume	-0.771	0.085	-0.686	-1.071	0.036	-1.035	0.825	0.020	0.845	0.615	0.023	0.638
International Import Volume	0.111	0.003	0.114	0.043	0.106	0.149	0.347	0.010	0.357	0.332	0.012	0.344
Balance of Trade (ordinary change)	-40.1	4.0	-36.1	-148.6	2.2	-146.4	860.7	19.9	880.6	672.0	26.1	698.1

Table 5.15 Decomposition of the Short-Run Effects Using the Johansen Procedure: Increased Production Capacity in the Automobile Industry (55% increase in the Northeast and 0.5% in the Center-South)

	North			Northeast			Center-South			Brazil		
	CS	NE	CS+NE	CS	NE	CS+NE	CS	NE	CS+NE	CS	NE	CS+NE
Real GDP/GRP	0.005	0.039	0.044	0.001	0.060	0.061	0.017	0.004	0.021	0.014	0.013	0.027
Real Household Consumption	0.006	0.057	0.063	0.003	0.031	0.034	0.013	0.005	0.018	0.011	0.012	0.023
Unemployment Rate (% point change)	-0.005	-0.050	-0.055	-0.002	-0.037	-0.039	-0.014	-0.004	-0.018	-0.010	-0.015	-0.025
Consumer Price Index	0.007	0.000	0.007	0.004	0.001	0.005	0.006	0.002	0.008	0.006	0.001	0.007
Regional/National Consumption Rate	-0.005	0.045	0.040	-0.008	0.020	0.012	0.002	-0.007	-0.005	--	--	--
Employment: Persons	0.005	0.052	0.057	0.002	0.038	0.040	0.014	0.004	0.018	0.010	0.015	0.025
Interregional Export Volume	0.021	0.029	0.050	0.027	0.123	0.150	-0.006	0.027	0.021	--	--	--
Interregional Import Volume	0.001	0.045	0.046	-0.009	0.062	0.053	0.026	0.048	0.074	--	--	--
International Export Volume	-0.077	0.085	0.008	-0.107	0.036	-0.071	0.083	0.020	0.103	0.062	0.023	0.085
International Import Volume	0.011	0.003	0.014	0.004	0.106	0.110	0.035	0.010	0.045	0.033	0.012	0.045
Balance of Trade (ordinary change)	-4.0	4.0	0.0	-14.9	2.2	-12.7	86.1	19.9	106.0	67.2	26.1	93.3

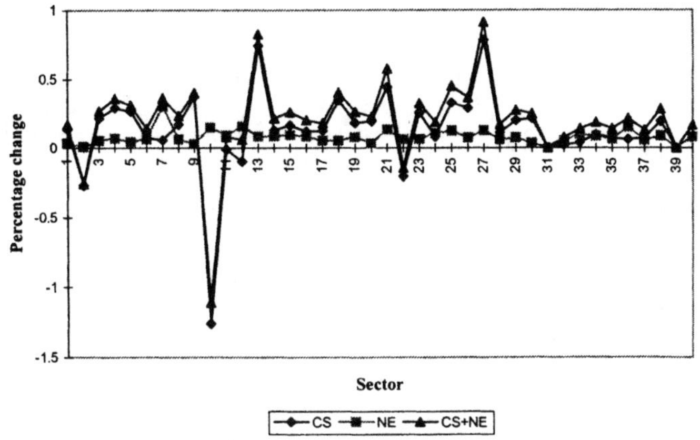

Figure 5.22 Decomposition of Short-Run Employment Effects of Increased Production Capacity in the Transportation Equipment Sector: North

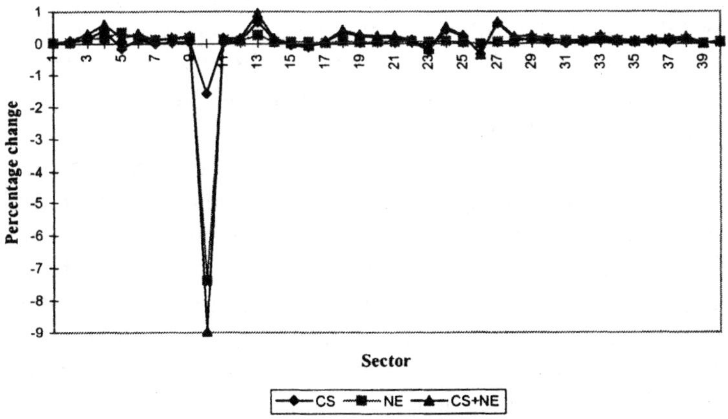

Figure 5.23 Decomposition of Short-Run Employment Effects of Increased Production Capacity in the Transportation Equipment Sector: Northeast

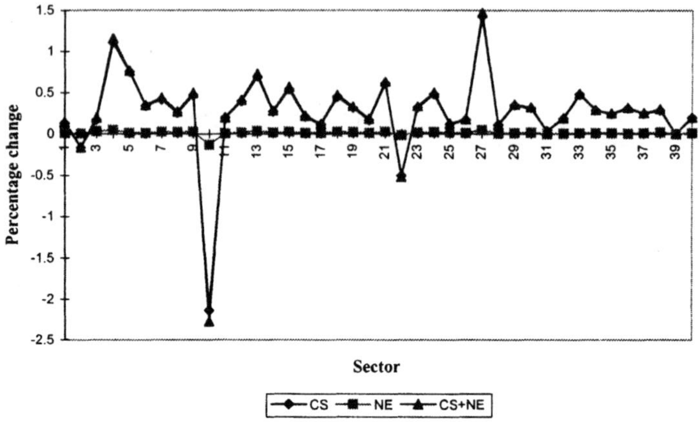

Figure 5.24 Decomposition of Short-Run Employment Effects of Increased Production Capacity in the Transportation Equipment Sector: Center-South

The estimates confirm the efficiency results suggested in the last section: investments carried out in the Center-South produce higher national growth (0.014% against 0.009% when the initial injection takes place in the Northeast).[15] However, investments originating in the Northeast improve the regional distribution of output; in this case, the results for GRP show the following (the number in parenthesis showing the estimates for investments originating in the Center-South): 0.024% (0.005%) in the North, 0.042% (0.001%) in the Northeast, and 0.002% (0.017%) in the Center-South.

The short-run output multiplier effect can be decomposed into its intraregional (internal multiplier) and interregional (external multiplier) components, the former representing the impacts on the outputs of sectors within the region where the investment change was generated, and the latter showing the impacts on the other regions of the system (interregional *spillover* effects). Figure 5.25 shows the short-run direct and indirect effects of a unit change in the current capital stock in the transportation sector in the Northeast and Center-South net of the initial injection, i.e., the output multiplier effect net of the initial change. The entries are shown in percentage terms, providing insights into the degree of dependence of each

[15] When compared to the figures presented in Table 5.15 (real GDP), these estimates give an idea of the extent of the linearization errors.

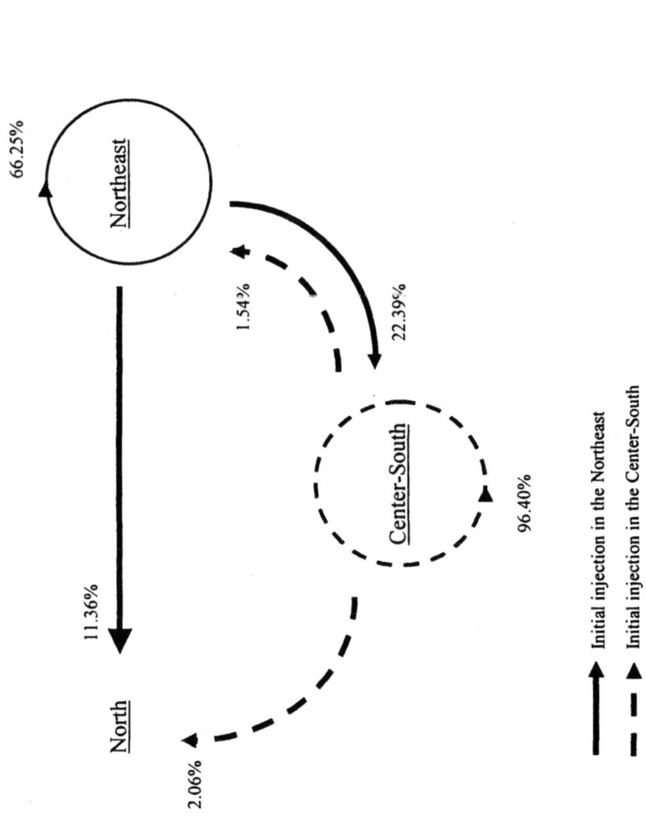

Figure 5.25 Percentage Distribution of Short-Run Output Multiplier Net of Initial Injection: Investments in the Automobile Industry

region on the other regions. The Center-South is by far the most self-sufficient region; the intraregional flow-on effects from a unit change in the investments in the automobile industry are in excess of 96%; for the Northeast, there is a lower degree of intraregional self-sufficiency, and the dominant interregional flows generated by the region usually end up in the Center-South.

Sensitivity Analysis The simulation described above is based on the assumption that new investments in the transportation equipment sector bring about technological changes producing increases in the capital-labor ratio of the industry. Moreover, it tries to cope with the empirical evidence that the increasing levels of production in the sector have been accompanied by reductions in the employment levels. To adapt the model to carry out impact analysis of such changes, it is assumed that exogenous changes occur in the current capital stocks of the industry, inducing substitution away from labor resources. However, the degree of this substitution, i.e., the labor-saving content of the new technology, depends heavily on the values assumed for the parameters determining the primary-factor elasticity of substitution in the model. The benchmark value, used in the previous exercise, equals 0.50. By varying the value of this parameter for the transportation equipment sector, one can achieve results representing the use of alternative technologies in the automobile industry. The value of the parameter was arbitrarily set at 0.05 and 5.00, defining different degrees of labor-saving content; 0.05 implies very low levels of labor saving, with the technology approaching the Leontief specification; 5.00, on the other hand, implies very high levels of substitution (the model was solved twice).

Figures 5.26-5.28 depict the differential impacts of the assumed technologies on the levels of employment in the industries. It is clear that employment expands at a greater rate when Leontief-type technology is assumed. The restriction imposed by the model on the movements of employment levels in each region is specified by the regional unemployment rates, defined by the relation between the initial level of employment and the labor supply.

The aggregate results for GRP/GDP employment, shown in Figures 5.29-5.30, indicate that the choice of technology is very relevant, especially to the regions where investments take place.

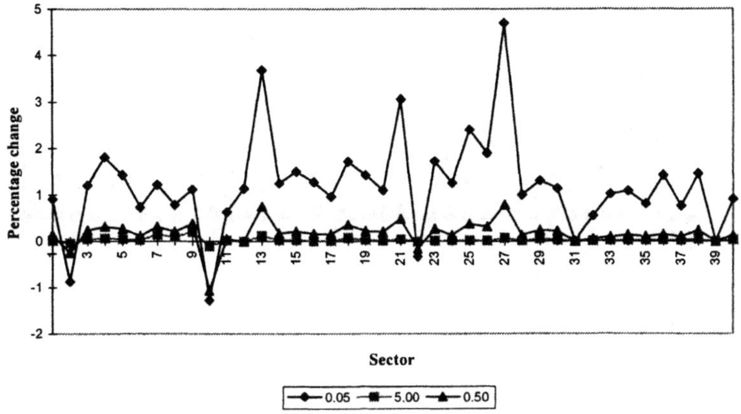

Figure 5.26 Short-Run Employment Effects of Different Technologies: North

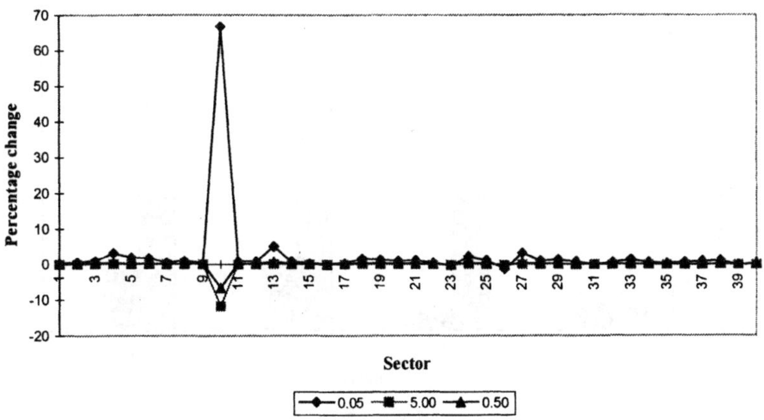

Figure 5.27 Short-Run Employment Effects of Different Technologies: Northeast

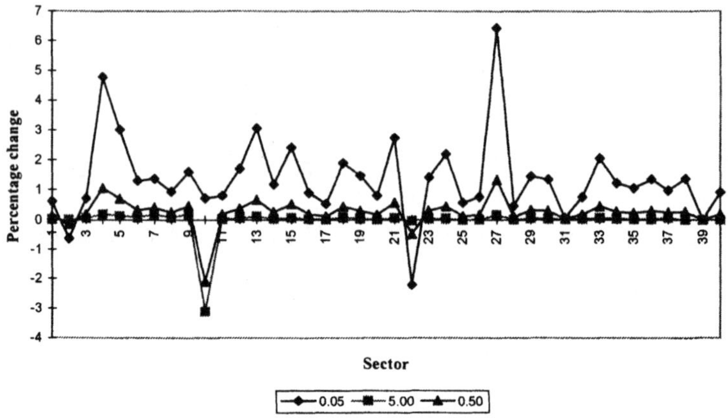

Figure 5.28 Short-Run Employment Effects of Different Technologies: Center-South

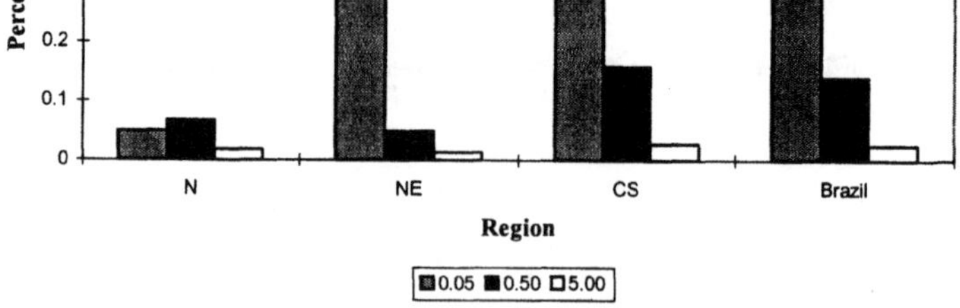

Figure 5.29 Regional and National Short-Run Effects of Different Technologies in the Transportation Equipment Sector: GDP/GRP

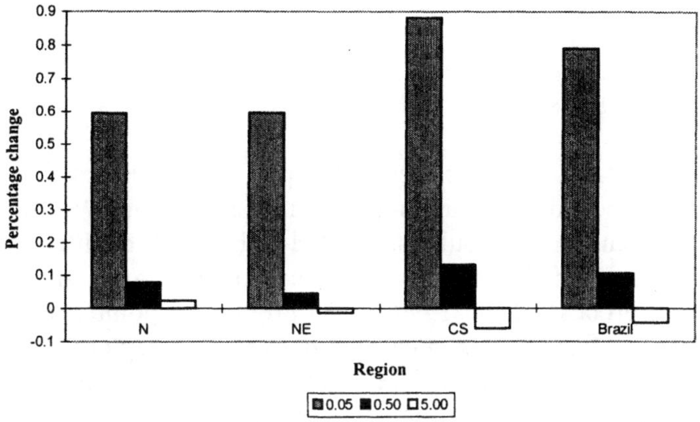

Figure 5.30 Regional and National Short-Run Effects of Different Technologies in the Transportation Equipment Sector: Employment

Finally, the results show that the concern of trade unions on the level of employment should be considered under two aspects. First, the spillover effects from the transportation sector are very strong, both intraregional and interregionally, and an increase in the investments in the industry are very likely to generate overall positive results, as the model projects. Secondly, the evaluation of the technology to be adopted should be perceived on the grounds of feasibility: given the available choices, what would be the impact on the variables of interest (e.g. employment). Technically, it reflects the use of appropriate values for the primary-factor substitution elasticity which represent the available technology.

6 Conclusion

Summary of Results

The simulation exercises described in Chapter 5 were intended to examine some of the aspects of the changing economic environment in Brazil in the 1990's. The quantitative results supported a thorough qualitative analysis of the evolution of Brazil's productive structure after the economic liberalization process of the 1990's. As previously pointed out, the goal was to use a formal analytical framework to capture the role of interindustrial and interregional relations in the economic development process through the evaluation of the regional impact of different economic policies. Attention was directed to the short-term and long-term analysis of different issues: the effects of trade liberalization, reductions in transportation costs reflecting specific changes in the so called *Custo Brasil*, and the regional impact of a development project. Theoretical and historical relevance to the Brazilian case motivated the choice of policies to be analyzed.

The choice of the CGE method to address the regional impact of macroeconomic, structural and sectoral policies is justified by its ability to address the issue of regional inequality and structural changes based on the theoretical framework of the dynamics of regional development described in Chapter 1. It borrows from the input-output framework the capability of handling details at the sectoral level, providing a detailed picture of the regional economies. Input-output linkages also incorporate the static dimension of regional development by revealing the strength of interregional spread effects through the specification of existing trade flows in the economy. However, the CGE approach goes one step further; regional competitiveness is captured by incorporating price effects in those models. Differential regional prices play a major role in the theories of regional development, in which regional competitive advantage is addressed through differential production costs and activities allocation.

Tables 6.1a and 6.1b summarize the results of the basic simulations carried out in the book; they show the direction of the effects of the different policies on the activity level of the regional industries and on the gross regional products, as well as similar estimates for the country as a whole.

Table 6.1a Summary of Simulations' Results: Activity Level

		Tariff Reduction							
	Sectors	Short-Run				Long-Run			
		N	NE	CS	BR	N	NE	CS	BR
S1	Agriculture	+	+	+	+	+	-	+	+
S2	Mining	+	+	+	+	+	-	+	-
S3	Nonmetallic Minerals	-	-	-	-	+	-	+	+
S4	Steel	+	+	+	+	+	-	+	+
S5	Nonferrous Metals	+	+	+	+	+	-	+	+
S6	Other Metal Products	+	+	+	+	+	-	+	+
S7	Machinery	+	+	+	+	+	-	+	+
S8	Electrical Equipment	+	-	+	+	+	-	+	+
S9	Electronic Equipment	+	-	-	+	+	-	+	+
S10	Transportation Equipment	+	+	+	+	+	-	+	+
S11	Wood Prod. and Furniture	+	+	+	+	-	-	+	+
S12	Paper Prod. and Printing	+	+	+	+	-	-	+	+
S13	Rubber	-	-	+	+	-	-	+	+
S14	Chemicals	-	-	-	-	-	-	-	-
S15	Petroleum Refining	-	+	-	-	+	-	+	-
S16	Other Chemicals	-	-	-	-	-	-	-	-
S17	Pharmaceuticals and Vet.	-	-	-	-	-	-	-	-
S18	Plastics	-	+	+	+	+	-	+	+
S19	Textiles	+	+	+	+	+	-	+	+
S20	Clothing	+	+	+	+	+	-	+	+
S21	Footwear	+	+	+	+	+	-	+	+
S22	Coffee	+	+	+	+	+	-	+	+
S23	Processed Vegetables	+	+	+	+	+	-	+	+
S24	Meat Packing Plants	+	+	+	+	+	-	+	+
S25	Dairy Products	+	+	+	+	+	-	+	+
S26	Sugar	-	+	-	+	-	-	+	-
S27	Vegetable Oil Mills	+	+	+	+	-	-	+	+
S28	Other Food Products	-	-	-	-	-	-	+	-
S29	Other Manufacturing	-	+	+	+	+	-	+	+
S30	Elec., Gas and Sanit. Serv.	+	+	+	+	+	-	+	+
S31	Construction	+	+	+	+	+	-	+	+
S32	Trade	+	+	+	+	+	-	+	+
S33	Transportation	+	+	+	+	+	-	+	+
S34	Communication	+	+	+	+	+	-	+	+
S35	Financial Institutions	+	+	+	+	+	-	+	+
S36	Personal services	+	+	+	+	+	-	+	+
S37	Business Services	+	+	+	+	+	-	+	+
S38	Real Estate	+	+	+	+	+	-	+	+
S39	Public Administration	0	0	0	0	+	-	+	+
S40	Community Services	+	+	+	+	+	-	+	+
	Real GDP/GRP	+	+	+	+	+	-	+	+

Table 6.1b Summary of Simulations' Results: Activity Level

		TFP Growth in S33				Investment in S10			
	Sectors	Long-Run				Short-Run			
		N	NE	CS	BR	N	NE	CS	BR
S1	Agriculture	+	-	+	+	+	+	+	+
S2	Mining	-	-	+	+	-	+	-	-
S3	Nonmetallic Minerals	+	-	+	+	+	+	+	+
S4	Steel	+	-	+	+	+	+	+	+
S5	Nonferrous Metals	+	-	+	+	+	+	+	+
S6	Other Metal Products	+	-	+	+	+	+	+	+
S7	Machinery	+	-	+	+	+	+	+	+
S8	Electrical Equipment	+	-	+	+	+	+	+	+
S9	Electronic Equipment	+	-	+	+	+	+	+	+
S10	Transportation Equipment	+	+	+	+	-	+	+	+
S11	Wood Prod. and Furniture	+	-	+	+	+	+	+	+
S12	Paper Prod. And Printing	+	-	+	+	-	+	+	+
S13	Rubber	+	+	+	+	+	+	+	+
S14	Chemicals	+	-	+	+	+	+	+	+
S15	Petroleum Refining	+	-	+	+	+	-	+	+
S16	Other Chemicals	+	-	+	+	+	-	+	+
S17	Pharmaceuticals and Vet.	-	-	+	+	+	+	+	+
S18	Plastics	+	-	+	+	+	+	+	+
S19	Textiles	+	-	+	+	+	+	+	+
S20	Clothing	-	+	+	+	+	+	+	+
S21	Footwear	+	-	+	+	+	+	+	+
S22	Coffee	+	-	-	-	-	+	-	-
S23	Processed Vegetables	+	-	+	+	+	-	+	+
S24	Meat Packing Plants	+	-	+	+	+	+	+	+
S25	Dairy Products	+	-	+	+	+	+	+	+
S26	Sugar	+	-	+	-	+	-	+	-
S27	Vegetable Oil Mills	-	-	+	+	+	+	+	+
S28	Other Food Products	+	-	+	+	+	+	+	+
S29	Other Manufacturing	+	-	+	+	+	+	+	+
S30	Elec., Gas and Sanit. Serv.	+	-	+	+	+	+	+	+
S31	Construction	+	-	+	-	+	+	+	+
S32	Trade	+	-	+	+	+	+	+	+
S33	Transportation	+	+	+	+	+	+	+	+
S34	Communication	+	-	+	+	+	+	+	+
S35	Financial Institutions	+	-	+	+	+	+	+	+
S36	Personal services	+	-	+	+	+	+	+	+
S37	Business Services	+	-	+	+	+	+	+	+
S38	Real Estate	+	-	+	+	+	+	+	+
S39	Public Administration	+	-	+	+	0	0	0	0
S40	Community Services	+	-	+	+	+	+	+	+
	Real GDP/GRP	+	-	+	+	+	+	+	+

In the tariff simulation exercise, industry activity results show that, in general, export sectors benefit most from the tariff cut, while import-competing sectors are the main losers in the short-run. As a general result, in the long-run, the industries that become exposed to higher levels of foreign competition, more precisely those of the chemical complex, are adversely affected in the three regions. It becomes clear that the performance of industries in the Northeast is weaker than the overall better performance of the Center-South. Regarding regional output, all the regions are positively affected in the short-run, and, in the long-run, only the Northeast presents negative results. In both cases, the tariff reduction worsens the Northeast's relative position in the country.

The experiment showing the effects of total factor productivity growth in the transportation sector also reveals a situation of increasing regional imbalances, in favor of the more developed region of the Center-South. This appears to be the case, not only at the aggregate output level, but also in most of the sectors. Finally, the policy simulation assessing the regional effects of the planned investments in the transportation equipment sector predicts a higher aggregate impact in the growth of the Center-South, contributing, again, to increasing regional disparities. At the sectoral level, traditional export sectors are the main losers in the three regions examined.

Policy Implications

The discussion of regional and sectoral impacts of alternative strategies of regional development in the present macroeconomic context of the Brazilian economy has shown that the open policies of the 1990's and the national strategies for increasing international competitiveness are very likely to increase regional imbalances in the country. The regional de-concentration trend verified in the period from the 1960's to the early 1980's was heavily induced by an active government intervention, manifested in actions such as direct investments in regional development projects and tax incentives in the less developed regions of the country. However, with the fiscal crisis generalized to all levels of government, little room for new public ventures was available.

The agreed agenda for the coming years includes the competitive integration of the country in the global trade network, with the domestic concern of sustainable stabilization. This implies the attraction of foreign investments and a responsible (balanced) budget policy for all levels of government. The latter precludes regional policies based on heavy redistributional expenditures, as was the case in the 1970s. Foreign investors search for better financial returns, and, therefore, are not concerned with regional equity; location is defined on a purely economic basis.

Haddad (1996) points out that the new growth cycle of the Brazilian economy will be intensive in technology, reflecting greater exposure to international competition. Conventional industrial location theory, in many cases, fails to explain the patterns of the new investments. Technical skills and urban agglomeration are two important factors that will influence the location of incoming investments in the regions, as interregional competition will be more heavily based on non-traditional locational factors such as quality of universities, educational attainment, and quality of life, than on conventional locational factors such as low wages and tax incentives.

Based on international comparisons, Malecki (1991) concludes that advanced technology has had some positive effects on national and local policy. It has prompted a more long-term perspective about economic development; and it has shown the significant advantages to be gained from investments in human capital, especially through education. The creation of new high-technology complexes will not be an everyday, or everywhere, occurrence. Large urban regions, especially those where university research is abundant, are the prime locations, in no small part because of the entrepreneurial "climate" and opportunities present. Other places, if they can attain some – even if not all – of the attributes of the large urban areas, might get at least a small development benefit. In the case of Brazil, the Center-South concentrates the human capital stock of the country, which is the most required factor to attract new investments.

The results of this book suggest that the interplay of market forces in the Brazilian economy favors the more developed region of the country. In other words, the trickling-down effects generated by market forces are still very unlikely to overtake the polarization effects from the Center-South. If regional equity is part of the country's development agenda, an active regional policy by the central government is still needed, in order to reduce regional economic disparities, and specifically to address the problems of the North and Northeast, traditionally backward areas reliant on low technology activities. The improvement of the economic infrastructure in those regions, as well as the establishment of enduring competitive advantages, through a consistent human capital policy, are necessary to attenuate the adverse regional effects of the development strategy pursued by the public authorities.

Nowadays, the regional policy carried out by the federal government consists of isolated subsidies and industrial incentives to growth centers. In the context of the fiscal adjustment process of the 1990s, the role of the central government in stimulating directly productive activities and enhancing the social overhead capital in the lagging regions is being neglected. In the conception of the *Real Plan*, there was no explicit concern about the formulation of a regional development policy for the country. The *Real Plan* was conceived as a global stabilization plan, which would include economic reforms (privatization, concessions and deregulation) and institutional reforms (tax system, social security and administrative), without proposing any strategy for medium and long-run development. However, with the benefits from the stabilization and the reforms, a new cycle of private investments emerged. These investments tended to concentrate in the South and Southeast regions, which provided a full range of non-traditional (e.g. technical skills and urban agglomeration) and traditional (e.g. friction of distance Mercosul) locational factors to attract the incoming capital. The lack of investments by the federal government, allied to the spurt in private investments, has led regional governments to engage in strong competition for private capital through fiscal mechanisms. In some cases, the political pressures by the representatives of the lagging regions produced elements of compensatory regional policies, as was the case of the special automotive regime promoted by the federal government for the less developed regions, which induced planned investments for the transportation equipment sector in the Northeast of over US$1 billion. The effects of such investments were shown to generate important effects in the region with a great extent of the benefits being transferred to the rest of the country. However, with the Asian crisis of the second half of 1997, there were doubts that these would be carried out.[1]

Regarding the less developed regions of the North and Northeast, regional development necessarily demands direct government intervention. Their economic structure should evolve to higher level of specialization in those activities where the regions present dynamic competitive advantage in order to define their role in the process of interregional and international integration. In the Northeast, different studies identified the regional competitive advantage in the productive transformation of the existing economic structure, based on the restructuring and modernization of

[1] Among the announced investment intentions of transnational automobile firms in 1997, two Korean firms were planning to invest over US$1 billion in an assembly plant to be located in the Northeastern state of Bahia.

specialized industrial complexes (e.g. the petrochemical complex in Bahia, and the mining complex in Maranhão); the modernization of the agricultural sector and the agriculturally-based industries; and the expansion of tourism and related activities. This strategy will need the active participation of public authorities through the adoption of regionally differentiated fiscal incentives, when necessary, and more important, through the provision of modern economic infrastructure and the formation and development of human resources in the region, emphasizing poverty alleviation and universal primary and secondary education (see Araújo, 1995, and Albuquerque and Gomes, 1996).

The positive results achieved by the North in the tariff-cut simulation were shown to be heavily influenced by the performance of the electric-electronic complex of Manaus. As already pointed out, the model's results overestimate the sectoral performance by neglecting substitution effects between regional and foreign electronic products for internal consumption, and by overestimating the cost reduction in the production of regional industries. In the first years of the 1990s, the reduction of tariff and non-tariff barriers adversely affected the electronic equipment sector in Manaus; however, the crisis was attenuated by compensatory tax incentives to the products produced in the *Zona Franca de Manaus* (Diniz and Santos, 1996). As international competitiveness is a fundamental part of the strategy of economic integration of the country in the new world order, palliative measures are not likely to be sustainable in the long-run. A development project emphasizing the strategies for the future consolidation of the industrial complex in Manaus is necessary, taking into account a long-run national development project. For the region as a whole, dynamic competitive advantages are identified, based on the new paradigm of international competitiveness, in activities where the environmentally responsible exploitation of the natural resources takes place.

Finally, the government has to identify priorities for investments in infrastructure. In this instance, the government will face conflicting choices in the allocation of the scarce resources. On the one hand, it is important to create and modernize the existing economic infrastructure in the lagging regions to facilitate the operation of the forces for the centrifugal spread of economic expansion in the more developed regions, and also to consolidate their regional competitiveness through the establishment of an effective stock of social overhead capital. On the other hand, demands for economic infrastructure are also perceived in the Southern part of the country, in the context of the free trade agreement between Brazil, Argentina, Paraguay and Uruguay. Increased trade among these countries will face significant transportation costs, and unless the transportation sector can be adjusted, the country will not face high gains in competitiveness both in the internal and external markets.

Methodological Issues and Future Research

The major research agenda for the next several years is to develop an analytical system to evaluate new policy initiatives and restructuring generated by market forces. As previously suggested, CGE models are not without their limitations – especially their limited ability to handle dynamics –, and they should be viewed as complement to existing models rather than as replacement. The integration of B-MARIA with a national macro model and regional input-output econometric models developed for the specific regions is viewed as a significant improvement in such modeling capability.[2] Complementary econometric models can generate forecasts to provide inputs to the CGE model, adopting the forecasting closure outlined, which also needs further development. Thus, a more complete range of policies can be evaluated in the light of the recent changes in the Brazilian economy. In this context, issues that might be considered include:

a) the macroeconomic policies during the 1990s: exchange rate policy, monetary policy, and fiscal policy;
b) the regional impact of Brazil's liberalization policies, of the *Real Plan*, and of the appreciation of the exchange rate;
c) the economic liberalization process during the 1990s: stages, and political and institutional mechanisms;
d) the impacts of the economic opening process and the exchange rate policy on the Brazil's current accounts; the evolution of the trade balance since 1990;
e) imports and exports penetration in the more recent years; impacts on the productive sectors of the Brazilian economy (income, output, and employment);
f) welfare evaluation of the economic opening process and its prospects.

---

[2] The use of regional input-output econometric models based on the CREIM specification (Israilevich *et al.*, 1997) might be the logical step, as the consistent theoretical structure of CREIM enables a great level of disaggregation and has already been successfully implemented for different Brazilian regions.

The second general aspect of the improvement of B-MARIA refers to the further development of the labor market dimension of the model. Global competition is increasingly focusing on differences in labor quality as well as labor cost from one country to another and from one region to another. The *occupational capital* from a region now plays an important role in attracting new investments and retaining existing industries. In an attempt to capture the position of the Brazilian economy and its regional economies in this context, some extensions of the model are proposed:

a) the disaggregation of labor by skills, based on consistent data, that will enable the analysis of issues related to endogenous growth theory, and skill-based shifts in labor demand;
b) the disaggregation of households by income level, considering the proper mapping from the labor categories, thus providing a framework for analysis of personal income distribution through changes in the economic structure;
c) changes in the model specification by endogenizing the labor market setting through the implementation of a theory of interregional migration.

Other proposed improvements and extensions to B-MARIA include:

a) immediate update and reevaluation of the input-output data base, as more recent published estimates become available;
b) specification of a higher level of regional disaggregation, whenever information will be available;
c) expansion of the foreign sector, including explicit modeling of trade relations with the main Brazilian partners (e.g. Mercosul); in this case, the specification can benefit from the work developed by Hertel (1996) in the Global Trade Analysis Project.

The field of regional CGE modeling is relatively recent and a line defining how regional CGE models' results differ from predictions obtained from alternative methods has yet to be drawn. The CGE approach provides improvement upon traditional fixed-price methods in the sense that the latter represent a limiting case within the CGE framework (Harrigan and McGregor, 1989; McGregor *et al.*, 1997). By incorporating price substitution effects, it also provides unique contributions to the broader field of regional modeling. However, in most applications, its contributions overlap with those provided by regional input-output econometric models, and the integration of both frameworks seems to be appealing.

Data limitations, especially the lack of estimates for the specified elasticities, and some unresolved theoretical issues in region specification which are important in the regional development literature, such as imperfect competition in regional markets and increasing returns to scale, give room for the future development of regional CGE models. To be sure, most of the relevant theoretical issues have already been tackled in national CGE models (see Gingsburgh and Keyzer, 1997) and regional scientists with a solid formation in economic theory will not face strong technical restrictions in the incorporation of the regional dimension to such models. However, because of data limitations, the implementation of regional CGE models carries a heavy burden which cannot be overcome unless more information at the regional level is available. That is a common issue of the broader field of regional modeling and researchers will have to face this bottleneck until the institutions responsible for data collection improve their process of collection and presentation of regional statistics.

The use of the CGE modeling approach has proved to be very relevant to the Brazilian case. Its ability to handle detail – both in terms of its disaggregation level and in terms of its theoretical specification – is useful for the analysis of policy issues and their effects on the economy. The further development of the Brazilian interregional CGE model, and the study of political and institutional aspects of the economic policies carried out in Brazil in the last years, with special attention to the regional impacts, still merit further research. The issues analyzed throughout the book and some of the issues outlined above, not addressed in the book, are also of interest for many Latin American countries. Further research may also be allocated towards comparative studies with other developing economies using the methodological approach proposed in this book. Thus, it is hoped that the lessons derived from the Brazilian experience will provide a benchmark for a better understanding of integrated interregional systems.

Technical Appendix

In this appendix, an overview of the specification of the linear form of the B-MARIA model is provided, based on the different groups of equations. The description is organized around the TABLO file, which implements the model in GEMPACK.[1] Attention is directed to the most relevant equations for the functioning mechanism of the model. The sets, variables and coefficients referring to each equation are explicitly declared. As already mentioned, there are five integrated modules of equations, which are explained in different subsections. The definition of the variables and coefficients of the model are encountered in the preceding sections of the TABLO input file. Variables are defined in percentage change form, unless specified otherwise.

The sets of descriptors for the components of vector variables are shown below.

```
SET IND # Industries # (S1-S40);
SET MARGIND # Margin industries # (S32,S33);
SUBSET MARGIND is subset of IND;
SET NONMARGIND # NonMargin industries # (S1-S31,S34-S40);
SUBSET NONMARGIND is subset of IND;
SET COM # Commodities # (S1-S40);
SET MARGCOM # Margin Commodities # (S32,S33);
SUBSET MARGCOM is subset of COM;
SET NONMARGCOM # NonMargin Commodities # (S1-S31,S34-S40);
SUBSET NONMARGCOM is subset of COM;
SET TEXP # Traditional Exports # (S1-S2,S22,S26);
SET NTEXP # Non-traditional Exports # (S3-S21,S23-S25,S27-S40);
SUBSET TEXP is subset of COM;
SUBSET NTEXP is subset of COM;
SET FAC # Primary Factors # (labor,capital,land);[2]
SET OCC # Occupation Types # SIZE 3;
SET ALLDEST # Destination of Goods #
(North,Northeast,CenterSouth,federal,foreign);
SET DOMDEST # Destination of Goods #
(North,Northeast,CenterSouth,federal);
SET REGDEST # 3 regional destinations #
(North,Northeast,CenterSouth);
SUBSET DOMDEST is subset of ALLDEST;
SUBSET REGDEST is subset of ALLDEST;
```

---

[1] The TABLO language is essentially conventional algebra, with names for variables and coefficients chosen to be suggestive of their economic interpretations. It is no more complex than alternative means of setting out the model.

[2] Because of data availability, only two primary factors were considered in the implementation of the model: labor and capital (including land).

```
SUBSET REGDEST is subset of DOMDEST;
SET ALLSOURCE # Origin of goods # (North,Northeast,CenterSouth,foreign);
SET REGSOURCE # 3 regional sources # (North,Northeast,CenterSouth);
SUBSET REGSOURCE is subset of ALLSOURCE;
SET TWOSOURCE # main sources # (domestic,foreign);
SUBSET MARGCOM is subset of MARGIND;
SUBSET MARGIND is subset of MARGCOM;
SUBSET REGSOURCE is subset of REGDEST;
SUBSET REGDEST is subset of REGSOURCE;
SUBSET COM is subset of IND;
SUBSET IND is subset of COM;
```

CGE Core Module

Demands by industries for intermediate inputs, User 1

The equations in this group describe the industry *j*'s demands for intermediate inputs. As discussed in chapter 3, the equations are derived under the assumption of Leontief technology with Armington nests (imperfect substitution between inputs of the same type from different sources). Equations E_x1a, E_x1c, and E_x1o specify that the percentage change in demand for commodity *i* from source *s* by industry *j* in region *q* for use as an input to current production depends on the activity level, and changes in prices and technology. Price-induced substitution between inputs of commodity *i* from different sources are captured through a substitution term which compares the percentage change in the price of input *i* to the percentage change in an index of all appropriate input prices. These price indices are calculated as weighted averages of the percentage changes in the prices to industry *j* of commodity *i* from the relevant sources. As described in equations E_p1o and E_p1c, the weights come from the cost structure of each individual industry.

```
VARIABLE
            (all,j,IND)(all,q,REGDEST)
a1(j,q)        # All input augmenting technical change #;
            (all,i,COM)(all,s,ALLSOURCE)(all,j,IND)(all,q,REGDEST)
p1a(i,s,j,q)  # Prices of inputs for current production #;
            (all,i,COM)(all,j,IND)(all,q,REGDEST)
p1c(i,j,q)     # Prices of composite inputs for current production #;
            (all,i,COM)(all,j,IND)(all,q,REGDEST)
p1o(i,j,q)     # Price, inputs for current production #;
            (all,i,COM)(all,s,ALLSOURCE)(all,j,IND)(all,q,REGDEST)
x1a(i,s,j,q)  # Demands for inputs for current production #;
            (all,i,COM)(all,j,IND)(all,q,REGDEST)
x1c(i,j,q)     # Demands for inputs for current production #;
            (all,i,COM)(all,j,IND)(all,q,REGDEST)
x1o(i,j,q)     # Demands for inputs for current production #;
```

```
        (all,j,IND)(all,q,REGDEST)
z(j,q)          # Activity level or value-added #;

COEFFICIENT
        (all,i,COM)
SIGMA1O(i)    # Armington import/domestic elast. of subst.: intermediate #;
        (all,i,COM)
SIGMA1C(i)    # Intra-domestic substitution elasticities: User 1 #;
        (all,s,ALLSOURCE)
IS_DOM(s)     # Binary dummy 1 #;
        (all,s,ALLSOURCE)
IS_IMP(s)     # Binary dummy 2 #;
TINY        # A very small number #;
        (all,i,COM)(all,j,IND)(all,q,REGDEST)
PVAL1O(i,j,q)  # Total purchase value for current production: dom. & imp. #;
        (all,i,COM)(all,s,ALLSOURCE)(all,j,IND)(all,q,REGDEST)
PVAL1A(i,s,j,q) # Purchase value for current production #;
        (all,i,COM)(all,aa,TWOSOURCE)(all,j,IND)(all,q,REGDEST)
PVAL1T(i,aa,j,q)    # Total purchase value for current production: dom. & imp. #;

EQUATION
E_x1a # Demand for goods by all source, User 1 #
        (all,i,COM)(all,s,ALLSOURCE)(all,j,IND)(all,q,REGDEST)
x1a(i,s,j,q) = IS_DOM(s)*(x1c(i,j,q)-SIGMA1C(i)*(p1a(i,s,j,q)-p1c(i,j,q)))
      + IS_IMP(s)*(x1o(i,j,q)-SIGMA1O(i)*(p1a(i,"foreign",j,q)-p1o(i,j,q)));
E_p1o # Price of domestic/foreign composite, User 1 #
        (all,i,COM)(all,j,IND)(all,q,REGDEST)
(TINY+PVAL1O(i,j,q))*p1o(i,j,q) = sum(s,ALLSOURCE,PVAL1A(i,s,j,q)*p1a(i,s,j,q));
E_p1c # Price of domestic composite, User 1 #
        (all,i,COM)(all,j,IND)(all,q,REGDEST)
(TINY+PVAL1T(i,"domestic",j,q))*p1c(i,j,q)
      = sum(s,REGSOURCE,PVAL1A(i,s,j,q)*p1a(i,s,j,q));
E_x1c # Demand for domestic composite, User 1 #
        (all,i,COM)(all,j,IND)(all,q,REGDEST)
x1c(i,j,q) = x1o(i,j,q) - SIGMA1O(i)*(p1c(i,j,q)-p1o(i,j,q));
E_x1o # Demands for composite inputs, User 1 #
        (all,i,COM)(all,j,IND)(all,q,REGDEST)
x1o(i,j,q) =  z(j,q) + a1(j,q);
```

Primary factor demands, prices and supplies

The equations in this group specify industry demands for labor, capital and land. They are derived under the assumption that industries choose their primary factor inputs to minimize primary factor costs subject to obtaining sufficient primary factor inputs to satisfy their technical requirements (nested Leontief/CES specification). Because it is assumed that there is no substitution between primary factors and other inputs, at the top of the nesting structure, industry *j*'s primary factor requirements are determined by its overall activity level, and by price-insensitive technology variables specifying the use of primary factors per unit of output (E_x1prim).

Following the nesting structure depicted in Figure 3.3, equations E_efflab, E_curcap and E_n define industry *j*'s demands for the composite occupational labor inputs, physical capital, and land, respectively. In these equations, factor demands are modeled to be proportional to overall regional industry's factor demand, technical changes, and price-induced substitution between primary factors. Equation E_xi_fac determine the price index term for these factor demand equations. At the lower level of the nesting structure, E_x1laboi specifies the occupational composition of industry *j*'s in region *q* labor input. In addition to the industry-region-specific expansion in the overall demand for labor, the demands for occupational inputs also respond to changes in the wage of each occupation relative to the average wage for labor in each regional industry, which is defined by E_p1lab. Equation E_labind gives the percentage change in industry *j*'s labor demand, by summing up the percentage changes in occupation-specific labor demands across occupations, weighted by the appropriate occupational structural coefficients.

```
VARIABLE
        (all,j,IND)(all,q,REGDEST)
a1cap(j,q)      # Capital augmenting technical change #;
        (all,j,IND)(all,q,REGDEST)
a1lab(j,q)  # Labor augmenting technical change #;
        (all,j,IND)(all,q,REGDEST)
a1land(j,q)     # Land augmenting technical change #;
        (all,j,IND)(all,q,REGDEST)
a1prim(j,q)     # All primary factor technical change #;
        (all,j,IND)(all,q,REGDEST)
curcap(j,q)     # Current capital stock #;
        (all,j,IND)(all,q,REGDEST)
efflab(j,q)  # Effective labor input #;
        (all,j,IND)(all,q,REGDEST)
labind(j,q)  # Employment by industry #;
        (all,j,IND)(all,q,REGDEST)
p1cap(j,q)      # Rental price of capital #;
        (all,j,IND)(all,q,REGDEST)
p1lab(j,q)  # Price of labor #;
        (all,j,IND)(all,q,REGDEST)
p1land(j,q)     # Rental price of land #;
        (all,j,IND)(all,q,REGDEST)
x1prim(j,q)     # Demand for the primary factor composite #;
        (all,j,IND)(all,q,REGDEST)
xi_fac(j,q)  # Index of factor costs #;
        (all,j,IND)(all,q,REGDEST)(all,m,OCC)
p1laboi(j,q,m)  # Wage of occupation type m in industry j #;
        (all,j,IND)(all,q,REGDEST)(all,m,OCC)
x1laboi(j,q,m)  # Employment of occupation type m in industry j #;
        (all,j,IND)(all,q,REGDEST)
n(j,q)          # Use of land #;
```

```
COEFFICIENT
        (all,m,OCC)(all,j,IND)(all,q,REGDEST)
LAB_OCC_IND(m,j,q)
                       # Labor in industry j #;
        (all,j,IND)(all,q,REGDEST)
CAPITAL(j,q)   # Total capital in industry j #;
        (all,j,IND)(all,q,REGDEST)
LAND(j,q)      # Total land use in industry j #;

        (all,j,IND)(all,q,REGDEST)
LABOR(j,q)     # Total labor bill in industry j #;
        (all,j,IND)(all,q,REGDEST)
TOTFACIND(j,q)   # Total factor input to industry j #;
        (all,j,IND)(all,q,REGDEST)
SIGMA1FAC(j,q)   # CES substitution elasticities for primary factors #;
        (all,j,IND)(all,q,REGDEST)
SIGMA1LAB(j,q)   # CES substitution elasticities between labor types #;

EQUATION
E_efflab # Industry demands for effective labor #
        (all,j,IND)(all,q,REGDEST)
efflab(j,q) = x1prim(j,q) + a1lab(j,q)
        - SIGMA1FAC(j,q)*[p1lab(j,q) + a1lab(j,q) - xi_fac(j,q)];
E_curcap # Industry demands for capital #
        (all,j,IND)(all,q,REGDEST)
curcap(j,q) = x1prim(j,q) + a1cap(j,q)
        - SIGMA1FAC(j,q)*[p1cap(j,q) + a1cap(j,q) - xi_fac(j,q)];
E_xi_fac # Effective price term for factor demand equations #
        (all,j,IND)(all,q,REGDEST)
(TINY+TOTFACIND(j,q))*xi_fac(j,q) = LABOR(j,q)*(p1lab(j,q)+a1lab(j,q))
                        + CAPITAL(j,q)*(p1cap(j,q)+a1cap(j,q))
                     + LAND(j,q)*(p1land(j,q)+a1land(j,q));
E_x1laboi # Demand for labor by industry and skill group #
        (all,m,OCC)(all,j,IND)(all,q,REGDEST)
x1laboi(j,q,m) = efflab(j,q) - SIGMA1LAB(j,q)*[p1laboi(j,q,m) - p1lab(j,q)];
E_p1lab # Price to each industry of labor in general #
        (all,j,IND)(all,q,REGDEST)
 (TINY+LABOR(j,q))*p1lab(j,q) = sum(m,OCC,LAB_OCC_IND(m,j,q)*p1laboi(j,q,m));
E_labind # Employment by industry #
        (all,j,IND)(all,q,REGDEST)
(TINY+LABOR(j,q))*labind(j,q) = sum(m,OCC,LAB_OCC_IND(m,j,q)*x1laboi(j,q,m));
E_x1prim # Demand for the primary-factor composite #
        (all,j,IND)(all,q,REGDEST)
x1prim(j,q) = z(j,q) + a1(j,q) + a1prim(j,q);
E_n # Industry demands for land #
        (all,j,IND)(all,q,REGDEST)
n(j,q) = x1prim(j,q) + a1land(j,q)
        - SIGMA1FAC(j,q)*[p1land(j,q) + a1land(j,q) - xi_fac(j,q)];
```

Demands by industries for capital creation, User 2

Units of capital stock are created for industry *j*, *at minimum cost*, in the same way depicted in the left portion of Figure 3.3, which shows the three-level technology for the use of intermediate inputs to current production. At the first level, commodities are combined via a Leontief function. At the second and third levels, domestic and imported, and regional commodities are combined, respectively, via a CES specification (Armington assumption). No primary factors are used in capital creation. The use of these inputs is recognized through the capital goods producing industries in the model: agriculture, other metal products, machinery, electrical equipment, electronic equipment, transportation equipment, wood products and furniture, other manufacturing, and construction. The equations describing the demand for the source-specific inputs, and for the composite inputs to capital creation are similar to the corresponding equations describing demands for intermediate inputs to current production.

Household demands for commodities, User 3

In deriving this group of equations, it is assumed that the household sector in each region behaves as if it is a single, budget-constrained, utility-maximizing entity.[3] The equations are derived in three stages, as described above, determining the optimal *composition* of household demand in each region. Total regional household consumption is determined in the government finance module.

Equations E_x3a and E_x3c specify the demands for the commodity bundles in the second and third levels of the nesting structure of household demand, following the CES pattern previously established, in which an activity variable and a price-substitution term play the major role. E_p3o and E_p3c provide the weighted price indices for the composite bundles.

Equation E_x3o specifies the demand for the composite commodities. Consumption of each commodity *i* depends on two components. First, for the subsistence component, which is defined as the minimum expenditure requirement for each commodity, changes in demand are generated by changes in the number of households and tastes. Second, for the luxury or supernumerary part of the expenditures in each good, demand moves with changes in the regional supernumerary expenditures, changes in tastes, and changes in the price of the composite commodity. The two components of household expenditures on the composite commodities are weighted by their respective shares in the total consumption of the composite commodity.

[3] It is assumed that the utility function is of the Klein-Rubin form. For details see Dixon *et al.* (1982).

```
VARIABLE
          (all,i,COM)(all,q,REGDEST)
a3lux(i,q)   # Change in household tastes, luxury #;
          (all,i,COM)(all,q,REGDEST)
a3sub(i,q)       # Change in household taste, subsistency #;
          (all,q,REGDEST)
luxexp(q)        # Total supernumerary household expenditure #;
          (all,i,COM)(all,s,ALLSOURCE)(all,q,REGDEST)
p3a(i,s,q)   # Purchasers prices by commodities and source for households #;
          (all,i,COM)(all,q,REGDEST)
p3c(i,q)     # Prices of composite inputs for households #;
          (all,i,COM)(all,q,REGDEST)
p3o(i,q)     # Price, inputs for households #;
          (all,q,REGDEST)
qhous(q)         # Number of households #;
          (all,i,COM)(all,s,ALLSOURCE)(all,q,REGDEST)
x3a(i,s,q)   # Household demand for goods #;
          (all,i,COM)(all,q,REGDEST)
x3c(i,q)     # Demands for inputs for households #;
          (all,i,COM)(all,q,REGDEST)
x3o(i,q)     # Demands for inputs for households #;

COEFFICIENT
          (all,i,COM)(all,q,REGDEST)
ALPHA_I(i,q)   # Supernumerary expenditure good i/total expenditure good i #;
          (all,s,REGSOURCE)
IS_DOM(s) = 1;
IS_DOM("foreign") = 0;
          (all,s,REGSOURCE)
IS_IMP(s) = 0;
IS_IMP("foreign") = 1;
          (all,i,COM)(all,s,ALLSOURCE)(all,q,REGDEST)
PVAL3A(i,s,q)  # Purchase value for household consumption #;
          (all,i,COM)(all,aa,TWOSOURCE)(all,q,REGDEST)
PVAL3T(i,aa,q)     # Total purchase value for household consumption: dom. & imp. #;
          (all,i,COM)(all,q,REGDEST)
PVAL3O(i,q)    # Total regional purchase value for household consumption #;
          (all,i,COM)
SIGMA3O(i)     # Armington import/domestic elast. of subst.: households #;
          (all,i,COM)
SIGMA3C(i)     # Intra-domestic substitution elasticities: User 3 #;

EQUATION
E_x3o # Household demand for composite commodities #
          (all,i,COM) (all,q,REGDEST)
x3o(i,q) =  [1-ALPHA_I(i,q)]*[qhous(q)+a3sub(i,q)]
        + ALPHA_I(i,q)*[luxexp(q) + a3lux(i,q) - p3o(i,q)];
E_x3a # Demand for goods by source, User 3 #
          (all,i,COM)(all,s,ALLSOURCE)(all,q,REGDEST)
x3a(i,s,q) =  IS_DOM(s)*(x3c(i,q)-SIGMA3C(i)*(p3a(i, s, q)-p3c(i,q)))
         + IS_IMP(s)*(x3o(i,q)-SIGMA3O(i)*(p3a(i,"foreign",q)-p3o(i,q)));
E_p3o # Price of domestic/foreign composite, User 3 #
          (all,i,COM)(all,q,REGDEST)
(TINY+PVAL3O(i,q))*p3o(i,q) = sum(s,ALLSOURCE,PVAL3A(i,s,q)*p3a(i,s,q));
```

```
E_p3c # Price of domestic composite, User 3 #
        (all,i,COM)(all,q,REGDEST)
(TINY+PVAL3T(i,"domestic",q))*p3c(i,q)
        = sum(s,REGSOURCE,PVAL3A(i,s,q)*p3a(i,s,q));
E_x3c # Demand for domestic composite, User 3 #
        (all,i,COM)(all,q,REGDEST)
x3c(i,q) = x3o(i,q) - SIGMA3O(i)*(p3c(i,q)-p3o(i,q));
```

Tax rates

Equations E_deltax1 to E_deltax6 specify the sales tax rates for different users. They allow for variations in tax rates across commodities, and their sources and destinations. Tax changes are expressed as percentage-point changes in the *ad valorem* tax rates.

```
VARIABLE
        (change)
deltax1all      # Overall percent-point change in indirect tax rates, user 1 #;
        (change)
deltax2all      # Overall percent-point change in indirect tax rates, user 2 #;
        (change)
deltax3all      # Overall percent-point change in indirect tax rates, user 3 #;
        (change)
deltax4all      # Overall percent-point change in indirect tax rates, user 4 #;
        (change)
deltax5all      # Overall percent-point change in indirect tax rates, user 5 #;
        (change)
deltax6all      # Overall percent-point change in indirect tax rates, user 6 #;
        (change)(all,i,COM)(all,s,ALLSOURCE)(all,j,IND)(all,q,REGDEST)
deltax1(i,s,j,q) # Percent-point change in tax rate on sales of interm. inputs #;
        (change)(all,i,COM)(all,s,ALLSOURCE)(all,j,IND)(all,q,REGDEST)
deltax2(i,s,j,q) # Percent-point change in tax rate on sales for capital creat. #;
        (change)(all,i,COM)(all,s,ALLSOURCE)(all,q,REGDEST)
deltax3(i,s,q)   # Percent-point change in tax rate on sales to households #;
        (change) (all,i,COM)(all,s,REGSOURCE)
deltax4(i,s)     # Percentage-point change in export tax rates #;
        (change)(all,i,COM)(all,s,ALLSOURCE)(all,q,REGDEST)
deltax5(i,s,q)   # Percent-point change: tax rate on sales to reg. gov. demand #;
        (change) (all,i,COM)(all,s,ALLSOURCE) (all,q,REGDEST)
deltax6(i,s,q)   # Percent-point change in sales tax rate, Fed. gov. demands #;
        (change) (all,i,COM)
deltax(i)    # Percentage-point change in the general sales tax rate #;
        (change) (all,q,ALLDEST)
deltaxdest(q)    # Regional tax shifter (percentage-point change) #;
        (change) (all,s,ALLSOURCE)
deltaxsource(s)      # Regional tax shifter (percentage-point change) #;

EQUATION
E_deltax1 # Tax rate on sales to User 1 #
        (all,i,COM)(all,s,ALLSOURCE)(all,j,IND)(all,q,REGDEST)
deltax1(i,s,j,q) = deltax(i) + deltax1all + deltaxsource(s)+deltaxdest(q);
```

```
E_deltax2 # Tax rate on sales to User 2 #
          (all,i,COM)(all,s,ALLSOURCE)(all,j,IND)(all,q,REGDEST)
deltax2(i,s,j,q) = deltax(i) + deltax2all + deltaxsource(s)+deltaxdest(q);
E_deltax3 # Tax rate on sales to User 3 #
          (all,i,COM)(all,s,ALLSOURCE)(all,q,REGDEST)
deltax3(i,s,q) = deltax(i) + deltax3all + deltaxsource(s)+deltaxdest(q);
E_deltax4 # Tax rate on sales to User 4 #
          (all,i,COM)(all,s,REGSOURCE)
deltax4(i,s)=deltax(i)+deltax4all+deltaxsource(s)+deltaxdest("foreign");
E_deltax5 # Tax rate on sales to User 5 #
          (all,i,COM)(all,s,ALLSOURCE)(all,q,REGDEST)
deltax5(i,s,q) = deltax(i) + deltax5all + deltaxsource(s)+deltaxdest(q);
E_deltax6 # Tax rate on sales to User 6 #
          (all,i,COM)(all,s,ALLSOURCE)(all,q,REGDEST)
deltax6(i,s,q) = deltax(i) + deltax6all + deltaxsource(s)+deltaxdest("federal");
```

Purchaser's prices of commodities

Equations E_p1a to E_p6a impose zero pure profits in the *distribution* of commodities to different users. Prices paid for commodity *i* from region *s* in industry *j* in region *q* by each user equate to the sum of its basic value and the costs of the relevant taxes and margins.

```
VARIABLE
natphi       # Exchange rate #;
          (all,i,COM)(all,s,ALLSOURCE)
p0a(i,s)     # Basic price of good i, source s #;
          (all,i,COM)(all,s,ALLSOURCE)(all,j,IND)(all,q,REGDEST)
p2a(i,s,j,q) # Prices of inputs for capital creation #;
          (all,i,COM)(all,s,ALLSOURCE)(all,q,REGDEST)
p5a(i,s,q)   # Purchasers prices for commodities (by source) by reg. gov. #;
          (all,i,COM)(all,s,ALLSOURCE)(all,q,REGDEST)
p6a(i,s,q)   # Purchasers prices paid for commodities by federal government #;
          (all,i,COM)(all,s,REGSOURCE)
p4r(i,s)     # F.O.B. foreign currency export prices #;

COEFFICIENT
          (all,i,COM)(all,s,ALLSOURCE)(all,j,IND)(all,q,REGDEST)
BAS1(i,s,j,q);  # Commodity inputs to the production process: basic values #
          (all,i,COM)(all,s,ALLSOURCE)(all,j,IND)(all,q,REGDEST)
BAS2(i,s,j,q);  # Commodity inputs to capital creation: basic values #
          (all,i,COM)(all,s,ALLSOURCE)(all,q,REGDEST)
BAS3(i,s,q);    # Commodity demands by regional households: basic values #
          (all,i,COM)(all,s,REGSOURCE)
BAS4(i,s);      # Commodity demands by foreigners: basic values #
          (all,i,COM)(all,s,ALLSOURCE)(all,q,REGDEST)
BAS5(i,s,q);    # Public good demands by regional governments: basic values #
          (all,i,COM)(all,s,ALLSOURCE)(all,q,REGDEST)
BAS6(i,s,q);    # Public good demands by the federal government: basic values #
          (all,i,COM)(all,s,ALLSOURCE)(all,j,IND)
          (all,q,REGDEST)(all,r,MARGCOM)
MAR1(i,s,j,q,r); # Demands for margins: user 1 #
```

```
        (all,i,COM)(all,s,ALLSOURCE)(all,j,IND)
        (all,q,REGDEST)(all,r,MARGCOM)
MAR2(i,s,j,q,r); # Demands for margins: user 2 #
        (all,i,COM)(all,s,ALLSOURCE)(all,q,REGDEST)(all,r,MARGCOM)
MAR3(i,s,q,r);   # Demands for margins: user 3 #
        (all,i,COM)(all,s,REGSOURCE)(all,r,MARGCOM)
MAR4(i,s,r);     # Demands for margins: user 4 #
        (all,i,COM)(all,s,ALLSOURCE)(all,q,REGDEST)(all,r,MARGCOM)
MAR5(i,s,q,r);   # Demands for margins: user 5 #
        (all,i,COM)(all,s,ALLSOURCE)(all,q,REGDEST)(all,r,MARGCOM)
MAR6(i,s,q,r);   # Demands for margins: user 6 #
        (all,i,COM)(all,s,ALLSOURCE)(all,j,IND)(all,q,REGDEST)
TAX1(i,s,j,q);   # Taxes on inputs to the production process #
        (all,i,COM)(all,s,ALLSOURCE)(all,j,IND)(all,q,REGDEST)
TAX2(i,s,j,q);   # Taxes on inputs to capital creation #
        (all,i,COM)(all,s,ALLSOURCE)(all,q,REGDEST)
TAX3(i,s,q);# Taxes on commodities demanded by regional households #
        (all,i,COM)(all,s,REGSOURCE)
TAX4(i,s);       # Taxes on commodities demanded by foreigners #
        (all,i,COM)(all,s,ALLSOURCE)(all,q,REGDEST)
TAX5(i,s,q);# Taxes on public goods demanded by regional governments (=0) #
        (all,i,COM)(all,s,ALLSOURCE)(all,q,REGDEST)
TAX6(i,s,q);# Taxes on public goods demanded by the federal government (=0) #
        (all,i,COM)(all,s,ALLSOURCE)(all,j,IND)(all,q,REGDEST)
PVAL2A(i,s,j,q) # Purchase value for capital creation #;
        (all,i,COM)(all,s,REGSOURCE)
PVAL4R(i,s)     # Purchase value for foreign exports #;
        (all,i,COM)(all,s,ALLSOURCE)(all,q,REGDEST)
PVAL5A(i,s,q)   # Purchase value for regional government demand #;
        (all,i,COM)(all,s,ALLSOURCE)(all,q,REGDEST)
PVAL6A(i,s,q)   # Purchase value for federal government demand #;

EQUATION
E_p1a # Purchasers prices - User 1 #
        (all,i,COM)(all,j,IND)(all,q,REGDEST)(all,s,ALLSOURCE)
(TINY+PVAL1A(i,s,j,q))*p1a(i,s,j,q) = [BAS1(i,s,j,q)+TAX1(i,s,j,q)]*p0a(i,s)
 + BAS1(i,s,j,q)*deltax1(i,s,j,q) + sum(r,MARGCOM,MAR1(i,s,j,q,r)*p0a(r,q));
E_p2a # Purchasers prices - User 2 #
        (all,i,COM)(all,j,IND)(all,q,REGDEST)(all,s,ALLSOURCE)
(TINY+PVAL2A(i,s,j,q))*p2a(i,s,j,q) = [BAS2(i,s,j,q)+TAX2(i,s,j,q)]*p0a(i,s)
 + BAS2(i,s,j,q)*deltax2(i,s,j,q) + sum(r,MARGCOM,MAR2(i,s,j,q,r)*p0a(r,q));
E_p3a # Purchasers prices - User 3 #
        (all,i,COM)(all,q,REGDEST)(all,s,ALLSOURCE)
(TINY+PVAL3A(i,s,q))*p3a(i,s,q) = [BAS3(i,s,q)+TAX3(i,s,q)]*p0a(i,s)
 + BAS3(i,s,q)*deltax3(i,s,q) + sum(r,MARGCOM,MAR3(i,s,q,r)*p0a(r,q));
E_p4r # Purchasers prices - User 4 #
        (all,i,COM)(all,s,REGSOURCE)
(TINY+PVAL4R(i,s))*(natphi+p4r(i,s)) = [BAS4(i,s)+TAX4(i,s)]*p0a(i,s)
 + BAS4(i,s)*deltax4(i,s) + sum(r,MARGCOM,MAR4(i,s,r)*p0a(r,s));
E_p5a # Purchasers prices - User 5 #
        (all,i,COM)(all,q,REGDEST)(all,s,ALLSOURCE)
(TINY+PVAL5A(i,s,q))*p5a(i,s,q) = [BAS5(i,s,q)+TAX5(i,s,q)]*p0a(i,s)
 + BAS5(i,s,q)*deltax5(i,s,q) + sum(r,MARGCOM,MAR5(i,s,q,r)*p0a(r,q));
```

```
E_p6a # Purchasers prices - User 6 #
        (all,i,COM)(all,s,ALLSOURCE) (all,q,REGDEST)
(TINY+PVAL6A(i,s,q))*p6a(i,s,q) = [BAS6(i,s,q)+TAX6(i,s,q)]*p0a(i,s)
 + BAS6(i,s,q)*deltax6(i,s,q) + sum(r,MARGCOM,MAR6(i,s,q,r)*p0a(r,s));
```

Tax revenues

Changes in tax revenues from indirect taxes levied on flows to different users are specified, for each region, in equations E_taxrev1 to E_taxrev6. Equations E_nattaxrev1 to E_nattaxrev6 provide the national aggregates. Percentage changes in tax revenues move with: 1) changes in the basic values of the corresponding commodity flows, which depends on changes in the basic price of the relevant commodity and the quantity flow; and 2) changes in the tax rates.

```
VARIABLE
nattaxrev1    # Aggregate revenue from indirect taxes on intermediate #;
nattaxrev2    # Aggregate revenue from indirect taxes on investment #;
nattaxrev3    # Aggregate revenue from indirect taxes on households #;
nattaxrev4    # Aggregate revenue from indirect taxes on exports #;
nattaxrev5    # Aggregate revenue from indirect taxes on regional government #;
nattaxrev6    # Aggregate revenue from indirect taxes on federal government #;
        (all,q,REGDEST)
taxrev1(q)    # Aggregate revenue, indirect taxes on intermediate #;
        (all,q,REGDEST)
taxrev2(q)    # Aggregate revenue, indirect taxes on investment #;
        (all,q,REGDEST)
taxrev3(q)    # Aggregate revenue, indirect taxes on households #;
        (all,s,REGSOURCE)
taxrev4(s)    # Aggregate revenue, indirect taxes on foreign exports #;
        (all,q,REGDEST)
taxrev5(q)    # Aggregate revenue, indirect taxes on regional government #;
        (all,q,REGDEST)
taxrev6(q)    # Aggregate revenue, indirect taxes on federal government #;

COEFFICIENT
        (all,q,REGDEST)
AGGTAX1(q)  # Sales tax on current production #;
        (all,q,REGDEST)
AGGTAX2(q)  # Sales tax on capital creation #;
        (all,q,REGDEST)
AGGTAX3(q)  # Sales tax on household consumption #;
        (all,s,REGSOURCE)
AGGTAX4(s)  # Sales tax on foreign exports #;
        (all,q,REGDEST)
AGGTAX5(q)  # Sales tax on regional government demand #;
        (all,q,REGDEST)
AGGTAX6(q)  # Sales tax on federal government demand #;
NATAGGTAX1     # Sales tax on current production: national total #;
NATAGGTAX2     # Sales tax on capital creation: national total #;
NATAGGTAX3     # Sales tax on household consumption: national total #;
NATAGGTAX4     # Sales tax on foreign exports: national total #;
```

```
NATAGGTAX5     # Sales tax on regional government demand: national total #;
NATAGGTAX6     # Sales tax on federal government demand: national total #;

EQUATION
E_taxrev1 # Aggregate revenue from indirect taxes levied on flows to User 1 #
        (all,q,REGDEST)
AGGTAX1(q)*taxrev1(q) =
sum(i,COM,sum(s,ALLSOURCE,sum(j,IND,TAX1(i,s,j,q)*{p0a(i,s)+x1a(i,s,j,q)}
                         + BAS1(i,s,j,q)*deltax1(i,s,j,q) )));
E_nattaxrev1 # National revenue from indirect taxes levied on flows to User 1 #
NATAGGTAX1*nattaxrev1 = sum(q,REGDEST,AGGTAX1(q)*taxrev1(q));
E_taxrev2 # Aggregate revenue from indirect taxes levied on flows to User 2 #
        (all,q,REGDEST)
AGGTAX2(q)*taxrev2(q) =
sum(i,COM, sum(s,ALLSOURCE, sum(j,IND;TAX2(i,s,j,q)*{p0a(i,s)+x2a(i,s,j,q)}
                         + BAS2(i,s,j,q)*deltax2(i,s,j,q) )));
E_nattaxrev2 # National revenue from indirect taxes levied on flows to User 2 #
NATAGGTAX2*nattaxrev2 = sum(q,REGDEST,AGGTAX2(q)*taxrev2(q));
E_taxrev3 # Aggregate revenue from indirect taxes levied on flows to User 3 #
        (all,q,REGDEST)
AGGTAX3(q)*taxrev3(q) =
sum(i,COM, sum(s,ALLSOURCE,TAX3(i,s,q)*{p0a(i,s)+x3a(I,s,q)}
                         + BAS3(i,s,q)*deltax3(i,s,q) ));
E_nattaxrev3 # National revenue from indirect taxes levied on flows to User 3 #
NATAGGTAX3*nattaxrev3 = sum(q,REGDEST,AGGTAX3(q)*taxrev3(q));
E_taxrev4 # Aggregate revenue from indirect taxes levied on flows to User 4 #
        (all,s,REGSOURCE)
AGGTAX4(s)*taxrev4(s) =  sum(i,COM,TAX4(i,s)*{p0a(i,s)+x4r(i,s)}
                                                + BAS4(i,s)*deltax4(i,s) );
E_nattaxrev4 # National revenue from indirect taxes levied on flows to User 4 #
NATAGGTAX4*nattaxrev4 = sum(s,REGSOURCE,AGGTAX4(s)*taxrev4(s));

E_taxrev5 # Aggregate revenue from indirect taxes levied on flows to User 5 #
        (all,q,REGDEST)
(TINY+AGGTAX5(q))*taxrev5(q) =
sum(i,COM, sum(s,ALLSOURCE,TAX5(i,s,q)*{p0a(i,s)+x5a(i,s,q)}
                          + BAS5(i,s,q)*deltax5(i,s,q) ));
E_nattaxrev5 # National revenue from indirect taxes levied on flows to User 5 #
(TINY+NatAGGTAX5)*nattaxrev5 = sum(q,REGDEST,AGGTAX5(q)*taxrev5(q));
E_taxrev6 # Aggregate revenue from indirect taxes levied on flows to User 6 #
        (all,q,REGDEST)
(TINY+AGGTAX6(q))*taxrev6(q) =
sum(i,COM,sum(s,ALLSOURCE,TAX6(i,s,q)*{p0a(i,s)+x6a(i,s,q)}
                         + BAS6(i,s,q)*deltax6(i,s,q) ));
E_nattaxrev6 # National revenue from indirect taxes levied on flows to User 6 #
(TINY+NATAGGTAX6)*nattaxrev6 = sum(q,REGDEST,AGGTAX6(q)*taxrev6(q));
```

Demands for international exports

As already mentioned, B-MARIA allows a different treatment of export demands for commodities in different categories: traditional and non-traditional exports. In E_x4r, the percentage change in traditional export demand for commodity *i* depends on the percentage changes in a price, and three shift variables which allow for vertical and horizontal movements in the demand curves. The price variable which influences export demands is the purchaser's price in foreign countries, which includes the relevant taxes and margins (see E_p4r). The parameter EXP_ELAST(i) controlls the sensitivity of export demand to price changes. E_nt_x4r defines non-traditional exports as a Leontief aggregate, and the demand for the non-traditional exports bundle is specified in E_aggnt_x4r, in a similar fashion to the demands for traditional exports. E_aggnt_p4r defines the average price of the composite commodity.

```
VARIABLE
          (all,s,REGSOURCE)
aggnt_x4r(s)    # Aggregate regional non-traditional exports #;
          (all,s,REGSOURCE)
aggnt_feq(s)    # Quant. shift non-traditional exports #;
          (all,s,REGSOURCE)
aggnt_fep(s)    # Price shift non-traditional exports #;
          (all,s,REGSOURCE)
aggnt_p4r(s)    # Aggregate foreign price non-traditional exports #;
          (all,i,NTEXP)
faggnt_i(i)  # Shifter by commodity #;
          (all,s,REGSOURCE)
faggnt_s(s)     # Shifter by region #;
          (all,i,NTEXP)(all,s,REGSOURCE)
faggnt_is(i,s)  # Shifter by commodity and region #;
          (all,i,COM)(all,s,REGSOURCE)
x4r(i,s)      # Export volume #;
          (all,i,COM)
fep(i)              # Price (upward) shift in export demands #;
          (all,i,COM)
feq(i)              # Quantity (right) shift in export demands #;
natfep        # Economy-wide shifter of export demand curves #;

COEFFICIENT
          (all,q,REGDEST)
AGGEXPNT(q)      # Total non-traditional export earnings #;
          (all,i,COM)
EXP_ELAST(i)      # Export demand elasticities: typical value -20.0 #;

EQUATION
E_x4r # Export demand functions #
          (all,i,TEXP)(all,s,REGSOURCE)
x4r(i,s) - feq(i) = EXP_ELAST(i)*[p4r(i,s) - fep(i) - natfep];
E_aggnt_x4r # Export demand functions, non-trad aggregate #
          (all,s,REGSOURCE)
aggnt_x4r(s) - aggnt_feq(s)
        = EXP_ELAST("S6")*[aggnt_p4r(s) - aggnt_fep(s) - natfep];
E_nt_x4r # Export demand functions, non-trad #
          (all,i,NTEXP)(all,s,REGSOURCE)
x4r(i,s) = aggnt_x4r(s) + faggnt_i(i) + faggnt_s(s) + faggnt_is(i,s);
```

```
E_aggnt_p4r # Export price, non-trad aggregate #
          (all,s,REGSOURCE)
AGGEXPNT(s)*aggnt_p4r(s) = sum(i,NTEXP,PVAL4r(i,s)*p4r(i,s)) + faggnt_p4r(s);
```

Demands for commodities for regional government expenditure

Regional governments consume only public goods provided by the public administration sector. Equation E_x5a shows the movement of regional government consumption in relation to movements in real regional household consumption.

```
VARIABLE
          (all,i,COM)(all,s,ALLSOURCE)(all,q,REGDEST)
f5a(i,s,q)   # Shift in regional government demand #;
natf5gen     # Overall shift term for regional government demand #;
          (all,q,REGDEST)
f5gen(q)          # Overall shift term for regional government demand #;
          (all,q,REGDEST)
cr(q)            # Real household consumption #;
          (all,i,COM)(all,s,ALLSOURCE)(all,q,REGDEST)
x5a(i,s,q)   # Regional government demand #;

EQUATION
E_x5a # Regional government demand #
          (all,i,COM)(all,s,ALLSOURCE)(all,q,REGDEST)
x5a(i,s,q) = cr(q) + f5a(i,s,q) + f5gen(q) + natf5gen;
```

Demands for commodities for federal government expenditure

Likewise, E_x6a shows the movement of federal government consumption in relation to the national private consumption.

```
VARIABLE
          (all,i,COM)(all,s,ALLSOURCE) (all,q,REGDEST)
f6a(i,s,q)   # Shift, federal government demand #;
natf6gen     # Overall shift term for federal government demand #;
          (all,q,REGDEST)
f6gen(q)          # Shifter, federal government demand  #;
natcR          # Real household consumption #;
          (all,i,COM)(all,s,ALLSOURCE)(all,q,REGDEST)
x6a(i,s,q)   # Federal government demand in each region #;

EQUATION
E_x6a # Federal government demand #
          (all,i,COM)(all,s,ALLSOURCE)(all,q,REGDEST)
x6a(i,s,q) = natcr + f6a(i,s,q) + f6gen(q) + natf6gen;
```

Margin usage of commodities

The role of margins is to facilitate flows of commodities from points of production or points of entry to either domestic users or ports of exit. Commodity margins include transportation and trade. Margins on commodities used by industry, investors, and households are assumed to be produced at the point of consumption. Margins on exports are assumed to be produced at the point of production. The margin demand equations (E_x1marg to E_x6marg) show that the demands for margins are proportional to the commodity flows with which the margins are associated.

```
VARIABLE
        (all,i,COM)(all,s,ALLSOURCE)(all,j,IND)
        (all,q,REGDEST)(all,r,MARGCOM)
x1marg(i,s,j,q,r)     # Margins - current production #;
        (all,i,COM)(all,s,ALLSOURCE)(all,j,IND)
        (all,q,REGDEST)(all,r,MARGCOM)
x2marg(i,s,j,q,r)     # Margins - capital creation #;
        (all,i,COM)(all,s,ALLSOURCE)
        (all,r,MARGCOM)(all,q,REGDEST)
x3marg(i,s,q,r)  # Margins - on sales to households #;
        (all,i,COM)(all,s,REGSOURCE)(all,r,MARGCOM)
x4marg(i,s,r)     # Margins - on exports #;
        (all,i,COM)(all,s,ALLSOURCE)(all,q,REGDEST)(all,r,MARGCOM)
x5marg(i,s,q,r)  # Margins - on sales to regional government demand #;
        (all,i,COM)(all,s,ALLSOURCE)(all,q,REGDEST) (all,r,MARGCOM)
x6marg(i,s,q,r)  # Margins - on sales to federal government demand #;
        (all,i,COM)(all,s,ALLSOURCE)(all,j,IND)(all,q,REGDEST)
x2a(i,s,j,q)  # Demands for inputs for capital creation #;

EQUATION
E_x1marg # Margins on sales to producers #
        (all,i,COM)(all,j,IND)(all,q,REGDEST)
        (all,s,ALLSOURCE)(all,r,MARGCOM)
x1marg(i,s,j,q,r)= x1a(i,s,j,q);
E_x2marg # Margins on sales to capital creators #
        (all,i,COM)(all,j,IND)(all,q,REGDEST)
        (all,s,ALLSOURCE)(all,r,MARGCOM)
x2marg(i,s,j,q,r)= x2a(i,s,j,q);

E_x3marg # Margins on sales to household consumption #
        (all,i,COM)(all,s,ALLSOURCE)(all,q,REGDEST)(all,r,MARGCOM)
x3marg(i,s,q,r) = x3a(i,s,q);
E_x4marg # Margins on exports: factory gate to port #
        (all,i,COM)(all,r,MARGCOM)(all,s,REGSOURCE)
x4marg(i,s,r) = x4r(i,s);
E_x5marg # Margins on sales to regional government demand #
        (all,i,COM)(all,s,ALLSOURCE)(all,q,REGDEST)(all,r,MARGCOM)
x5marg(i,s,q,r) = x5a(i,s,q);
```

```
E_x6marg # Margins on sales to federal government demand in each region #
        (all,i,COM)(all,r,MARGCOM)(all,s,ALLSOURCE)(all,q,REGDEST)
x6marg(i,s,q,r) = x6a(i,s,q);
```

Supply equals demand for domestic and imported commodities

The equations in this group impose the equilibrium conditions in the markets of margin commodities (E_mkt_clear_margins), nonmargin commodities (E_mkt_clear_nomarg) and imported commodities (E_x0impa, at the regional level, and E_natx0imp, at the national level). Notice that margin commodities are assumed to be produced in the destination region for users 1, 2, and 3.

```
VARIABLE
        (all,i,COM)
natx0imp(i)     # Import volume #;
        (all,i,COM)(all,q,REGDEST)
x0imp(i,q)      # Import volumes #;

COEFFICIENT
        (all,i,COM)
NATIMPORTS(i)   # Total basic-value imports of good i #;
        (all,i,COM)(all,q,REGDEST)
IMPORTS(i,q)  # Total basic-value imports of good i #;
        (all,i,COM)(all,s,REGSOURCE)
SALES(i,s)      # All usage #;

EQUATION
E_mkt_clear_margins # Demand equals supply for margin commodities #
        (all,r,MARGCOM)(all,s,REGSOURCE)
(TINY+SALES(r,s))*z(r,s) =
         sum(j,IND, sum(q,REGDEST,  BAS1(r,s,j,q)*x1a(r,s,j,q)
         + BAS2(r,s,j,q)*x2a(r,s,j,q)))
    + sum(q,REGDEST,BAS3(r,s,q)  *x3a(r,s,q))
    + BAS4(r,s)*x4r(r,s)
    + sum(q,REGDEST,  BAS5(r,s,q)  *x5a(r,s,q))
    + sum(q,REGDEST,  BAS6(r,s,q)  *x6a(r,s,q))
   + sum(j,IND, sum(i,COM, sum(ss,ALLSOURCE,MAR1(i,ss,j,s,r)*x1marg(i,ss,j,s,r)
         + MAR2(i,ss,j,s,r)*x2marg(i,ss,j,s,r))))
   + sum(i,COM, sum(ss,ALLSOURCE,MAR3(i,ss,s,r)*x3marg(i,ss,s,r)))
   + sum(i,COM, MAR4(i,s,r)*x4marg(i,s,r))
   + sum(i,COM, sum(ss,ALLSOURCE,MAR5(i,ss,s,r)  *x5marg(i,ss,s,r)  ))
   + sum(i,COM, sum(ss,ALLSOURCE,MAR6(i,ss,s,r)  *x6marg(i,ss,s,r)  ));
E_mkt_clear_nomarg # Demand equals supply for nonmargin commodities #
        (all,r,NONMARGCOM)(all,s,REGSOURCE)
(TINY+SALES(r,s))*z(r,s) =
    sum(j,IND, sum(q,REGDEST,  BAS1(r,s,j,q)*x1a(r,s,j,q)) )
       + sum(j,IND, sum(q,REGDEST,  BAS2(r,s,j,q)*x2a(r,s,j,q)) )
       + sum(q,REGDEST,  BAS3(r,s,q)  *x3a(r,s,q)  )
       + BAS4(r,s)   *x4r(r,s)
       + sum(q,REGDEST, BAS5(r,s,q)  *x5a(r,s,q) )
       + sum(q,REGDEST, BAS6(r,s,q)  *x6a(r,s,q) );
```

```
E_x0impa # Import volume of commodities by region #
        (all,i,COM)(all,q,REGDEST)
(TINY+IMPORTS(i,q))*x0imp(i,q) =
sum(j,IND,BAS1(i,"foreign",j,q)*x1a(i,"foreign",j,q)
                + BAS2(i,"foreign",j,q)*x2a(i,"foreign",j,q))
                + BAS3(i,"foreign",q)*x3a(i,"foreign",q)
                + BAS5(i,"foreign",q)*x5a(i,"foreign",q)
                + BAS6(i,"foreign",q)*x6a(i,"foreign",q);
E_natx0imp # Import volume #
        (all,i,COM)
(TINY+NATIMPORTS(i))*natx0imp(i) = sum(q,REGDEST, IMPORTS(i,q)*x0imp(i,q));
```

Basic prices

In this group of equations, zero pure profits in current production, capital creation, and importing are assumed. The price received for any activity is equal to the costs per unit of output. As can be noticed, the assumption of constant returns to scale adopted here precludes any activity variable from influencing basic prices, i.e., unit costs are independent of the scale at which activities are conducted.

Equations E_p0a and E_a impose zero pure profits in current production. The former defines the percentage change in the price received by producers in regional industry *j* per unit of output as being equal to the percentage change in *j*'s costs, which are affected by changes in technology and changes in input prices. Technological changes are defined by E_a, in which the different types of technical changes appear with weights reflecting their influence on *j*'s unit costs.

E_pi imposes zero pure profits in capital creation. The percentage change in the price of new units of capital is determined by the percentage change in the effective average cost of producing them.

Finally, E_p0ab imposes zero pure profits in importing. The basic price of a unit of imported commodity – the revenue earned per unit by the importer – depends on the foreign-currency C.I.F. price, the exchange rate, and the power of the tariff applying to imports of commodity *i*.

```
VARIABLE
        (all,j,IND)(all,q,REGDEST)
a(j,q)          # Average of technical change terms, prod. #;
        (all,j,IND)(all,q,REGDEST)
a1oct(j,q)  # Other cost ticket techncal change #;
        (all,j,IND)(all,q,REGDEST)
a2ind(j,q)  # Neutral technical change, capital creation #;
        (all,j,IND)(all,q,REGDEST)
p1oct(j,q)  # Price of other cost tickets #;
        (all,j,IND)(all,q,REGDEST)
pi(j,q)         # Costs of units of capital #;
```

```
        (all,i,COM)
pm(i)          # C.I.F. foreign currency import prices #;
        (all,i,COM)
powtaxm(i)     # Power of tariffs #;

COEFFICIENT
        (all,j,IND)(all,q,REGDEST)
COSTS(j,q)     # Total costs in industry j in region q #;
        (all,j,IND)(all,q,REGDEST)
OTHCOST(j,q)       # Other cost tickets paid by industry j #;
        (all,j,IND)(all,q,REGDEST)
INVEST (j,q)   # Total capital created for each industry #;

EQUATION
E_p0a # Zero pure profits in current production #
        (all,j,IND)(all,q,REGDEST)
(TINY+COSTS(j,q))*{p0a(j,q) - a(j,q)} =
    sum(i,COM,sum(s,ALLSOURCE,PVAL1A(i,s,j,q)*p1a(i,s,j,q)))
        + sum(m,OCC,LAB_OCC_IND(m,j,q)* p1laboi(j,q,m))
        + CAPITAL(j,q)*p1cap(j,q) + LAND(j,q)*p1land(j,q) + OTHCOST(j,q)*p1oct(j,q);
E_a # Technical change by industry-current production #
        (all,j,IND)(all,q,REGDEST)
(TINY+COSTS(j,q))*[a(j,q) - a1(j,q)] = TOTFACIND(j,q)*a1prim(j,q)
                        + LABOR(j,q)*a1lab(j,q)
                        + CAPITAL(j,q)*a1cap(j,q)
                        + LAND(j,q)*a1land(j,q)
                        + OTHCOST(j,q)*a1oct(j,q);
E_pi # Zero pure profits in capital creation #
        (all,j,IND)(all,q,REGDEST)
(TINY+INVEST(j,q))*(pi(j,q) - a2ind(j,q)) =
        sum(i,COM,sum(s,ALLSOURCE,PVAL2A(i,s,j,q)*p2a(i,s,j,q) ));
E_p0ab # Zero pure profits in importing #
        (all,i,COM)
p0a(i,"foreign") = pm(i) + natphi + powtaxm(i);
```

Components of regional GDP, real and nominal

This group of equations contain the definitions of the income and expenditure components of gross regional product. In the income side, equations E_caprev, E_labrev, E_lndrev, and E_octrev define percentage changes in nominal regional factor income payments. Total payments to factors are determined by the sum of the payments of the j industries in region q, where the industry payments are the product of the unit price of the factor and the respective number of units employed.

```
VARIABLE
        (all,q,REGDEST)
caprev(q)      # Aggregate payments to capital #;
        (all,q,REGDEST)
labrev(q)      # Aggregate payments to labor #;
        (all,q,REGDEST)
lndrev(q)      # Aggregate payments to land #;
```

```
        (all,q,REGDEST)
octrev(q)        # Aggregate other cost ticket payments #;
        (all,j,IND)(all,q,REGDEST)
x1oct(j,q)  # Demand for other cost tickets #;

COEFFICIENT
        (all,q,REGDEST)
AGGLAB(q)    # Total payments to labor #;
        (all,q,REGDEST)
AGGCAP(q)    # Total payments to capital #;
        (all,q,REGDEST)
AGGLND(q)    # Total payments to land #;
        (all,q,REGDEST)
AGGOCT(q)    # Total other cost ticket payments #;

EQUATION
E_caprev # Aggregate payments to capital #
        (all,q,REGDEST)
caprev(q) = (1.0/AGGCAP(q))* sum(j,IND,CAPITAL(j,q)*{p1cap(j,q)+curcap(j,q)});
E_labrev # Aggregate payments to labor #
        (all,q,REGDEST)
labrev(q) = (1.0/AGGLAB(q))*
   sum(j,IND,sum(m,OCC,LAB_OCC_IND(m,j,q)*{p1laboi(j,q,m)+x1laboi(j,q,m)}));
E_lndrev # Aggregate payments to land #
        (all,q,REGDEST)
lndrev(q) = (1.0/AGGLND(q))* sum(j,IND,LAND(j,q)*{p1land(j,q)+n(j,q)});
E_octrev # Aggregate other cost ticket payments #
        (all,q,REGDEST)
octrev(q) = (1.0/AGGOCT(q))* sum(j,IND,OTHCOST(j,q)*{p1oct(j,q)+x1oct(j,q)});
```

E_taxrevm determines tariff revenue in each region; E_taxind specifies the variable taxind(q), the aggregate revenue from all indirect taxes, as a weighted average of the percentage change in the commodity tax revenue raised from the purchases of different users.

Other definitional equations are available for the expenditure side components of the GRP, specifying percentage changes in nominal expenditure aggregates. They are derived from the level definitions of each component, which shows the nominal expenditure aggregate as the product of purchaser's price and the quantity in each aggregate category. In percentage change form, these definitions are presented in equations E_in, E_othnom5, E_othnom6, E_export, and E_imp. Equation E_c_a does not define nominal household consumption, which is defined by a consumption function. It only plays the role of a budget constraint on household expenditure. The quantity counterparts of the nominal equations are: E_cr, E_ir, E_othreal5, E_othreal6, E_expvol, and E_impvol. Quantity indices for interregional exports and imports are also defined: E_int_exp, and E_int_imp.

```
VARIABLE
          (all,q,REGDEST)
c(q)              # Nominal total household consumption #;
          (all,q,REGDEST)
export(q)         # Foreign currency value of exports #;
          (all,q,REGDEST)
expvol(q)         # Export volume #;
          (all,q,REGDEST)
in(q)             # Aggregate nominal investment #;
          (all,q,REGDEST)
ir(q)             # Aggregate real investment expenditure #;
          (all,q,REGDEST)
imp(q)        # Foreign currency value of imports #;
          (all,q,REGDEST)
impvol(q)         # Import volume index #;
          (all,q,REGDEST)
othnom5(q)        # Aggregate nominal regional government demand #;
          (all,q,REGDEST)
othnom6(q)        # Aggregate nominal federal government demand #;
          (all,q,REGDEST)
othreal5(q)       # Aggregate real regional government demand #;
          (all,q,REGDEST)
othreal6(q)       # Aggregate real federal government demand #;
          (all,s,REGSOURCE)
psexp(s)          # Price indices for interregional exports #;
          (all,q,REGDEST)
psimp(q)          # Price indices for interregional imports #;
          (all,s,REGSOURCE)(all,q,REGDEST)
psflo(s,q)    # Price index - interregional trade flows #;
          (all,q,REGDEST)
taxind(q)     # Aggregate revenue from all indirect taxes #;
          (all,q,REGDEST)
taxrevm(q)        # Aggregate tariff revenue #;
          (all,q,REGDEST)
xi2(q)        # Investment price index #;
          (all,q,REGDEST)
xi3(q)        # Consumer price index #;
          (all,q,REGDEST)
xi4(q)        # Exports Price Index #;
          (all,q,REGDEST)
xi5(q)        # Regional government demand price index #;
          (all,q,REGDEST)
xi6(q)        # Federal government demand price index #;
          (all,q,REGDEST)
xim(q)        # Imports price index #;
          (all,s,REGSOURCE)
xsexp(s)          # Exports volume in interregional trade #;
          (all,q,REGDEST)
xsimp(q)          # Imports volume in interregional trade #;
          (all,s,REGSOURCE) (all,q,REGDEST)
xsflo(s,q)    # Volume of interregional trade flows #;
          (all,j,IND)(all,q,REGDEST)
y(j,q)            # Capital creation by using industry #;
```

```
COEFFICIENT
        (all,q,REGDEST)
AGGCON(q)   # Total purchases by households #;
        (all,q,REGDEST)
AGGEXP(q)    # Total export earnings #;
        (all,q,REGDEST)
AGGIMP(q)    # Total foreign currency import costs #;
        (all,q,REGDEST)
AGGINV(q)    # Investment #;
        (all,q,REGDEST)
AGGOTH5(q)        # Value of regional government demand #;
        (all,q,REGDEST)
AGGOTH6(q)        # Total value of federal demand #;
        (all,q,REGDEST)
AGGTAXM(q)        # Tariffs #;
        (all,q,DOMDEST)
AGGTAX(q)    # Aggregate indirect tax revenue collected by region #;
        (all,s,REGSOURCE) (all,q,REGDEST)
C_XSFLO(s,q)      # Trade: interregional trade flows #;
        (all,s,REGSOURCE)
C_XSEXP(s)   # Interregional exports #;
        (all,q,REGDEST)
C_XSIMP(q)    # Interregional imports #;
        (all,i,COM)(all,q,REGDEST)
IMPCOST(i,q)  # Total ex-duty imports of good r #;

EQUATION
E_taxrevm # Aggregate tariff revenue #
        (all,q,REGDEST)
AGGTAXM(q)*taxrevm(q) = sum(i,COM,Tariff(i,q)*{pm(i) + natphi + x0imp(i,q)}
                  + IMPORTS(i,q)*powtaxm(i));
E_taxind # Aggregate value of indirect taxes #
        (all,q,REGDEST)
taxind(q) = (1.0/AGGTAX(q))*( AGGTAX1(q)*taxrev1(q) + AGGTAX2(q)*taxrev2(q)
            + AGGTAX3(q)*taxrev3(q) + AGGTAX5(q)*taxrev5(q));
E_c_a # Household budget constraint #
        (all,q,REGDEST)
AGGCON(q)* c(q) =
      sum(i,COM, sum(s,ALLSOURCE, PVAL3A(i,s,q)*{x3a(i,s,q)+p3a(i,s,q)} ));
E_cr # Real (total) household consumption #
        (all,q,REGDEST)
cr(q) = c(q) - xi3(q);
E_in # Total nominal investment #
        (all,q,REGDEST)
in(q) = ir(q) + xi2(q);
E_ir # Total real investment #
        (all,q,REGDEST)
ir(q) = (1.0/AGGINV(q))*sum(j,IND,INVEST(j,q)*y(j,q));
E_othnom5 # Aggregate nominal value of regional government demand #
        (all,q,REGDEST)
othnom5(q) = othreal5(q) + xi5(q);
E_othreal5 # Aggregate real regional government demand #
        (all,q,REGDEST)
othreal5(q) = (1.0/AGGOTH5(q))*
    sum(i,COM,sum(s,ALLSOURCE,PVAL5A(i,s,q)*x5a(i,s,q) ));
```

```
E_othnom6 # Nominal federal government demand #
        (all,q,REGDEST)
othnom6(q) = othreal6(q) + xi6(q);
E_othreal6 # Real federal government demand #
        (all,q,REGDEST)
AGGOTH6(q) * othreal6(q) =
    sum(i,com, sum(s,ALLSOURCE,PVAL6A(i,s,q) * x6a(i,s,q)));
E_export # Foreign currency value of exports #
        (all,q,REGDEST)
export(q) =(1.0/AGGEXP(q))*sum(i,COM,PVAL4R(i,q)*[p4r(i,q) + x4r(i,q)] );
E_expvol # Export volume index #
        (all,q,REGDEST)
expvol(q) = export(q) + natphi - xi4(q);
E_imp # Foreign currency value of imports #
        (all,q,REGDEST)
imp(q) = (1.0/AGGIMP(q))*sum(i,COM,IMPCOST(i,q)*[pm(i)+ x0imp(i,q)]);
E_impvol # Import volume index #
        (all,q,REGDEST)
impvol(q) = imp(q) + natphi - xim(q);
E_int_exp # Interregional exports #
        (all,s,REGSOURCE)
(TINY + C_XSEXP(s)) * (psexp(s) + xsexp(s))
  = sum(q,regdest, C_XSFLO(s,q) * (psflo(s,q) + xsflo(s,q)))
   - C_XSFLO(s,s) * (psflo(s,s) + xsflo(s,s));
E_int_imp # Interregional imports #
        (all,q,REGDEST)
(TINY + C_XSIMP(q)) * (psimp(q) + xsimp(q))
  = sum(s,regsource, C_XSFLO(s,q) * (psflo(s,q) + xsflo(s,q)))
   - C_XSFLO(q,q) * (psflo(q,q) + xsflo(q,q));
```

National GDP, real and nominal, and its components

In this block of equations, the national GDP components are obtained from the aggregation of regional results.

Regional and national price indices

Aggregate price indices for regional and national aggregates play an important role in the functioning of the model. They are defined in this section following a standard specification: price indices are defined as weighted averages of the percentage changes in the relevant prices. A decomposition of the movements in the interregional terms of trade, is covered in this block of equations. It basically decomposes the change in terms of trade in each region into three parts: the world price effect, the export price effect, and the import price effect.

Money wage settings

These equations define the wage settings available in B-MARIA, which allow for alternative perspectives on wage determination. They include movements in real wages from the view points of consumers and employers. In the first case, movements in the consumer real wage rate, i.e., the average nominal wage rate divided by the consumer price index, represent a key factor in wage negotiations; equation E_pwagei provides a flexible setting for money wage determination, in which deviations in the growth of wages relative to the growth of the national consumer price index are allowed. E_pwage presents the regional aggregation of E_pwagei. E_pwage_p shows the regional aggregation of the variable p1lab (price of *hiring* labor) across industries, which is critical for the outcome for employment. Movements in regional wage differentials are defined as the difference between the movements in the aggregate regional real wage received by workers, and the national real wage (E_wage_diff) .

```
VARIABLE
          (all,q,REGDEST)
fwage(q)          # Overall real wage shifter #;
          (all,j,IND)(all,q,REGDEST)
fwagei(j,q)       # Industry-specific wage shifter #;
          (all,q,REGDEST)
pwage(q)          # Region-wide nominal wage received by workers #;
          (all,q,REGDEST)
pwage_p(q)        # Region-wide nominal wage paid by producers #;
          (all,j,IND)(all,q,REGDEST)
pwagei(j,q)       # Nominal wage rates #;
natfwage          # Overall wage shifter #;
natrealwage       # National consumer real wage #;
natxi3        # Consumer price index #;
          (all,q,REGDEST)
wage_diff(q)      # Regional real wage differential #;

EQUATION
E_pwagei # Flexible setting of money wages #
          (all,j,IND)(all,q,REGDEST)
pwagei(j,q)= natxi3  + natfwage + fwage(q) + fwagei(j,q);
E_pwage # Region-wide nominal wage received by workers #
          (all,q,REGDEST)
AGGLAB(q)*pwage(q) = sum(j,IND,LABOR(j,q)*pwagei(j,q));
E_pwage_p # Region-wide nominal wage paid by producers #
          (all,q,REGDEST)
AGGLAB(q)*pwage_p(q) = sum(j,IND,LABOR(j,q)*p1lab(j,q));
E_wage_diff # Region real-wage diff #
          (all,q,REGDEST)
wage_diff(q) = pwage(q) - natxi3 - natrealwage;
```

Miscellaneous definitions of factor prices

Other factor-market variables are defined in this section. Most of them are aggregations of previously defined industry and regional variables. An important definition to understand the simulations results is provided by equation E_xiplpk_ind, which indicates the changes in the relative prices of hiring labor and acquiring new units of capital, for each industry. Definitions of interregional terms of trade (E_totdom), and foreign terms of trade (E_totfor) are also important.

```
VARIABLE
          (all,q,REGDEST)
reg_p1cap(q)   # Regional rental price of capital #;
          (all,q,REGDEST)
totdom(q)         # Domestic terms of trade #;
          (all,q,REGDEST)
totfor(q)      # Foreign terms of trade #;
          (all,q,REGDEST)
xiplpk(q)      # Index of relative price of labor and capital #;

EQUATION
E_totdom # Domestic terms of trade #
          (all,q,REGDEST)
totdom(q) = psexp(q) - psimp(q);
E_totfor # Foreign terms of trade #
          (all,q,REGDEST)
totfor(q) = xi4(q) - xim(q);
E_xiplpk # Index of relative price of labor and capital #
          (all,q,REGDEST)
xiplpk(q) = pwage_p(q) - reg_p1cap(q);
```

Employment aggregates

Two equations define the regional and national demands for each of the three types of labor, by aggregating industry results.

Government Finance Module

The government finance module incorporates equations determining the gross regional product (GRP), for each region, through the decomposition and modeling of its components. A similar approach is adopted for the value added components. GRP is defined from both the expenditure and the income side.

The budget deficits of regional governments and the federal government are also determined here. Regional governments are comprised of the state and municipal levels of direct administration within each region. At both levels of government, productive activities are not considered; they are included in the production sectors. The structure of the government accounts used in the model is heavily based on the State Fiscal Data Base developed by Dinsmoor and Haddad (1996). Some changes were carried out to accommodate the federal and the municipal administrations. Definitions of the main revenue and expenditure components of the government accounts are also available in this module of equations.

Another important definition in this block of equations refers to the specification of the regional aggregate household consumption functions. They are defined as a function of household disposable income, which is disaggregated into its main sources of income, and the respective tax duties.

Value-added components of regional product

The equations in this group disaggregate further the four components of regional value added determined in the CGE core, in order to separate production taxes from payments to factors. The wage bill is separated into wages, salaries and supplements, imputed wages, and payroll taxes; capital rentals into returns to fixed capital and property taxes; land rentals into returns to land, and land taxes; and "other cost tickets" into three components. There is an equation specifying the movements of each one of these ten components of value added. They move proportionally to appropriate price and quantity variables determined in the CGE core module.

Equations E_rpr and E_rpri are important for the computation of the difference between the wage rate received by the workers and the price of hiring labor (employment cost), which is driven by changes in the payroll tax rate in each industry in a region. This difference is used to define the after-tax wage rate in the CGE core. Other definitions include: regional gross operating surplus, production taxes, and national aggregates.

```
VARIABLE
           (all,j,IND)(all,q,REGDEST)
arpri(j,q)    # Payroll tax adjustment factor #;
           (all,j,IND)(all,q,REGDEST)
frpri(j,q)    # Payroll tax rate shifter #;
           (all,j,IND)(all,q,REGDEST)
rpri(j,q)           # Payroll tax rate (in per cent) #;
           (all,q,REGDEST)
rpr(q)        # Payroll tax rate #;
```

```
COEFFICIENT
          (all,j,IND)(all,q,REGDEST)
C_Z01_I_R(j,q) # Wages, salaries and supplements by region and industry #;
          (all,j,IND)(all,q,REGDEST)
C_Z02_I_R(J,Q)    # Imputed wages by region and industry #;
          (all,j,IND)(all,q,REGDEST)
C_Z03_I_R(J,Q)    # Payroll taxes by region and industry #;

EQUATION
E_rpr # Payroll tax adjustment #
          (all,j,IND) (all,q,REGDEST)
C_Z03_I_R(j,q) * rpri(j,q) =
           (C_Z01_I_R(j,q) + C_Z02_I_R(j,q) + C_Z03_I_R(j,q) + TINY) * arpri(j,q);
E_rpri # Setting of payroll tax rates #
          (all,j,IND) (all,q,REGDEST)
rpri(j,q) = rpr(q) + frpri(j,q);
```

Gross regional product and its components

This block of equations defines the components of GRP, from the income and expenditure side. The definitions use variables mapped from the CGE core and value added block. The income-side components are defined in three main groups of equations. First, wage income, which is composed by wage, salaries and supplements, and PAYE taxes, is directly linked to the value added block through wages, salaries and supplements. Second, non-wage income, also decomposed into a gross revenue component and a direct tax component, is linked to the value added block via the regional gross operating surplus. Finally, a group of indirect taxes provides direct links to the CGE core – tariffs, and other commodity taxes less subsidies –, and to the value added block – production taxes. Equation E_dompy000 defines GRP at market prices (income side) based on these three broad definitions.

From the expenditure side, GRP at market prices is defined as the sum of domestic absorption (private consumption, private investment, regional government consumption, federal government consumption, and government investment), and interregional and international trade balances (E_dompq000). All the components of GRP, expenditure side, are mapped from the CGE core module.

```
VARIABLE
          (all,q,REGDEST)
dompy000(q)   # GRP at market prices (income side) #;
          (all,q,REGDEST)
dompy100(q)   # Wages, salaries and supplements #;
```

```
        (all,q,REGDEST)
dompy200(q)   # GOS: non-wage primary factor income #;
        (all,q,REGDEST)
dompy300(q)   # Indirect taxes less subsidies #;
        (all,q,REGDEST)
dompq000(q)   # GRP at market prices (expenditure side) #;
        (all,q,REGDEST)
dompq100(q)   # (all,q,REGDEST) domestic absorption #;
        (all,q,REGDEST)
dompq200(q)   # Interregional trade balance #;
        (all,q,REGDEST)
dompq300(q)   # International trade balance #;

COEFFICIENT
        (all,q,REGDEST)
C_DOMPY000(Q)  # GRP at market prices (income side) #;
        (all,q,REGDEST)
C_DOMPY100(Q)  # Wages, salaries and supplements #;
        (all,q,REGDEST)
C_DOMPY200(Q)  # GOS: non-wage primary factor income #;
        (all,q,REGDEST)
C_DOMPY300(Q)  # Indirect taxes less subsidies #;
        (all,q,REGDEST)
C_DOMPQ000(Q)  # GRP at market prices (expenditure side) #;
        (all,q,REGDEST)
C_DOMPQ100(Q)  # Domestic absorption #;
        (all,q,REGDEST)
C_DOMPQ200(Q)  # Interregional trade balance #;
        (all,q,REGDEST)
C_DOMPQ300(Q)  # International trade balance #

EQUATION
E_dompy000 # GDP at market prices (income side) - regions #
        (all,q,REGDEST)
C_DOMPY000(q) * dompy000(q) =  C_DOMPY100(q) * dompy100(q)
                             + C_DOMPY200(q) * dompy200(q)
                             + C_DOMPY300(q) * dompy300(q);
E_dompq000 # GRP at market prices (expenditure side) #
        (all,q,REGDEST)
C_DOMPQ000(q) * dompq000(q) =  C_DOMPQ100(q) * dompq100(q)
                             + C_DOMPQ200(q) * dompq200(q)
                             + C_DOMPQ300(q) * dompq300(q);
```

Intermediary variables

These equations define a group of variables to be used as a link between the value added and GRP blocks, and the components of government finances. The variables defined here represent aggregation of previously defined variables.

Income and expenditure components of government finances

This group of equations defines the components of the federal and regional governments accounts, for the direct administration. Regional government estimates are calculated through the aggregation of the state and municipalities accounts in each region. Given differences in the budget structure of the three levels of administration, a common structure was used, as follows:

- Total Revenue =
  - \+ Direct taxes
  - \+ Indirect taxes
  - \+ Interest received
  - \+ Federal transfers to the regions
  - \+ Other revenue
- Financing Transactions = Total Revenue – Total Outlays =
  - \+ Net borrowing
  - \+ Increase in provisions
  - \+ Other financing transactions
- Total Outlays =
  - \+ Expenditures on goods and services
  - \+ Personal transfers
  - \+ Subsidies
  - \+ Interest payments
  - \+ Federal transfers to the regions
  - \+ Other outlays

A further disaggregation of some of the revenue and expenditure components is available. The government accounts are driven by variables determined in the other groups of equations. Mapping variables from the CGE core for tariffs, government consumption, and government investment are specified. In the same manner, mappings from the GRP equations group determine movements in income taxes, and other commodity taxes in the regions. Payroll taxes changes in the regions are mapped from the value added block; and unemployment benefits and personal benefits payments in the regions are mapped from the household disposable income block.

Other components of governments budgets are assumed to move with the economic activity of the regions (for regional governments), or of the country (for the federal government). This default option can be overridden, in many cases, by the use of shift variables. The GRP-GDP-driven components include: other direct taxes; property taxes; land taxes; other indirect taxes; interest received; federal government transfers to the regions; other revenue; and interest payments.

Subsidies from the regional governments are assumed to maintain a constant ratio with commodity tax revenue. Nominal budget deficits are defined from the structural relations outlined above. Real budget deficits are defined by deflating the nominal deficits with the regional and national consumer prices. Other equations define revenue and expenditure aggregates.

Household income and its components

These equations provide the disaggregation and sources of the components of household disposable income. Equation E_hhldy000 defines household disposable income in each region as the sum of four components:

a) primary factor income (wage and non-wage income), which is defined in the value added block;
b) personal benefits, which isolates unemployment benefits from other personal benefits; the former being indexed to the national CPI and moving positively with increases in labor supply, and negatively with increases in the level of employment, and the latter also indexed by the national CPI and following population changes;
c) income from other sources, which follows the general growth in the regional economies;
d) direct taxes on household income, which are comprised of taxes on wage and non-wage income, assumed to move proportionally to their incidence counterparts, and other direct taxes, derived in the government accounts block.

The remaining equations are mapping equations to be used elsewhere in the model.

```
VARIABLE
          (all,q,REGDEST)
hhldy000(q)    # Disposable income #;
          (all,q,REGDEST)
hhldy100(q)    # Primary factor income #;
          (all,q,REGDEST)
hhldy200(q)    # Personal benefit receipts #;
          (all,q,REGDEST)
hhldy300(q)    # Other income (net) #;
          (all,q,REGDEST)
hhldy400(q)    # Direct taxes #;
```

```
COEFFICIENT
          (all,q,REGDEST)
C_HHLDY000(Q)   # Disposable income #;
          (all,q,REGDEST)
C_HHLDY100(Q)   # Primary factor income #;
          (all,q,REGDEST)
C_HHLDY200(Q)   # Personal benefit receipts #;
          (all,q,REGDEST)
C_HHLDY300(Q)   # Other income (net) #;
          (all,q,REGDEST)
C_HHLDY400(Q)   # Direct taxes #;

EQUATION
E_hhldy000 # Disposable income #
          (all,q,REGDEST)
C_HHLDY000(q) * hhldy000(q) =  C_HHLDY100(q) * hhldy100(q)
                             + C_HHLDY200(q) * hhldy200(q)
                             + C_HHLDY300(q) * hhldy300(q)
                             - C_HHLDY400(q) * hhldy400(q);
```

Miscellaneous equations of the government finance module

In addition to some definitions to be used to drive expenditure components of the government accounts (government consumption and investment), mapped from the CGE core block, there are two important equations. First, equation E_c_b specifies a *Keynesian* regional household consumption function, which determines regional household expenditure as a function of disposable income. Second, an equation defining the relative tax rates on wage and non-wage income is provided in E_rl.

```
VARIABLE
          (all,q,REGDEST)
miscf001(q)      # Shift variable : consumption function #;
miscf002         # Shift variable : relative income tax rates #;
rl               # Tax rate - wages, salaries and supplements #;
rk               # Tax rate - non-wage primary factor income #;
          (all,q,REGDEST)
yd_r(q)      # Household disposable income #;

EQUATION
E_c_b # Consumption function #
          (all,q,REGDEST)
c(q) = yd_r(q) + miscf001(q);
E_rl # Relative income tax rates #
rl = rk + miscf002;
```

Capital Accumulation and Investment Module

Capital stock and investment relationships are defined in this module. Comparative-static and forecasting versions of the model contain different equations. The forecasting equations were derived in B-MARIA for purposes of its future developments. As explained below, at this stage, only the comparative-static version of the model produces reliable results, restricting the use of the model to short-run and long-run policy analysis. When running the model in the comparative-static mode, there is no fixed relationship between capital and investment. The user decides the required relationship on the basis of the requirements of the specific simulation.

The theory of the allocation of investment across industries in B-MARIA is represented by this group of equations. Equation E_r0 defines the percentage change in the current rate of return on fixed capital in industry *j*, in region *q*. Rates of return are defined as the ratio between the rental values and the cost of a unit of capital in each industry, minus the rate of depreciation (notice that the coefficient QCOEF(j,q) refers to the ratio of the gross to the net rate of return). E_f_rate_xx says that if the percentage change in the rate of return in a regional industry grows faster than the national average rate of return, capital stocks in that industry will increase at a higher rate than the average national stock. For industries with lower-than-average increase in their rates of return to fixed capital, capital stocks increase at a lower-than-average rate, i.e., capital is attracted to higher return industries. The shift variable, f_rate_xx(j,q), exogenous in long-run simulation, allows shifts in the industry's rates of return. Equation E_naty establishes that total real investment in each sector equals the sum of the respective sectoral investments across the regions.

Equations E_curcapT1 and E_yT allows for users to jump from comparative-static to forecasting experiments. FRED and PRIOD are defined by users. In the comparative-static simulations, FRED was set equal to 1 and PRIOD equal to 2.[4] For these values, E_curcapT1 implies that the percentage change in an industry's capital stock in year *T* is the same as the percentage change in its capital stock in year *T+1*; E_yT implies that the percentage change in an industry's capital stock in year *T* is equal to the percentage change in industry's investments in year *T*.

[4] For forecasting simulations, FRED = PRIOD = number of years of the forecast. For a detailed interpretation of E_curcapT1 and E_yT used in forecast experiments, see Horridge *et al.* (1993), and Peter *et al.* (1996b).

```
VARIABLE
        (change) (all,j,IND)(all,q,REGDEST)
delf_rate(j,q)   # A change shifter in capital_accum equation #;
        (change)
delkfudge        # Dummy variable to switch on capital accumulation equation #;
        (all,j,IND) (all,q,REGDEST)
f_rate_xx(j,q)   # Shifter, rate of return eq. #;
        (all,j,IND) (all,q,REGDEST)
curcap_t1(j,q)        # Capital stock in period T+1 #;
natr_tot         # Average rate of return #;
        (all,q,REGDEST)
kt(q)            # Aggregate capital stock, rental weights #;
        (all,j,IND)(all,q,REGDEST)
r0(j,q)          # Current rates of return on capital #;
        (all,j,IND)
naty(j)      # Capital creation by using industry #;

COEFFICIENT
        (all,j,IND)(all,q,REGDEST)
BETA_R(j,q)   # Parameter to distribute investment #;
        (all,j,IND)
DEP(j)      # Depreciation factor, uniform across regions #;
K_TERM        # A constant in T+1 capital equation #;
        (all,j,IND)
NATINVEST(j) # Total capital created for each industry #;
        (all,j,IND)(all,q,REGDEST)
QCOEF(j,q)    # Ratio, gross to net rate of return #;
        (all,j,IND)(all,q,REGDEST)
VALKT(j,q)    # Assest-value of capital stock in period T #;
        (integer)
FRED          # Switch variable, forecast to comparative statatic #;
        (integer)
PRIOD         # Number of years in a forecast period #;
        (all,j,IND) (all,q,REGDEST)
VALK_0(j,q)   # Base-year asset value of capital stock #;
        (all,j,IND)(all,q,REGDEST)
VALK_T1(j,q)  # Value of capital stock in period T+1 #;
        (all,j,IND)(all,q,REGDEST)
INVEST_0(j,q) # Base-year value of investment #;

EQUATION
E_r0 # Definition of rates of return to capital #
        (all,j,IND)(all,q,REGDEST)
r0(j,q) = QCOEF(j,q)*(p1cap(j,q) - pi(j,q));
E_f_rate_xx # Capital growth rates related to rates of return #
        (all,j,IND)(all,q,REGDEST)
(r0(j,q) - natr_tot) = BETA_R(j,q)*[curcap(j,q) - kt(q)] + f_rate_xx(j,q);
E_naty # Total real investment #
        (all,j,IND)
(Tiny+NATINVEST(j))*naty(j) = sum(q,REGDEST,INVEST(j,q)*y(j,q));
E_curcapT1 # Capital stock in period T+1 #
        (all,j,IND)(all,q,REGDEST)
 IF(FRED ne PRIOD, curcap_t1(j,q) - curcap(j,q))
+ IF(FRED eq PRIOD, curcap_t1(j,q) - K_TERM*curcap(j,q)) =0;
```

```
E_yT # Investment in period T #
        (all,j,IND)(all,q,REGDEST)
 IF(FRED ne PRIOD, curcap(j,q) - y(j,q)- 100*delf_rate(j,q))
+ IF(FRED eq PRIOD, + VALKT(j,q)*DEP(j)*curcap(j,q)
            + (Tiny + INVEST(j,q))*y(j,q)
            - 100*(VALK_0(j,q)*(1-DEP(j))-INVEST_0(j,q))*delkfudge
            + 100*delf_rate(j,q) - VALK_T1(j,q)*curcap_t1(j,q)) = 0;
```

Foreign Debt Accumulation Module

This module is based on the specification proposed in ORANI-F (Horridge *et al.*, 1993), in which the nation's foreign debt is linearly related to accumulated balance-of-trade deficits. In summary, trade deficits are financed by increases in the external debt (E_delbt and E_deldebt).

```
VARIABLE
        (change)
deldfudge      # Dummy variable in equation E_delDebt #;
        (change)
delbt       # Ordinary change in the real trade deficit #;
        (change)
deldebt     # Ordinary change in foreign debt  #;
natexpvol      # Export volume #;
natxi4      # Exports price index #;
natxim      # Imports price index #;
natimpvol      # Import volume #;

COEFFICIENT
B0            # Original real trade deficit #;
DEBT0         # Original real foreign debt #;
M_DEBT        # A constant #;
N_DEBT        # A constant#;
P_GLOBAL      # Converts Cr$ into 'real' terms #;
R_WORLD       # World interest rate: number like 1.06 #;
NATAGGEXP        # National exports #;
NATAGGIMP        # National foreign currency import costs #;

EQUATION
E_delbt # Ordinary change in real trade deficit #
100*P_GLOBAL*delbt =  NATAGGIMP*(natimpvol)
            - NATAGGEXP*(natexpvol + natxi4 - natxim);
E_deldebt # Ordinary change in foreign debt #
deldebt = {DEBT0*(R_WORLD^PRIOD-1)+B0*N_DEBT}*deldfudge+M_DEBT*delbt;
```

Labor Market and Regional Migration Module

In this module, regional population is defined through the interaction of demographic variables, including interregional migration. Links between regional population and regional labor supply are provided. Demographic variables are usually defined exogenously, and together with the specification of some of the labor market settings, labor supply can be determined together with either interregional wage differentials or regional unemployment rates. In summary, either labor supply and wage differentials determine unemployment rates, or labor supply and unemployment rates determine wage differentials.

Equations E_del_labsup defines the percentage-point change in regional unemployment rates in terms of percentage changes in labor supply and persons employed; labor supply moves with regional workforce participation rate and population of working age (E_wpop). In E_Pop, it is assumed that the regional population of working age is proportional to the regional population. Regional aggregate employment in wage bill weights and in number of persons are assumed to be proportional (E_rempl_interf); number of households in a region is assumed to be proportional to the regional population (E_Pop_interf).

Equation E_del_RM is implemented in comparative-static experiments by assigning a value of zero to delrpfudge(q); regional population growth moves with natural growth and migration forecasts. Finally, the remaining equations define national aggregates based on summing regional variables.

```
VARIABLE
          (change)(all,q,REGDEST)
del_fm(q)        # Ordinary changes in foreign migration: regions #;
          (change)(all,q,REGDEST)
del_g(q)         # Ordinary changes in natural pop. (births-deaths): regions #;
          (change)(all,q,REGDEST)
del_rm(q)        # Ordinary change in interregional migration #;
          (change)(all,q,REGDEST)
delrpfudge(q)  # Dummies in equation E_del_RM #;
          (change) (all,q,REGDEST)
del_unr(q)       # Percentage-point changes in regional unemployment rate #;
          (all,q,REGDEST)
employ(q)        # Regional employment: persons #;
          (all,q,REGDEST)
f_l(q)           # Shifter in regional employment #;
          (all,q,REGDEST)
f_pop(q)         # Shifter in equation E_del_RM #;
          (all,q,REGDEST)
f_wpop(q)        # Shifter in equation E_WPop #;
          (all,q,REGDEST)
labsup(q)  # Labor supply #;
```

```
          (all,q,REGDEST)
l(q)           # Aggregate employment - wage bill weights #;
          (all,q,REGDEST)
pop(q)       # Regional population #;
          (all,q,REGDEST)
          (all,q,REGDEST)
pr(q)        # Regional workforce participation rate #;
wpop(q)          # Regional population of working age #;

COEFFICIENT
          (all,q,REGDEST)
C_LABSUP(q)      # regional labor supply #;
          (all,q,REGDEST)
C_EMPLOY(q)      # regional employment: persons #;
C_PA2            # Coefficient in population accumulation equation #;
          (all,q,REGDEST)
C_POP(q)         # Regional population #;
          (all,q,REGDEST)
C_PR1(q)         # Constant term in regional population accumulation equation #;

EQUATION
E_del_labsup # Percentage-point changes in regional unemployment rates #
          (all,q,REGDEST)
C_LABSUP(q)*del_unr(q)=C_EMPLOY(q)*(labsup(q)-employ(q));
E_Pop # Regional working age population #
          (all,q,REGDEST)
wpop(q) = pop(q) + f_wpop(q);
E_rempl_interf # Interface employ and l #
          (all,q,REGDEST)
l(q) = employ(q) + f_l(q);
E_del_RM # Accumulation of regional population #
          (all,q,REGDEST)
C_POP(q)*pop(q) =  C_PR1(q)*delrpfudge(q)
              + C_PA2*(del_rm(q)+del_fm(q)+del_g(q))+f_pop(q);
E_Pop_interf # Interface Pop and qhous #
          (all,q,REGDEST)
qhous(q) = pop(q) + f_qhous(q);
E_wpop # Regional labor supply #
          (all,q,REGDEST)
labsup(q) = pr(q) + wpop(q);
```

Bibliography

Adams, P. D. and Dixon, P. B. (1995). Prospects For Australian Industries, States And Regions: 1993-94 To 2001-02. *Australian Bulletin of Labour*, vol. 21, no. 2, June.

Adelman, I. and Robinson, S. (1978). **Income Distribution Policy In Developing Countries: A Case Study of Korea**. Stanford University Press, Stanford, CA.

AERI/CNT (1996). **O Impacto do MERCOSUL Sobre os Sistemas de Transportes do Brasil**. Análise Econômica Regional e Internacional Ltda. and Confederação Nacional dos Transportes, Brasília, D.F..

Agénor, P. R. and Montiel, P. J. (1996). **Development Macroeconomics**. Princeton University Press, Princeton, New Jersey.

"A Indústria Automobilística no Brasil a Mil Por Hora", *Rumos*, July 1997, pp. 24-31.

Albuquerque, R. C. and Gomes, R. M. (1996). Nordeste: Os Desafios de uma Dupla Inserção. In Fórum Nacional: *O Real, o Crescimento e as Reformas*, Ed. J. P. R. Velloso, José Olympio Editora, Rio de Janeiro.

Alonso, W. (1968). Urban and Regional Imbalances in Economic Development. *Economic Development and Cultural Change*, vol. 17, pp. 1-14.

Amos, O. (1989). An Inquiry into the Causes of Increasing Regional Income inequality in the United States. *The Review of Regional Studies*, vol. 19, no. 2, pp. 1-13.

Anselin, L. and Madden, M. (1990). **New Directions In Regional Analysis: Integrated And Multi-Regional Approaches**. Belhaven Press, London.

Araújo, T. B. (1995). Nordeste, Nordestes: Que Nordeste? In *Federalismo no Brasil: Desigualdae Regionais e Desenvolvimento*, Eds. R. B. A. Affonso and P. L. B. Silva, FUNDAP, São Paulo.

Armington, P. S. (1969). A Theory Of Demand For Products Distinguished By Place Of Production. *International Monetary Fund Staff Papers*, 16, pp. 159-178.

Arocena, M. (1995). Common Market of the Southern Cone: MERCOSUR. *Working Papers Series 204*, Inter-American Development Bank, September.

Arrow, K. J. and Hahn, F. H. (1971). **General Competitive Analysis**. Holden-Day, Inc., San Francisco.

Azzoni, C. R. (1995). Economic Growth and Convergence of Regional Income: New Evidence on the Brazilian Case. *Paper presented at the 42nd Annual North American Meeting of the Regional Science Association International*, Cincinnati, OH, November.

Azzoni, C. R. (1996). Distribuição Pessoal de Renda Interna aos Estados e Desigualdade de Renda entre os Estados no Brasil: 1960, 70, 80 e 90. *Unpublished manuscript*, copy from the author.

Baer, W. (1965). **Industrialization and Economic Development in Brazil**. Richard D. Irwin, Inc., Homewood, Illinois.

Baer, W. (1995). **The Brazilian Economy: Growth and Development**. Praeger, Westport, 4th edition.

Baer, W. and Maloney, W. (1997). Neoliberalism and Income Distribution in Latin America. *World Development*, vol. 25, no. 3, pp. 311-327.

Baer, W., Haddad, E. A. and Hewings, G. J. D. (1998). The Regional Impact of Neo-Liberal Policies in Brazil. *Revista de Economia Aplicada*, vol. 2, no. 2, pp. 219-241.

Barro, R. and Sala-i-Martin, X. (1991). **Economic Growth**. McGraw Hill, New York.

Batten, D. (1982). The International Linkages Between National And Regional Input-Output Models. *International Regional Science Review*, vol. 7, no. 1, pp. 53-68.

Batten, D. and Westin, L. (1988). Modelling Commodity Flows On Trade Networks: Retrospect And Prospect. *Working Paper from CERUM*, 1988:30, Umea, October.

BNB (1992). **Matriz de Insumo-Produto do Nordeste 1980 e 1985: Metodologia e Resultados**. Banco do Nordeste do Brasil, S.A., Fortaleza.

Bolton, R. (1980). Symposium On Multiregional Forecasting And Policy Simulation Models. *Journal of Regional Science*, vol. 20, no. 2, pp. 131-142.

Boudeville, J.-R. (1961). **Les Espaces Économiques**. Presses Universitaires de France, Paris.

Braga, H. C., Santiago, G. M. C. and Ferro, L. C. M. (1988). Estrutura da Proteção Efetiva no Brasil: 1985. *Pesquisa e Planejamento Econômico*, vol. 18, no. 3, December.

Bruno, M. (1987). Opening Up: Liberalization with Stabilization. In *The Open Economy: Tools for Policymakers in Developing Countries*, Eds. R. Dornbusch and L. Helmers. EDI Series in Economic Development, Oxford University Press.

Buarque, S. C., Lopes, A. D., and Rosa, T. C. (1995). Integração Fragmentada e Crescimento da Fronteira Norte. In *Federalismo no Brasil: Desigualdae Regionais e Desenvolvimento*, Eds. R. B. A. Affonso and P. L. B. Silva, FUNDAP, São Paulo.

Buckley, P. H. (1992). A Transportation-Oriented Interregional Computable General Equilibrium Model of the United States. *The Annals of Regional Science*, 26: 331-348.

Cella, G. (1984). The Input-Output Measurement of Interindustry Linkages. *Oxford Bulletim of Economics and Statistics*, 70: 705-712.

Chenery, H. B. and Watanabe, T. (1958). International Comparisons of the Structure of Production. *Econometrica*, 26: 487-521.

Clements, B. J. (1990). On the Decomposition and Normalization of Interindustry Linkages. *Economic Letters*, 33: 337-340.

Clements, B. J. and Rossi, J. W. (1990). Interindustry Linkages and Economic Development: The Case of Brazil Reconsidered. *The Developing Economies*, 29: 166-187.

Clements, B. J. and Rossi, J. W. (1992). Ligações Interindustriais e Setores-Chave na Economia Brasileira. *Pesquisa e Planejamento Econômico*, 22: 101-124

CNI (1995). **Custo Brasil**. Ano 28, no. 289, June.

Deaton, A. and Muellbauer, J. (1980). **Economics And Consumer Behavior**. Cambridge University Prees, 1996 reprint.

Debreu, G. (1959). **Theory of Value**. Wiley, New York.

De Melo, J. (1988). Computable General Equilibrium Models For Trade Policy Analysis In Developing Countries: A Survey. *The World Bank WP53*, April.

Denslow, D. (1978). As Exportações e a Origem do Padrão de Industrialização Regional do Brasil. In *Dimensões do Desenvolvimento Brasileiro*, Eds. W. Baer, P. P. Geiger and P. R. Haddad Editora Campus Ltda., Rio de Janeiro.

Dervis, K. J., De Melo, J. and Robinson, S.(1982). **General Equilibrium Models For Development Policy**. A World Bank Research Publication. Cambridge University Press, Cambridge.

Despotakis, K. A. and Fisher, A. C. (1988). Energy In A Regional Economy: A Computable General Equilibrium Model For California. *Journal of Environmental Economics and Management*, 15, pp. 313-330.

Diniz, C. C. and Santos, F. B. T. (1996). Manaus: Uma “Satellite Platform” na Região Amazônica. *ANPEC*, XXIV Encontro Nacional de Economia, Dezembro.

Dinsmoor, J. and Haddad, E. A. (1996). Brazil: The Use of State Fiscal Data Bases for Financial Projections. *Region I Technical Note*, Inter-American Development Bank, August.

Dixon, P. B. (1996). **The MONASH Model**. Material prepared for the 1996 MONASH Model Course, Monash University, Australia, 24 November to 6 December.

Dixon, P. B., Bowles, S. and Kendrick, D. (1983). **Teoría Microeconómica: Notas Y Problemas**. Hispano Europea, S. A., Barcelona (Notes and Problems in Microeconomic Theory).

Dixon, P. B., Madden, J. R. and Peter, M. W. (1993). The Effects Of Reallocating General Revenue Assistance Among The Australian States. *The Economic Record*, vol. 69, no. 207, pp. 367-381, December.

Dixon, P. B. and Parmenter, B. R. (1994). Computable General Equilibrium Modelling. *Preliminary Working Paper no. IP-65*, IMPACT Project, Monash University, Clayton, July.

Dixon, P. B., Parmenter, B. R., Powell, A. A. and Wilcoxen, P. J. (1992). **Notes And Problems In Applied General Equilibrium Economics**. Advanced Textbooks in Economics 32, Eds. C. J. Bliss and M. D. Intriligator, North-Holland, Amsterdam.

Dixon, P. B., Parmenter, B. R., Sutton, J. and Vincent, D. P. (1982). **ORANI: A Multisectoral Model Of The Australian Economy**. North-Holland, Amsterdam.

Eatwell, J., Milgate, M. And Newman, P. (1989). **The New Palgrave: General Equilibrium**. W. W. Norton & Company, New York.

Edgeworth F. Y. (1881). **Mathematical Psychics**. C. Kegan Paul, London.

FIBGE (1995). **Matriz de Insumo-Produto Brasil - 1985**. Departamento de Contas Nacionais, Fundação Instituto Brasileiro de Geografia e Estatística, Rio de Janeiro, February.

Frankel, J. E. (1998). **The Regionalization of the World Economy**. National Bureau of Economic Research, The University of Chicago Press, Chicago and London.

Furtado, C. (1963). **The Economic Growth of Brazil**. University of California Press, Berkeley and Los Angeles.

Gazel, R. C. (1994). **Regional and Interregional Economic Effects of the Free Trade Agreement Between the US and Canada**. Ph.D. dissertation. University of Illinois at Urbana-Champaign.

Ginsburgh, V. and Keyzer, M. (1997). **The Structure of Applied General Equilibrium Models**. The MIT Press, London.

Guilhoto, J. J. M.(1986). **A Model for Economic Planning and Analysis for the Brazilian Economy**. University of Illinois at Urbana-Champaign, Ph.D. dissertation.

Guilhoto, J. J. M. (1995). **Um Modelo Computável de Equilíbrio Geral para Planejamento e Análise de Políticas Agrícolas (PAPA) na Economia Brasileira**. ESALQ, Piracicaba, Tese de Livre Docência, June.

Guilhoto J. J. M. and Fonseca, M. A. R. (1990). As Principais Correntes de Modelagem Econômica e o Caso Brasileiro. *Anais do XII Encontro Brasileiro de Econometria, Brasília*, December 03-06.

Guilhoto, J. J. M., Haddad, E. A., Sonis, M., and Hewings, G. J. D. (1997). Comparative Analysis of Brazilian Regional Economic Structure. *Regional Economics Applications Laboratory*, University of Illinois at Urbana-Champaign.

Guimarães Neto, L. (1995). Desigualdades Regionais e Federalismo. In *Federalismo no Brasil: Desigualdae Regionais e Desenvolvimento*, Eds. R. B. A. Affonso and P. L. B. Silva, FUNDAP, São Paulo.

Guimarães Neto, L. (1996). Ciclos Econômicos e Desigualdades Regionais no Brasil. *ANPEC*, XXIV Encontro Nacional de Economia, Dezembro.

Haddad, E. A. (1995). **The Economic Structure of Minas Gerais: An Input-Output Approach**. University of Illinois at Urbana-Champaign, M.A. thesis.

Haddad, E. A. and Hewings, G. J. D. (1997). The Theoretical Specification of B-MARIA. Discussion Paper REAL 97-T-5, *Regional Economics Applications Laboratory*, University of Illinois at Urbana-Champaign, November.

Haddad, E. A., Hewings, G. J. D. and Peter, M. (1998). Input-Output Systems in Regional and Interregional CGE Models. Discussion Paper REAL 98-T-11,

Regional Economics Applications Laboratory, University of Illinois at Urbana-Champaign.

Haddad, P. R. (1978). As Políticas de Desenvolvimento Regional no Brasil: Notas Para Uma Avaliação. In *Dimensões do Desenvolvimento Brasileiro*, Eds. W. Baer, P. P. Geiger and P. R. Haddad Editora Campus Ltda., Rio de Janeiro.

Haddad, P. R. (1996). Os Impactos do Novo Ciclo Sobre os Desequilíbrios Regionais. In Fórum Nacional: *O Real, o Crescimento e as Reformas*, Ed. J. P. R. Velloso, José Olympio Editora, Rio de Janeiro.

Haddad, P. R. (1997). A Questão Regional em Três Ciclos de Expansão do Brasil. *Idéias e Debates*, Instituto Teotônio Vilela, Brasília.

Harrigan, F. and McGregor, P. G. (1988a). **Recent Advances in Regional Economic Modelling**. London Papers in Regional Science 19, Pion, London.

Harrigan, F. and McGregor, P. G. (1988b). Price and Quantity Interaction in Regional Economic Models: The Importance of "Openness" and "Closures". In London Papers in Regional Science 19: *Recent Advances in Regional Economic Modelling*, Eds. F. Harrigan and P. G. McGregor, Pion, London.

Harrigan, F. and McGregor, P. G. (1989). Neoclassical and Keynesian Perspectives on the Regional Macro-Economy: A Computable General Equilibrium Approach. *Journal of Regional Science*, vol. 29, no. 4, pp. 555-573.

Harrigan, F., McGregor, P. G., Swales, J. K. and Dourmashkin, N. (1992). Imperfect Competition in Regional Labour Markets: A Computable General Equilibrium Analysis. *Environment and Planning A*, vol. 24, pp. 1463-1481.

Harris Jr., C. C. (1988). From General Spatial Equilibrium Theory to Multiregional Operational Models. In London Papers in Regional Science 19: *Recent Advances in Regional Economic Modelling*, Eds. F. Harrigan and P. G. McGregor, Pion, London.

Harrison, W. J. and Pearson, K. R. (1994). Computing Solutions for Large General Equilibrium Models Using GEMPACK. *Preliminary Working Paper no. IP-64*, IMPACT Project, Monash University, Clayton.

Harrison, W. J. and Pearson, K. R. (1996). An Introduction to GEMPACK. *GEMPACK User Documentation GPD-1*, IMPACT Project and KPSOFT, third edition, September.

Harrison, W. J., Pearson, K. R. and Powell, A. A. (1994). Multiregional And Intertemporal AGE Modelling Via GEMPACK. *Preliminary Working Paper no. IP-66*, IMPACT Project, Monash University, Clayton, September.

Hertel, T. W. (1996). **Global Trade Analysis: Modeling and Applications**. Cambridge University Press.

Hewings, G. J. D. (1985). **Regional Input-Output Analysis**. Sage Publications, Beverly Hills.

Hewings, G. J. D. and Jensen, R. C. (1986). Regional, Interregional And Multiregional Input-Output Analysis. In *Handbook of Regional and Urban Economics*, vol. 1, Ed. P. Nijkamp, North-Holland, Amsterdam.

Higgins, B. and Savoie, D. J. (1995). **Regional Development Theories and Their Application**. Transaction Publishers, New Brunswick.

Higgs, P. J., Parmenter, B. R. and Rimmer, R, J. (1988). A Hybrid Top-Down, Bottom-Up Regional Computable General Equilibrium Model. *International Regional Science Review*, vol. 11, no. 3, pp. 317-328.

Hirschman, A. O. (1958). **The Strategy of Economic Development**. Yale University Press, New Haven.

Horridge, J. M., Parmenter, B. R., Cameron, M., Joubert, R., Suleman, A. and De Jongh, D. (1995). The Macroeconomic, Industrial, Distributional And Regional Effects Of Government Spending Programs In South Africa. *General Paper no. G-109*, IMPACT Project, Monash University, Clayton, April.

Horridge, J. M., Parmenter, B. R. and Pearson, K. R. (1993). ORANI-F: A General Equilibrium Model of the Australian Economy. *Economic and financial Computing*, vol. 3, no. 2, Summer.

Hulu, E. and Hewings, G. J. D. (1993). The Development And Use Of Interregional Input-Output Models For Indonesia Under Conditions Of Limited Information. *Review of Urban and Regional Development Studies*, 5.

Israilevich, P., Hewings, G. J. D., Schindler, G. R. and Mahidhara, R. (1996). The Choice Of An Input-Output Table Embedded In Regional Econometric Input-Output Models. *Papers in Regional Science*, 75, 2, pp.103-119.

Israilevich, P., Hewings, G. J. D., Sonis, M., and Schindler, G. R. (1997). Forecasting Structural Change with a Regional Econometric Input-Output Model. *Journal of Regional Science*, forthcoming.

Johansen, L. (1960). **A Multi-Sectoral Study Of Economic Growth**. North-Holland/Ameraican Elsevier, Second Enlarge Edition (1974).

Jones, R. and Whalley, J. (1988). Regional Effects Of Taxes In Canada: An Applied General Equilibrium Approach. *Journal of Public Economics*, 37, pp. 1-28.

Jones, R. and Whalley, J. (1989). A Canadian Regional General Equilibrium Model And Some Applications. *Journal of Urban Economics*, 25, pp. 368-404.

Kenderes, M. (1990). IMPACT Project Documentation: The First Fifteen Years, 1975-89. IMPACT Project, Melbourne, February.

Kimbell, L. J. and Harrison, G. W. (1984). General Equilibrium Analysis Of Regional Fiscal Incidence. In *Applied General Equlibrium Analysis*, Eds. H. E. Scarf and J. B. Shoven, Cambridge University Press, chapter 7.

Ko, S. (1985). **A Regional Computable General Equilibrium Model For Korea**. Ph.D. dissertation. University of Illinois at Urbana-Champaign.

Ko, S. and Hewings, G. J. D. (1986). A Regional Computable General Equilibrium Model for Korea. *The Korean Journal of Regional Science*, vol. 2, December, pp. 45-57.

Koh, Y., Schreiner, D. F. and Shin, H. (1993). Comparisons Of Regional Fixed Price And General Equilibrium Models. *Regional Science Perspectives*, vol. 23, no. 1, pp. 33-80.

Kraybill, D. S., Johnson, T. G. and Orden, D. (1992). Macroeconomic Imbalances: An Multiregional General Equilibrium Analysis. *American Journal of Agricultural Economics*, vol. 74, no. 3, pp. 726-736.

Krugman, P. (1991a). **Geography and Trade**. MIT Press, Cambridge.

Krugman, P. (1991b). Increasing Returns and Economic Geography. *Journal of Political Economy*, 99: 483-499.

Lavinas, L., Garcia, E. H., and Amaral, M. R. (1997). Desiguladades Regionais: Indicadores Socioeconômicos nos Anos 90. *Texto para Discussão 460*, IPEA, Rio de Janeiro, February.

Leontief, W., Morgan, A., Polenske, K., Simpson, D. and Tower, E. (1965). The Economic Impact - Industrial And Regional - Of An Arms Cut. *The Review of Economics and Statistics*, vol. XLVII, no. 3, pp. 217-241.

Leontief, W. and Strout, A. (1963). Multiregional Input-Output Analysis. In *Structural Interdependence and Economic Development*, Ed. T. Barna, McMillan, London.

Liew, L. H. (1982). Regional Disaggregation Of A National Economic Model: The "Bottoms-Up" Approach. *Preliminary Working Paper no. OP-34*, IMPACT Project, Melbourne, August.

Liew, L. H. (1984a). A Johansen Model For Regional Analysis. *Regional Science and Urban Economics*, 14, pp. 129-146.

Liew, L. H. (1984b). "Tops-Down" Versus "Bottoms-Up" Approaches To Regional Modeling. *Journal of Policy Modeling*, vol. 6, no. 3, pp. 351-367.

Liew, L. H. (1995). Modelling Inter-Regional Strategic Interactions Within A General Equilibrium Framework. In *1995 IFAC/IFIP/IFOR/SEDC Symposium on Modelling and Control in National and Regional Economies*, preprint vol. 2.

Maimon, D., Baer, W., and Geiger, P. P. (1977). O Impacto Regional das Políticas Econômicas no Brasil. *Revista Brasileira de Geografia*, 39 (3): 3-53, July/September.

Malecki, E. J. (1991). **Technology and Economic Development: The Dynamics of Local, Regional and National Change**. Longman Scientific and Technical, Essex.

Markusen, A. (1987). **Regions: The Economics And Politics Of Territory**. Rowman and Littlefield, Totowa, NJ.

Mas-Colell, A., Whinston, M. D. and Green, J. R. (1995). **Microeconomic Theory**. Oxford University Press, New York.

McGregor, P. G., Swales, J. K. and Yin, Y. P. (1996). AMOS-RUK: An Interregional Computable General Equilibrium Model Of Scotland And Rest Of The UK. *Paper prepared for the 5th World Congress of Regional Science Association*, Tokyo, May.

McGregor, P. G., Swales, J. K. and Yin, Y. P. (1997). Spillover and Feedback Effects ni General Equilibrium Interregional Models of the National Economy: A Requiem for Interregional Input-Output? *Unpublished manuscript*, copy from the author, November.

Miller, R. E. and Blair, P. D. (1985). **Input-Output Analysis: Foundations and Extensions**. Prentice Hall, Englewood Cliffs.

Moreira, A. R. B. and Urani, A. (1994). Um Modelo Multissetorial de Consistência para a Região Nordeste. *Texto para Discussão 352*, IPEA, Brasília, October.

Morgan, W., Mutti, J. and Partridge, M. (1989). A Regional General Equilibrium Model Of The United States: Tax Effects On Factor Movements And Regional Production. *The Review of Economics and Statistics*, 71, pp. 626-635.

Myrdal, G. (1957). **Rich Lands and Poor: the Road to World Prosperity**. Harper and Brothers, New York.

Naqvi, F. and Peter, M. W. (1995). Notes On The Implementation Of MONASH-MRF: A Multiregional Model Of Australia. *Working Paper no. OP-82*, IMPACT Project, Monash University, Clayton, April.

Naqvi, F. and Peter, M. W. (1996). A Multiregional, Multisectoral Model of The Australian Economy With An Illustrative Application. *Australian Economic Papers*, June.

Nijkamp, P., Rietveld, P. and Snickars, F. (1986). Regional And Multiregional Economic Models: A Survey. In *Handbook of Regional and Urban Economics*, vol. 1, Ed. P. Nijkamp, North-Holland, Amsterdam.

Parmenter, B. R. (1983). Multiregional Modelling Of The Australian Economy: Experience From The Impact Project. *General Paper no. G-50*, IMPACT Project, Melbourne, August.

Parmenter, B. R., Pearson, K. R. and Jagielski, R. (1985). Bottoms-Up, Tops-Down And Hybrid Methods For Regionalizing Computable General Equilibrium Models: Some Comparisons. *Preliminary Working Paper no. OP-52*, IMPACT Project, Melbourne, February.

Peebles, G. H. (1995). **Lean Production, Sub Contracting, and Industrial Development: The Case of the Brazilian Automobile Industry**. University of Illinois at Urbana-Champaign, Ph.D. dissertation.

Perroux, F. (1955). A Note on the Notion of Growth Pole, *Économie Appliquée*, nos. 1 and 2.

Peter, M. W. (1996). An Illustrative Application: The Economic Effects Of A Regional-Government Infrastructure Project. IMPACT Project, Monash University, Clayton, *mimeo*, 01/09/96.

Peter, M. W. (1997). Notes on comparative Static closures for MONASH-MRF. *Unpublished manuscript*, copy from the author.

Peter, M. W., Han, S. H., Meagher, G. A. and Naqvi, F. (1996a). The Database Of MONASH-MRF. IMPACT Project, Monash University, Clayton, *mimeo*, July.

Peter, M. W., Horridge, M., Meagher, G. A., Naqvi, F. and Parmenter, B. R. (1996b). The Theoretical Structure Of MONASH-MRF. *Preliminary Working Paper no. OP-85*, IMPACT Project, Monash University, Clayton, April.

Rasmussen, P. N. (1956). **Studies in Inter-Sectoral Relations**. North Holland, Amsterdam.

Rolim, C. F. C., Machado, C. C., Lavinas, L., Lemos, M. B., Magina, M., and Rios-Neto, E. (1996). Saldo Comercial, Transferências Governamentais e Movimento de Capitais Inter-Regional. *Estudos Econômicos*, vol. 26, no. 1, pp. 5-19.

Round, J. I. (1978). An Interregional Input-Output Approach To The Evaluation Of Nonsurvey Methods. *Journal of Regional Science*, vol. 18, no. 2, pp. 179-194.

Round, J. I. (1983). Nonsurvey Techniques: A Critical Review Of The Theory And The Evidence. *International Regional Science Review*, vol. 8, no. 3, pp. 189-212.

Sachs, J. D. and Warner, A. (1995). Economic Reform and the Process of Economic Integration. In *Brookings Papers on Economic Activity*, Eds. W. C. Brainard and G. L. Perry, Brookings Institution, Washington D.C..

Savedoff, W. D. (1990). Os Diferenciais Regionais de Salários no Brasil: Segmentação Versus Dinamismo da Demanda. *Pesquisa e Planejamento Econômico*, vol. 20, no. 3, December.

Scarf, H. (1967). The Approximation Of Fixed Points Of A Continuous Mapping. *SIAM Journal of Applied Mathematics*, vol. 15, no. 5, pp. 1328-1343.

Scarf, H. (1973). **The Computation Of Economic Equilibria**. Yale University Press, New Haven.

Shoven, J. B. and Whalley, J. (1984). Applied General-Equilibrium Models Of Taxation And International Trade: An Introduction And Survey. *Journal of Economic Literature*, vol. XXII, pp. 1007-1051, September.

Shoven, J. B. and Whalley, J. (1992). **Applying General Equilibrium**. Cambridge Surveys of Economic Literature. Cambridge University Press.

Sonis, M., Guilhoto, J. J. M., Hewings, G. J. D., and Martins, E. B. (1995). Linkages, Key Sectors and Structural Change: Some New Perspective. Developing Economies, vol. XXXIII, no. 3.

Sonis, M., Guo, J., and Hewings, G. J. D. (1994). Comparative Analysis of China's Metropolitan Economies: An Input-Output Perspective. *Discussion Paper REAL 94-P-3*, Regional Economics Applications Laboratory, University of Illinois at Urbana-Champaign, October.

Sonis, M. and Hewings, G. J. D. (1989). Error and Sensitivity Input-Output Analysis: A New Approach. In *Frontiers of Input-Output Analysis*, Eds R. E. Miller, K. R. Polenske, and A. Z. Rose, Oxford University Press, New York.

Sonis, M. and Hewings, G. J. D. (1993). Hierarchies of regional Sub-Structures and Their Multipliers Within Input-Output Systems: Miyazawa Revisited. *Hitotsubashi Journal of Economics*, 34: 33-44.

Sonis, M., Hewings, G. J. D., and Guo, J. (1996). Sources of Structural Change in Input-Output Systems: A field of Influence Approach. *Economic Systems Research*, vol. 8, no. 1.

Sousa, M. C. S. (1987). Proteção, Crescimento e Distribuição de Renda no Brasil – Uma Abordagem de Equilíbrio Geral. Revista Brasileira de Economia, vol. 41, n. 1, Jan-Mar, pp. 99-116.

Spencer, J. E. (1988). Computable General Equilibrium, Trade, Factor Mobility, And The Regions. In London Papers in Regional Science 19: *Recent Advances in Regional Economic Modelling*, Eds. F. Harrigan and P. G. McGregor, Pion, London.

SUDAM (1994). **Matriz de Insumo-Produto do Norte 1980 e 1985: Metodologia e Resultados**. Superintendência de Desenvolvimento da Amazônia, Belém.

Varian, H. R. (1992). **Microeconomic Analysis**. W. W. Norton & Company, New York. Third edition.

Walras, L. (1874). Éléments d'Économie Politique Pure. 4me Édition Définitive et Augmentée par l'Auteur (1926), R. Pichon et R. Durand-Auzias Editeurs, Paris.

Watanuki, M. (1996). Regional Development Policy Analysis Of Indonesia: Interregional CGE Modeling Approach. *Paper presented at the 43rd North American Meeting of the Regional Science Association International*, Washington DC, November.

West, G. (1995). Comparison of Input-Output, Input-Output + Econometric and Computable General Equilibrium Impact Models at the Regional Level. *Economic Systems Research*, vol. 7, no. 2.

Whalley, J. and Trela, I. (1986). **Regional Aspects Of Confederation**. Vol. 68 for the Royal Commission on the Economic Union and Development Prospects for Canada. University of Toronto Press, Toronto.

Williamson, J. (1965). Regional Inequality and the Process of National Development: A Description of the Patterns. *Economic Development and Cultural Change*, vol. 13, pp. 3-84.

World Bank (1996). *Brazil: The Custo Brasil Since 1990-1992*. World Bank Report No. 15663-BR, Latin america and the Caribbean Region, December.

Zini Jr., A. A. and Sachs, J. (1996). Regional Income Convergence in Brazil. *Unpublished manuscript*, copy from the author, April.

Index

About the Author

Dr. Eduardo A. Haddad (1970) holds a bachelor degree in Economics from the Federal University of Minas Gerais, Brazil (1993). In January 1995 he received a M.A. degree in Economics from the University of Illinois at Urbana-Champaign, USA; he successfully defended his Ph.D. dissertation, at the same institution, in December 1997. In the calendar year of 1998, he was engaged in post-doctoral research at the University of Oxford, in the UK. He is currently a Research Professor of Economics at *Fundação Instituto de Pesquisas Econômicas* (FIPE) at the University of São Paulo, Brazil, and also holds a position as Adjunct Research Assistant Professor at the Regional Economics Applications Laboratory (REAL) at the University of Illinois at Urbana-Champaign, USA.

Dr. Haddad has published on regional and interregional input-output analysis, general equilibrium modeling, and various aspects of regional economic development in Brazil and other developing countries, in both national and international journals; he has also contributed with chapters in international books in the fields of Regional Science and Economic Development.

For Product Safety Concerns and Information please contact our EU representative GPSR@taylorandfrancis.com Taylor & Francis Verlag GmbH, Kaufingerstraße 24, 80331 München, Germany

Batch number: 10725901

Printed by Printforce, the Netherlands